HISTORY
vs
HOLLYWOOD

HISTORY
vs
HOLLYWOOD
HOW THE PAST IS FILMED

M J TROW

PEN & SWORD
HISTORY

AN IMPRINT OF PEN & SWORD BOOKS LTD.
YORKSHIRE – PHILADELPHIA

First published in Great Britain in 2024 by
Pen & Sword History
An imprint of
Pen & Sword Books Ltd
Yorkshire - Philadelphia

Copyright © M.J. Trow, 2024

ISBN 978 1 39906 650 1

The right of M.J. Trow to be identified as the Author of this work has been asserted by him in accordance with the Copyright, Designs and Patents Act 1988.

A CIP catalogue record for this book is available from the British Library

All rights reserved. No part of this book may be reproduced or transmitted in any form or by any means, electronic or mechanical including photocopying, recording or by any information storage and retrieval system, without permission from the Publisher in writing.

Typeset in INDIA by IMPEC eSolutions
Printed and bound in England by CPI Group (UK) Ltd, Croydon, CR0 4YY

Pen & Sword Books Limited incorporates the imprints of Archaeology, Atlas, Aviation, Battleground, Digital, Discovery, Family History, Fiction, History, Local, Local History, Maritime, Military, Military Classics, Politics, Select, Transport, True Crime, After the Battle, Air World, Claymore Press, Frontline Publishing, Leo Cooper, Remember When, Seaforth Publishing, The Praetorian Press, Wharncliffe Books, Wharncliffe Local History, Wharncliffe Transport, Wharncliffe True Crime and White Owl.

For a complete list of Pen & Sword titles please contact

PEN & SWORD BOOKS LIMITED
47 Church Street, Barnsley, South Yorkshire S70 2AS, United Kingdom
E-mail: enquiries@pen-and-sword.co.uk
Website: www.pen-and-sword.co.uk

or

PEN AND SWORD BOOKS
1950 Lawrence Rd, Havertown, PA 19083, USA
E-mail: Uspen-and-sword@casematepublishers.com
Website: www.penandswordbooks.com

This book is dedicated

to the thousands of men and women,

on both sides of the camera

who have brought history

so vibrantly to life.

Contents

Overture	Lights! Camera! Action!	viii
Chapter 1	Swords and Sandals: From Genesis to the Fall of Rome	1
Chapter 2	The Dark Ages: From the Fall of Rome to Alfred the Great	27
Chapter 3	The Middle Ages: From Hastings to Bosworth	32
Chapter 4	The Renaissance: From Bluff King Hal to Gloriana	52
Chapter 5	The Swashbucklers: From the Musketeers to the Pirates	66
Chapter 6	The New World: From the Halls of Montezuma to Uncle Sam	79
Chapter 7	The Age of Empire: From Bonaparte to Ekaterinburg	99
Chapter 8	Westerns: Heading Them Off at the Past	133
Chapter 9	To Hell and Back: War from the Trenches to the Killing Fields	165
Chapter 10	Shoot! Crime Films: From Cain to Bundy	199
Chapter 11	Ice-Cream and Popcorn	223
Chapter 12	The One-Eyed Monster	235
Bibliography		243
Index		245

Overture

Lights! Camera! Action!

'On 14 February 1900, a party of schoolgirls went on a picnic at Hanging Rock near Mount Macedon in the Australian state of Victoria ... During the afternoon, several members of the party disappeared without trace.'

Except that they didn't.

The compelling film made by director Peter Weir perfectly captures turn of the century Australia, the tweeness of the girls at a private school, a thin veneer of their burgeoning sexuality. The heat, the sun, the very silence of the Hanging Rock combines to form a mesmerising backdrop to a film that tantalises, but in the end offers no answers. The film is based on Joan Lindsay's 1967 novel, which offers no resolution either. But such was the grip of the extraordinarily atmospheric film that thousands believed that it was based on fact. Accordingly, various versions of the story were written up in books and magazines of the supernatural and the occult. The movie was 'a ghost story without ghosts, a puzzle without a solution and a story of sexual repression without the sex' according to one critic.

This is the problem with movies; they tell stories for entertainment. And stories are made up.

Thousands of books have been written on what history is (or isn't) but essentially, it is an interpretation of the past. And where there is one interpretation, there are often dozens. As Clint Eastwood's fictional detective Harry Callaghan says in *The Dead Pool* (1988), 'Opinions are like assholes; everybody's got one.' So, was Moses sent by God or was he just a clever conjuror? Was Jesus the son of God or a rabble-rousing troublemaker for the Romans? Was El Cid, Spain's national hero, fighting for justice or for money? Was Scotland's William Wallace a freedom fighter or a horse thief? The interpretations are endless and they are all based on the evidence of history. There is, however, a world of difference between an historian's interpretation and a film-maker's.

Most people who watch historical films – and even those who make them – aren't historians. They may be buffs and know that the Roman cavalry didn't have stirrups and that Lieutenant Bromhead (Michael Caine in *Zulu*) couldn't have used the Webley revolver he carries in the film because it hadn't been invented yet. But most people are unaware of any of these niceties. They want a straightforward story, exciting adventure, love interest, dash and fire. If there's a little bit of a moral dilemma, that's fine, but it shouldn't be overdone. As audiences, we have to *identify* with one side or the other; if we're ambivalent, the film has failed.

Let me give you one example I've mentioned already. In 1995, Mel Gibson made *Braveheart*, the 'true' story of William Wallace, who led the Scots in their bid for freedom from the overlordship of Edward I of England. I saw the film in the cinema and was delighted. The acting, the costumes, the scenery, the music – it was all epic in every sense – and the battle scenes were among the best ever made. I am a Welshman. Perhaps some of my ancestors made up the longbowmen who fought for Edward against the Scots. That was the same Edward who had already defeated my people and built massive castles everywhere to make sure they behaved themselves. So I came out of the cinema buoyed up. At last they were making epics again, sweeping stories from the past that sang the praises of heroes. Films of my childhood, like *Spartacus*, *El Cid*, *Ben-Hur* and dozens of others swept into my filmic memory. I could see them all, as surely as I could see William Wallace's claymore hurtling through the air against the sullen sky of the Battle of Bannockburn that ends *Braveheart*.

Then, in the harsh light of day, doubts crept in as realism hit home. Bannockburn was a dazzling victory for the Scots, although we don't see it on screen and the impression we have is that the new leader who replaced the dead Wallace, Robert the Bruce, only reluctantly and at the last minute, prepares to take on the generally superior English. In fact, he had decided that days or weeks earlier and the only reason he won Bannockburn is that his men dug concealed pits on the field into which the unsuspecting English cavalry charged headlong. It was a brilliant tactic, but it was not in accord with the starving, downtrodden peasantry of *Braveheart*. And Robert the Bruce, as king, certainly didn't become a man of the people, as the film implies. That is pure late twentieth-century nonsense.

Randall Wallace, a descendant of William, who wrote the screenplay, cleverly opens the film's narrative with, 'I will tell you of William Wallace. Historians from England will say I am a liar. But history is written by those who have hung [*sic*] heroes.' This is clever because it puts Wallace's opponents on the back foot. I am not calling Mr Wallace a liar, but I am saying that he has chosen a very different interpretation from the one I would choose and the historical record suggests. Another, equally brilliant, film could be made from the angle of the English and Edward I. What would not work is to make a film that tried to tell both sides together, with any kind of balance. That would make it a documentary, fascinating and valuable in its own right but not a movie in the accepted sense. When movies try this – as in *Zulu Dawn* (see Chapter 7) – they inevitably fail.

Omar Sharif's debut was in David Lean's *Lawrence of Arabia* (1962) (see Chapter 9) and he said of the film, 'Four hours long, with no stars, and no women, and no love story and not much action either.' The movie worked spectacularly well, winning seven Oscars, but Sharif makes an interesting point. Movie-makers in the past rarely contemplated making a film without a love interest and often, it has been shoe-horned in to a story that is essentially about men. As I say elsewhere in this book, dozens, perhaps hundreds, of movies have, as their tag lines 'for the love of a woman', as if this gives us reason for a million acts of stirring heroism. As E.C. Bentley said, 'The art of biography is different from geography. Geography is about maps, but biography is about chaps.' And that, feminist readers excuse me, is the problem.

History is about chaps too, largely because most of it was written by men. In the pantheon of movies, women usually serve as arm candy or motivation for the hero. We'll meet examples later, but Doris Day as *Calamity Jane* (see Chapter 8) is interesting because she dresses, rides and drinks like a man. El Cid's wife, Ximene (Sophia Loren) is almost lost to him because of the male world of politics in which he is caught up. Only when accidents of royal birth produce a queen, rather than a king, are women allowed centre stage. So Eleanor of Aquitaine (Katharine Hepburn), Elizabeth (umpteen actresses), Catherine the Great (ditto) and Victoria (ditto again) have all had movies made about them, many of them excellent, but they aren't the norm. Neither are films about genuine heroines – the Second World War agents Violette Szabo (Virginia McKenna) and Odette Churchill (Anna Neagle); the slave Harriet Tubman (Cynthia Erivo) and the Medieval enigma Joan of Arc (several actresses) are all superb examples, but they are in the tiny minority.

Then, there is the hoary question of historical accuracy, which this book is all about. The French have made at least four epic movies about William of Normandy's invasion of England in 1066; as far as I am aware, Britain hasn't made one. In reality, William and his knights spoke Norman French, itself an admixture of Danish/Viking dialect. Harold Godwinson's thegns and fyrds spoke Old English – Beowulf's Saxon overlaid (again) with Viking. For a film to be made with that accuracy, we'd need subtitles or (usually unconvincing) dubbing, neither of which really works. For that reason, I have not included 'foreign' films in this book, with one or two notable exceptions. We shouldn't have to *work* to be entertained. No doubt, some readers will be annoyed by this, as the omission excludes some first-rate movies, but for reasons of length, I have chosen to draw it.

Which raises the vexed problem of dialogue. The recent Netflix series *The Crown* has been criticized (rightly) because it offers casual chats between lead-players, e.g. Prince Charles and Princess Diana, which can only be guesswork. We cannot *know* what was said behind palace doors and in the context of real people still alive, this is inflammatory and irresponsible. With dead characters, too, we have no idea of conversation. All we know is that Oliver Cromwell never came face to face with Charles I; nor did Elizabeth I ever meet her cousin, Mary, Queen of Scots. In both cases (*Cromwell* and *Mary, Queen of Scots*) the film-makers would have you believe otherwise. The older movies threw out 'thees' and 'thous' all over the place, as in Tony Curtis' immortal 'Yondah lies duh castle of my fodduh' (*The Black Shield of Falworth* 1954). Mercifully, nobody does it that way any more!

And always remember that Hollywood (and any other movie-making centre in the world) is all about fakery. No one would go and see a Western directed by Sean Aloysius O'Fearna, until they realized he was John Ford. Who in their right minds would latch on to the heroism of Bernie Schwartz, Maurice Micklewhite and Marion Morrison unless they knew that they were Tony Curtis, Michael Caine and John Wayne? Viewer, beware!

There are gaffes galore in historical movies, often for the reasons of cost or because the producer/director has other priorities. Everybody guffawed at the amphibious motorized vehicles sneakily used by the French invading armies in Russell Crowe's *Robin Hood* (2010) but didn't turn a hair at the *curved* sabres (as opposed to straight blades) carried by the Scots Greys in Sergei Bondarchuk's *Waterloo* (1970). Neither were they overly perturbed when director Tony Richardson equipped his entire Light Brigade in crimson overalls (trousers) rather than just the 11th Hussars, who actually wore them (*The Charge of the Light Brigade* 1968).

In this book, I have made my selection of movies based on actual characters taking part in the action. I am very aware that that leaves out some excellent films, which accurately convey a sense of place and time. Today, with the domination of television over the silver screen, historical films are still being made and are still popular. As I write, there are plans to make not one, but two series on gladiators in ancient

Rome. In one of them, Anthony Hopkins is to play Vespasian, one of the most impressive generals and emperors that Rome produced. Today's doyen of the epic, Ridley Scott, is about to release a new version of Napoleon, the most-filmed character in history. But it would be remiss of me to discuss the subject without reference to 'woke'. In the interests of diversity and inclusion, actual history is being increasingly ignored and/or rewritten. So, recently, there were objections to Angelina Jolie playing Cleopatra on the extremely spurious grounds that Cleopatra was black. The last pharaoh of Egypt had a Greek father and we have no idea who her mother was. She *may* have been an African slave, but equally, she may not. None of this stopped Jodie Turner-Smith, a black actress, from playing the English girl Anne Boleyn in the mini-series of the same name in 2021 on Channel 5. Cultural appropriation doesn't extend much further than this. And actually, none of it is new. The actress Sarah Bernhardt wowed Parisian audiences as the perfectly male Hamlet in a stage production in 1899. In the movie world, Laurence Olivier not only 'blacked up' as *Othello* in his filmed version of the Shakespeare, but 'browned up' as Muhammad Ahmad, the tribal leader known as the Mahdi, in *Khartoum* (1966) (see Chapter 7). Such appropriation might make some of us cringe today. It makes me cringe because of its lack of veracity; contrast the burnt-corked suave Englishman Rex Harrison in *King Richard and the Crusaders* (1954) with the authentic Syrian actor Ghassan Massoud in Ridley Scott's *Kingdom of Heaven* (2005). Both played the Muslim leader Salah-ed-Din, the Lionheart's dignified adversary in the land that was holy to them both.

The depressing news is that, of the thousands of historical films I have seen during a lifetime of addiction to the cinema and television, *not one* has actually told the whole truth. I have spent far too many hours transported back in time by the movies reviewed in this book. This was, for me, more than entertainment; it led me to read history at university and to write about the past, even in the fiction I now write with my wife. Incidentally, she is probably the only person I know who did a more than passable impression of Charlton Heston in *El Cid* holding up an imaginary two-handed sword and grating 'To whom does Calahora belong?' Unfortunately, she was balancing on a church pew at the time, fell off and broke her arm. Greater love hath no woman.

Chapter 1

Swords and Sandals: From Genesis to the Fall of Rome

The Early Years

'In the beginning,' says Genesis, the opening verse of the first book of the Bible, 'God created the heaven and the earth.' Hollywood, the 'tinsel town' that became the centre of the moving picture world, came along a little later.

Like other life-changing technology, the birth of the moving picture was fought over by America, France, Germany and Italy. Britain, that had the largest empire the world has ever seen at the time, was slightly behind. In 1894, Thomas Edison set up the Kinetoscope in New York, a slot machine that showed moving pictures on an endless belt. Each 'film' lasted a minute and people queued for hours to have a peep. There was, no doubt, an element of voyeurism about all this because in July of that year, Senator Bradley banned the showing of one of these – *The Serpentine Dance* by W.K. Laurie Dickson – because it showed dancer Annabelle Moore's underwear. Censorship is older than Hollywood. The same director filmed 'Buffalo Bill' Cody's rodeo in October, a contemporary event, of course, at the time, but pointing in the direction of the most popular brand of film entertainment – the Western (see Chapter 8).

In France, the Lumière brothers patented a system which 'synthesizes colour by a rapid succession of monochrome images'. By December, Laurie Dickson was already publishing a *History of the Kinetograph*, proving how quickly the 'magic' new phenomenon was catching on. Edison had been working on a variety of 'moving picture' gadgets in West Orange, New Jersey, since 1887. Auguste and Louis Lumière patented their own machine in February 1895. Charles Pathé, Henri Joly and Leon Gaumont built on early research, setting up film companies left, right and centre. The grand opening of the Lumières' Cinematograph took place on 28 December in the Indian Salon in the basement of the spectacular Grand Café. The price of entry was 1 franc.

By then, however, the first historical movie had already been made. At the end of August 1895, Edison produced *The Execution of Mary Stuart,* directed by Alfred Clark and starring Robert Thomas. It was one of the first films to use trained actors, although, since the running time was only 18 seconds, they clearly weren't called upon to do much! As the executioner's axe swings, Mary's body is substituted by a mannequin and her severed head is held up for the prurient delight of the audience. How horrified they were by what must have looked real, we don't know. Neither do we know why Edison chose this topic. As we shall see in Chapter 4, Mary Stuart, Queen of Scots, was beheaded at Fotheringhay Castle, Northamptonshire, on 8 February 1587. Edison's version, despite a reasonable attempt at English sixteenth-century costume, has it happening outside, which saved on lighting costs and technical difficulties.

In the actual event, Mary's wig fell off to reveal her bald head, which horrified the select audience as much as the decapitation. To add to the terror of the moment, her little lapdog scampered out from under her skirts as her body flopped. It's unlikely that Edison knew any of this – such drama, which would thrill audiences worldwide in the decades ahead, would have to wait.

As the 1890s progressed, ugly controversy arose between film companies over rights and patents, but in 1898 Edison raided the Bible for the first time with his filming of the Oberammergau Passion Play, which had appeared every ten years in Bavaria since 1634 (with a few exceptions) and featured the crucifixion of Christ. As with his depiction of Mary, it was dramatic, heartrending stuff. The Church, which had looked scornfully on the early cinema (in France, Georges Méliès showed naked bathing scenes in the previous year and the Catholic clergy were very upset) now warmed to the idea – Christianity could reach new masses. 'True to life' said Edison's posters, even though Bavaria (itself a substitute for the Middle East) was actually the roof of the grand Central Palace in New York. Not to be outdone, the Lumières came out with *The Life and Passion of Christ* and Gaumont *Life of Christ*. Even when Méliès produced his short travelogue on the sea, he had to include Christ walking on it. The historical figure filmed more than any other is Napoleon Bonaparte, but Jesus Christ was the first cinema star.

Inevitably, the early producers and directors chose themes which would have a resonance with their audiences. In 1900, when the world was wowed by the impressive World's Fair in Paris, Victorin-Hippolyte Jasset produced *Vercingetorix*, a glorified horse show. The real Vercingetorix was a Gallic chieftain who fought against Julius Caesar, and was defeated and executed in 46 BC. Three years after the film, although it didn't contain any real characters, Edison's company produced the first Western, *The Great Train Robbery*, the most memorable scene of which was a cowboy pointing his six-gun at the camera and firing. There were screams in every theatre where it was shown and a considerable amount of ducking and flinching. *The Great Train Robbery* appeared in the same year as *The Virginian* by Owen Wister, which many consider to be the first genuine Western novel.

Crime appeared on the screen (apart from robbing trains) in 1905 with *The Life of Charles Peace* by William Haggar in London. Peace still captivates today, perhaps because of his extraordinary ability to disguise himself by dislocating his jaw. A cat burglar and murderer, he was hanged at Armley gaol, Leeds, in February 1879. Not to be outdone, Australian director Charles Tait went one better a year later with *The Story of Ned Kelly*. Its running time was an astonishing seventy minutes (compare this with Edison's seconds long *Mary Stuart* only twelve years earlier). Kelly was the son of an Irish immigrant, a horse thief and bush ranger who was hanged in 1880. The bizarre home-made breastplate and helmet he wore during his robberies was lent to Tait's company by Victoria's state museum. The star, in what may have been an early publicity stunt, 'disappeared' before filming was finished and adjustments had to be made accordingly.

Hooray for Hollywood

In the United States, New York and Chicago were the centres of early film production, but from 1909, a 'sleepy little town' on the outskirts of Los Angeles, California, began to dominate. The Sunshine State offered just that – bright sun which made camera work easy and wide-open spaces to build studio lots and film epic scenes. Producer William Selig set up a company here as did G.M. Anderson who transformed for the silver screen into 'Bronco Billy', the lead in literally hundreds of Western 'shorts'. Ironically, he lost his first part in *The Great Train Robbery* because he couldn't ride! He improved rapidly.

In 1912, German immigrant Carl Laemmle set up Universal in the Hollywood hills, opening his new $165,000 studio with a golden key as the paparazzi snapped away. The money and the organization stayed on the East Coast for years but increasingly, production itself happened in the far West. Three years after opening, Universal were making 250 films a year.

Interestingly, in view of the extraordinary power of the studios in later years, it was the actors (now called 'stars') who called the shots. Mary Pickford was picking up $10,000 a week by 1915. She set up Paramount four years later, along with the heart-throb Douglas Fairbanks, comedian Charlie Chaplin and director D.W. Griffith.

In February 1910, far from Hollywood, director Louis Feuillades began a Biblical series for Gaumont, the first of which was *Balthazar's Feast*. Vitagraph in Chicago went one better with a five-reel epic, *The Life of Moses*, 'a reverent and dignified portrayal', including the miracle of the Red Sea which cost $10,000 to film and looks dreadful today. By now, there were regular magazines for cinema-goers and *Moving Picture World* wrote that the film was 'a graphic reproduction of the main events in the life of Moses, corresponding closely to the conception which has been inculcated in those who have attended church and Sunday school'.

And that, of course, was the problem. Adding to the glitz of what would become 'Tinseltown', the premise of Biblical film was wrong from the start. To be fair, historical Biblical studies had barely advanced beyond the universities, and the Bible, unlike the Koran, had a mystic iconicism of its own. It had a plethora of people from all over the Middle East who were assumed to be real historical characters. The Good Book had once been God's Spell, the literal words of God and Christ. The fact that the work had gone through umpteen translations over 1,500 years, from Hebrew to Greek to Latin to English, passed most people by. In Victorian England, Jesus was portrayed as a blue-eyed white man with long auburn hair. He invariably wore white and was more or less a public schoolboy, albeit with a unique spiritual dimension. In the New Testament, the baddies were Judas Iscariot and various scheming Pharisees, aided and abetted by the cold indifference of the Roman governor of Judea, Pontius Pilate, and the psychopathic King Herod. The goody was Jesus and, far below him in terms of piety and courage, his disciples. Incidentally, the only 'good' woman was Mary, Jesus' mother.

Since the Old Testament was essentially a ludicrously garbled history of the Hebrews, Moses, Joshua and the rest are the good guys. Everybody else, but especially Rameses II and his Egyptians, are the villains. To see it any other way bordered on blasphemy. When the Monty Python team made the spoof *Life of Brian* (1979) – 'He's not the Messiah. He's a very naughty boy!' – there were howls of protest from the churches and the conservative world. In the ultra-touchy 'Bible belt' of South Carolina, the show was cancelled after one night and the Liberal Left were gunning for Senator Thurmond who spearheaded the campaign against the film. In Britain, an exasperated Malcolm Muggeridge argued on television with the Python actors and lost resoundingly. Such a film would not have reached the storyboard stage in earlier decades. All this played perfectly into the hands of Hollywood producers; simple stories told from one angle only, with right and wrong, good and bad, clearly delineated. Add to that casts of thousands (cheaply hired extras in bad costumes before the days of computer-generated images (CGI)) and you have box office dynamite.

Out of Eden

What follows is a look at the movies that have depicted the world of the Old Testament, a vast chronological timespan glossed over in the Bible by various 'begetting' of people you've never heard of and centring geographically on the Middle East. Because of the accident of the Bible's Hebrew origins and the absorption of the much later Christianity by the West, all the stories and virtually all the movies of the Old Testament focus on that. The problem is that a huge percentage of the Old Testament is myth. Every civilization has its creation stories – Adam and Eve are everywhere, only the names have been changed – and once a literal interpretation was abandoned by almost everybody, film-makers were not inclined to spend much time on forbidden trees, serpents and the concept of original sin. Far more interesting to see how God's chosen people (and there are several examples of those, too) fared in the outside world beyond the beautiful paradise the world's first couple had thrown away.

As author George MacDonald Fraser says in his *The Hollywood History of the World*, 'Hollywood is not a school for teaching history; its business is making money out of entertainment.' And the sheer scope of the Old Testament defeats everybody. *The Bible* (1966) is a hugely misleading title, even with its subtitle of 'In the Beginning', because, even at nearly four hours long, it doesn't get beyond Genesis 22 (17 pages out of 777 in the version I'm using). Undeterred, the film trots out a number of Hollywood greats – Richard Harris was the fratricidal Cain; John Huston, who also directed, was Noah, starring in his own disaster movie by building an ark. Stephen Boyd (always a baddie) was Nimrod, trying to climb the tower of Babel. Peter O'Toole was not one but three angels! The critics were dismissive. David Robinson wrote, 'An Old Testament spectacular like any other,' and Rex Reed, 'At a time when religion needs all the help it can get, John Huston may have set its cause back a couple of thousand years.'

Our problem is that not only are the stories of the Old Testament hopelessly child-like (and were unleashed on children as indoctrination in the past) but we have no idea whether any of these people were real. You will look in vain for any of them outside the Bible and whereas Noah's flood may have its basis in any or several actual natural geological disasters, that doesn't make his ark look any more likely. The recent attempt to make the Noah story by Russell Crowe *without* the God dimension and punishment for the sins of the world merely leaves us with a run-of-the-mill disaster movie that has been better done by almost everybody.

Attempting to place these Old Testament epics into a chronological order and give them a date is brave in the extreme, but Baird Searles does it in *Epic! History on the Big Screen*. There are no real characters in *Sodom and Gomorrah* (1962) but Searles places the action in the twentieth century BC, which is a neat little mathematical pattern. We don't really have to go any further than Anouk Aimee's immortal line – 'Greetings, Sodomites and Israelites!' – to see the problem that lies in store for the uninitiated. Sodom and Gomorrah were the cities of the plain in Canaan, destroyed by God because of the sexual depravity that went on there. Sodomy (anal intercourse) was a major criminal offence in most western countries for centuries, leading in some cases to the death penalty. The heart-throb Stewart Granger was Lot, whose wife turns into a pillar of salt (as you do!) but nothing, the 'swinging sixties' notwithstanding, was made of Lot's incest with his daughters. Stanley Baker was the baddie, of course, despite being the good guy once or twice in his career.

The Egyptian (1954), set approximately in the fourteenth century BC, deals with the problems of leadership in one of the greatest civilizations in the ancient world. Akhenaton is real enough (Michael Wilding in the film), a fascinating pharaoh who abandoned the rich pantheon of gods we all know about today – Horus, Bast, Osiris etc. – in favour of a single god. Monotheism was suicide in ancient Egypt and not only Akhenaton but his son Tutankhamun met sticky ends at the hands of the pharaoh wannabe, General Horemheb (Victor Mature). The costumes are pretty awful, but in this, as in earlier movies, the sets, with pyramids, columns and marble deities, are largely impressive. Halliwell, *the* critic of movies for years, sums it up pretty well – 'makes an excellent example of the pictures they don't make 'em like any more'.

Mature was cast again, this time as a hero, in *Samson and Delilah* (1949). He doesn't really look strong enough, with or without God's help, to knock down buildings, but we have the Hollywood pairing of the good man and the bad woman (Delilah was Hedy Lamarr), which adds a frisson to the whole thing. This, too, is straight out of the historical playbook as written by men. *Every* woman from Eve onwards is weakness and sinfulness personified, in literature as well as film, because the Church said so. The only exception is Mary, the mother of Christ. Richard Mallett of *Punch* wrote, 'To ignore so enormous, over-coloured, over-stuffed, flamboyant an "epic" would be almost as absurd as taking it seriously.'

Probably the film that encapsulates the Old Testament best is *The Ten Commandments,* set in the thirteenth century BC and dealing with Moses leading his 'children' out of Egyptian slavery into the 'land flowing with milk and honey', Canaan. This is the story of Exodus, seminal as far as today's Jews and Israelis are concerned, but there is no record of it in Egyptian history and the Egyptians kept good records. There had already been one *Ten Commandments* film before Cecil B. DeMille made his version in 1923. It was still in the silent era, despite various experiments with sound having gone on for a quarter of a century, and the undertaking was epic. A massive set of gates, complete with bas-reliefs of chariots and pharaohs was built, costing a fortune, not to mention the wages of the extras, hauling giant statues into place or hurtling across the desert in pursuit of Moses' people making for the Red Sea. DeMille went way over budget to reach $1.5 million and critics were left bemused that nearly half the film is set in modern America as a morality tale. When he came to remake it, DeMille got it right.

The souvenir programme which was sold at the film's premiere in 1956 contains paintings that are a reminder of the frequent source of Biblical movies. The great Victorian canvases of artists like Leighton, Alma-Tadema and Burne-Jones often depicted scenes from the Bible, and Hollywood copied them faithfully. As DeMille wrote in the programme, 'That relationship between God and man is the greatest drama in the world – a drama in which we are the actors.' The actors themselves are interesting. Moses was played by Charlton Heston, who would become, more than any other actor, Hollywood's 'Mr Epic'. When Heston got to DeMille's studio, to discuss auditioning for the part, he found it stuffed full of paintings borrowed from museums, historical artefacts and books. He mugged up on a recent history of Egypt and plunged into Exodus and Deuteronomy. 'Then of course, I had to be circumcised,' he joked in *In the Arena*. 'What actors won't do for a good part (Nah ... only kidding).'

DeMille's dilemma was rather superficial. 'Can we be worthy of its theme?' he asked rhetorically. 'That demanded adherence to the Bible and to facts.' But there were no facts. Most scholars today place Moses historically during the reigns of Seti I and his son Rameses II. Cedric Hardwicke, Shakespearean stalwart, played the former, and the enigmatic Yul Brynner was Rameses, even giving up his Broadway success of *The King and I* to take on the role. These two men are the only ones in the genuinely historical record – everybody else is fiction. DeMille was right in proclaiming the pious hope that Christians (not invented of course in Moses' day), Jews and Muslims could find harmony in the fact that Moses is a common hero to all three faiths. He was wrong in making the assumption that he ever existed.

The 'book of the film' was *Moses and Egypt* by Henry S. Noerdlinger and published by the University of Southern California Press, in which he researched extensively in the Bible, the Koran and the Midrash (a rabbinical commentary from the twelfth century AD). Research, of course, is only as good as its original sources – all three of Noerdlinger's were seriously flawed. The Americans in particular lapped all this up. Around the rim of Boston's Liberty Bell, icon of the stand against colonial Britain, are the words, 'Proclaim liberty throughout all the land, unto all the inhabitants thereof'. These, supposedly, are Moses' words.

'I am the Lord thy God,' said Heston as the Lord spoke to Moses before giving him the tablets of the Ten Commandments. We almost believed that God was American and were able to ignore the fact that the Egyptians, the Sumerians, the Greeks, the Romans and just about every ancient civilization also had similar laws handed down by their gods.

There is no doubt that DeMille's *Ten Commandments* was *the* epic of the ancient world but look again at the special effects of the parting of the Red Sea; they are dreadful. That is because the director used the same footage from his 1923 version, when no doubt they seemed stunning. As an appropriate footnote to this film, Charlton Heston joked that he once tried to part the waters of his swimming pool at home – and nothing happened at all!

The Old Testament has a number of fascinating couples, tailormade for the big screen. One of these, in 1951, was *David and Bathsheba*. She was the beautiful wife of Uriah the Hittite (sent by David to die in battle so he could have her for himself) and he was one of the foremost kings of Israel, seen as a founding figure of his people. Gregory Peck had the gravitas to play him in 1951 and the adulterous Bathsheba was Susan Hayward. Unlike many of the Old Testament sirens in the cinema (Sheba, Delilah, Cleopatra) she is spared the inevitable belly dancing scene – cue whirling slaves, ostrich fans, calypso-style drumming and a few veils. 'For this woman, he broke God's own commandments! The fire and tempest of their love still flames across 3,000 years!' Er … no, not really.

In 1930, largely under pressure from the Catholic church, the Motion Picture Producers and Distributors of America under its chairman, Will Hays, pushed for reforms to clean up Hollywood's act in what came to be called the Production Code. There were too many bad guys, loose women and nudity for some people and F.D. Roosevelt's New Deal, federal power overriding freedom, was pushing in the same direction. Hays was every bit as restrictive as Joseph Goebbels in Nazi Germany, where every film studio was under direct government control. Not until 1967 would a new (and fairer) rating system replace Hays' new Puritans, over twenty years after Goebbels' censorship disappeared. 'Law,' said Hays, 'natural or human, shall not be ridiculed,' – so anything Moses said was fine – this, of course, in a country that once made it illegal to criticize the president. 'The sanctity of marriage and the home shall be upheld,' which should have put the kibosh on most of the Old Testament. Sexual perversion (homosexuality) was out of the question, so no one *quite* knew why Sodom was such a hellhole. 'Miscegenation' (mixed-race sexuality) was outlawed in a country obsessed with its racial legacy. 'Indecent movements' was tricky – the court dancers referred to above had to be careful. 'The treatment of bedrooms must be governed by good taste and delicacy.' Compare stills of Betty Blythe as Sheba in 1921 with Susan Hayward as Bathsheba and you'll get the point. Betty is festooned with 1920s Art Nouveau/Deco pearls and sequins, but her nipples are clearly visible, as are her bare arms (unthinkable to the Victorians) and her top is open almost to the waist. Susan, by contrast, despite having enraptured David when he sees her bathing, is dressed for the Arctic. She *does* have a low-cut gown, but her breasts are completely covered by the pointy bra of the 1950s and the only part of her body on display are her toes, peering out from the inevitable sandals. Interestingly, the same couple in Richard Gere's *King David* (1985) are wearing even more clothes, Cherie Lunghi's all bleached linen. This is presumably more in accord with *actual* historical research rather than Hays-inspired bigotry, although Halliwell still didn't like it. 'Astonishingly tedious, confused and inept telling of familiar tales' is the verdict.

In *Solomon and Sheba* (1959), the late Gina Lollobrigida shimmered with her astonishing figure and even had a bath and took part in an orgy sequence, but it was all terribly tactful. Incidentally, rather than Sheba being the lover of Solomon, the historical record tells us that she may have gone to Israel once, on a state visit. As Baird Searles puts it, 'something like Margaret Thatcher visiting George Bush' (and I don't remember any orgy scenes then!) The film's tag line read, 'Only once in 3,000 years has there been anything like it'; for which we must be grateful. Halliwell described it as 'alternating between pretentiousness and cowboys and Indians'.

No one could fault these Old Testament epics for their sets. They were universally brilliant, D.W. Griffith's *Intolerance* (1916) perhaps the granddaddy of them all. Everybody copied this, whether the storyline involved real characters or not and audiences who had no knowledge of ancient Middle Eastern culture believed all of it.

The Glory That Was Greece

The other historical theme that influenced film-makers was ancient Greece, the culture that would eclipse that of Egypt and Israel and lay down the foundations, at least, of western democracy. Unfortunately, too many such films dealt with Troy, but every character in that monumental siege story is fictional. When the archaeologist Heinrich Schliemann excavated Hissarlik in 1870, he decided it was Troy itself, for no good archaeological reason. He also found elsewhere a beaten gold face which he called the mask of Agamemnon. But Schliemann was an unprincipled treasure hunter, a sort of rogue Indiana Jones and nobody accepts his theories today. Agamemnon was overlord of the Greek city states, but he, the Spartan king Menelaus, the Trojan king Priam, in fact the city of Troy itself come to us from Homer's *Iliad*, which is, in fact, an early novel. There were certainly wars between the

Greeks and the Persians which went on intermittently for centuries, but there was no single Trojan war.

The film *300 Spartans* (1962) was a little more like it, but only a little. It was remade in 2007 as *300* in which the star was not Gerard Butler as King Leonidas, but CGI, complete with more fake blood and artificial pecs than anybody knew what to do with. The original, with not very accurate Greek hoplite armour, deals with the heroic stand of 300 Spartans at the Battle of Thermopylae in 480 BC. Richard Egan is suitably stoic as Leonidas and we see the phalanx wedge formation of the Spartans, the most formidable military force in the fifth century BC, slicing through the Persian ranks of King Xerxes I. There is no hint of the homosexual pairings among the Spartans (lovers fighting side by side); 1962 may have been the early Sixties, but the decade wasn't as swinging as all that. Both versions of the film are a bit of a cop out, of course, and it's not their fault. There may have been only 300 Spartans, but they had almost 10,000 allies with them at Thermopylae and might well have won. But mankind has never let things like figures and facts get in the way of a good story – 'Go, stranger, to Sparta; tell/that here, defending her great laws, we fell.' Which, incidentally, spawned another fictional movie set in a different war – Vietnam – called *Go Tell the Spartans* (1978).

The greatest military figure to come out of Greece in the pre-Christian era was not Greek at all; he was Macedonian. Alexander the Great was the son of the one-eyed Philip and both men had dreams of destroying the Persian empire (today's Iran and Iraq). Alexander was a boy wonder, achieving astonishing military successes and carving an empire from Egypt to India. His death, perhaps by poisoning, at the age of 32, ended the pipe dream as fast as it had developed. Someone of Alexander's brilliance and scope is very difficult to deal with on the big screen and he has been badly served. Richard Burton in *Alexander the Great* (1956) doesn't impress in a blond wig and the script is a mess. Critic Andrew Sarris wrote, '[Director Robert] Rossen has aimed for greatness and lost honourably.' *Alexander* (2004) with Colin Farrell in the title role, is even worse – how can you trust a man whose eyebrows are a different colour from his hair and a Macedonian with an Irish accent? Both films suffer from the fact that they cannot leave out the supernatural of the Greek gods, whom the Greeks believed interfered constantly in people's lives. Alexander may have believed all that, but we don't and the end result is rather silly.

The Grandeur That Was Rome

As far as film-makers and their audiences are concerned, the ancient world comes to an end with the fall of the Roman empire. The film of that name (1964) is one of the worst in the cinema's long attempt to get things right. No one has ever really explained why a small settlement along the river Tiber in central Italy could grow to dominate the world in such a way that it still resonates today. Sensibly, film-makers take the story a step at a time.

The Punic Wars of the third century BC saw Rome at the heart of a power struggle with Carthage, in what is today Tunisia. The Carthaginian leader who nearly toppled Rome was Hannibal, famous for attacking the city from the north (he should have come in from the south-west) and crossing the Alps with elephants, animals largely unknown in Italy. Military experts still argue over how useful these animals were. They are unpredictable and the African breed is less biddable than the Indian. Even so, the sheer terror of seeing them unleashed on a battlefield was probably enough. It was, perhaps, unfortunate that the 1960 *Hannibal* was Victor Mature, a bit long in the tusk by now and he fails to convince. It didn't help either that the star was famously afraid of animals, even horses, so all the elephants are blue screen superimpositions and it shows. No wonder the Romans eventually beat him!

A movie of an altogether different calibre was Stanley Kubrick's *Spartacus*, produced in the same year as *Hannibal*. The man was a slave, probably from Thrace (today's Bulgaria) who became a gladiator and led a slave revolt (one of three in a thirty-year period) against Rome in 71 BC. The story had a universal appeal – a wronged, humiliated man of the people standing up against one of the most brutal societies in history in the dying days of the Roman republic. Karl Marx and Friedrich Engels, co-writers of the *Communist Manifesto* (1848) regarded Spartacus as the greatest man in ancient history. Such was his reputation that in Germany after the First World War, a group of socialists called themselves the Spartacus League and opposed the rising Right of the Nazi party. The author of the best-known novel about him, Howard Fast, was a Communist too and the film's screenplay was written by yet another writer of the Left, Dalton Trumbo (see Chapter 11).

This was at a time when America was obsessed with 'Reds under the bed', a nonsensical notion that the entire country was being undermined by Socialist ideals. In a mad crusade led by Senator Joe McCarthy of Wisconsin, many Hollywood players on both sides of the camera lined up to accuse their Left-wing colleagues. The House Un-American Activities Committee put these people on trial live on television.

Typical of the Right's attitude to *Spartacus* was that of the gossip columnist Hedda Hopper, who made and broke Hollywood careers. 'It has acres of dead people, more blood and gore than you ever saw in your whole life … That story was sold to Universal from a book written by a Communist [Fast] and the screenscript was written by a Communist [Trumbo] so don't go and see it.'

People ignored her in their thousands. In Hollywood's internecine squabbling, Yul Brynner had decided on making a Spartacus movie and had a budget of $5.5 million. Not to be outdone, Kirk Douglas sent him a telegram. 'We are spending five million, five hundred thousand and two dollars on Spartacus. Your move, Kirk.' Douglas' venture cost $12 million in the end. 'Who cares?' he asked the press. 'If *Spartacus* is a thrilling experience, twelve million is a drop in the bucket. If not, twelve dollars is too much.'

It was certainly thrilling. With 'early Greek style' music by Alex North and charismatic leads from Douglas as the gladiator-slave and

Laurence Olivier as the haughty Roman general, Marcus Licinius Crassus, it has rightly been acclaimed as one of the best historical films of all time. Douglas chose the 31-year-old Stanley Kubrick as director – they had worked together previously on the First World War film *Paths of Glory* (1957). Two stars who provided superb supporting roles were Peter Ustinov and Charles Laughton. Ustinov quipped at dinner parties, 'You have to be careful not to act too well' in a Kirk Douglas movie. He nevertheless acted most of the others off the screen. As the real-life trainer of Capua's gladiatorial school, however, he lacked realism. Every part of Ustinov's being suggested that he didn't know one end of a sword from another. Laughton said that he 'glanced at the script. Really, a piece of shit,' but he played the fictional senator Gracchus anyway. There were 1,400 pages of rewrites and Kubrick's first cut was six hours long.

In terms of history, 'Mrs Spartacus' was almost certainly a Thracian slave, like her husband, and was allegedly an acolyte of the cult of Bacchus, later outlawed by Rome for its flagrant sexuality. In the movie, she was the rather more chaste Jean Simmons, playing Varinia, a British slave girl. As for Crassus, he was not the brilliant general outlined in the film, but a devious (and obscenely rich) politician anxious to control Rome before they had emperors. Fighting was simply part of the job and he let Spartacus get away from him, despite building a wooden wall across the whole Italian peninsula.

The gladiatorial scenes are excellent, even if the actual arena at Capua, which I visited in 2005, was far more spectacular than Kubrick's 'wooden O'. Two things stand out in the film. First is the automaton-like precision of the Roman legions on the battlefield. In an age before CGI, the extras move as one, fronting their shields, levelling their spears and advancing at a steady pace in absolute silence, exactly as they did. Second, the magical scene in which Spartacus' defeated army has the chance to live if they surrender Spartacus himself. Before Douglas can get to his feet, Tony Curtis beats him to it. Another rebel joins him, and another, and another, all of them shouting, 'I am Spartacus!' It became a catchphrase and T-shirt logo for years afterwards.

For the historical record, although the Romans tried to downplay being beaten by a slave, Spartacus destroyed six armies sent against him before Crassus finally got lucky. Whereas in the film, Douglas' aim is to reach the Alps and so gain freedom for himself and his people, the real Spartacus turned back from the mountains, presumably because the lure of loot and plunder from Roman villas proved too great. An estimated 6,000 of the rebel slaves were crucified along the Appian Way into Rome, no doubt to 'discourage the others' (to misquote Voltaire). All accounts agree that Spartacus was not among them; he had been killed in battle.

A minor character in *Spartacus* was played by John Gavin, who said, of working with Olivier and Laughton, 'I received the best set of free dramatic lessons in show business history.' He was playing the young Julius Caesar (and was *far* too good-looking for the emperor-wannabe, called 'the greatest Roman of them all').

Which leads us neatly (and chronologically) into the imperial Roman period which began with civil war and violence, centring at first on Egypt. This was not the Egypt of the Nile and the old dynasties, but a 'modern' state under Roman control. For the city on the Tiber, Egypt was a breadbasket, providing the corn that Rome itself could not supply. It was important, therefore, to keep its ruler, Cleopatra, sweet. The Romans hated her, as they hated all powerful women. Roman society was completely patristic; the only women venerated were the Vestal Virgins, a group of Mother Theresas whose sole function was to maintain a sacred flame to the gods. Cleopatra was called *monstrum fatale* (deadly monster) by virtue of her sex alone. And Rome, slavishly copied centuries later by Hollywood, made sex what she was all about. She was Greek, not Egyptian, and wore her (light brown) hair in cornrows, the latest Roman style. She spoke umpteen languages and owned the biggest library in the world at Alexandria. None of this is apparent in the movies. From Theda Bara in 1917 to Elizabeth Taylor in 1963, she wears over-the-top Egyptian make-up and a black wig.

The sets of all the *Cleopatra* films (the central one, time-wise, was the 1934 version) were all sumptuous with colossal fans, hundreds of black slaves and as much nudity as the censor would allow. Theda Bara played the last pharaoh as a vamp, smouldering at the camera. Cecil B. DeMille's effort seventeen years later featured the latest heart-throb, Claudette Colbert. She wore the wig, of course, to disguise her 1930s hair and her famous gilded barge featured heavily. The 1963 version outshone anything that had gone before, then the most expensive film ever made. The director was Joseph L. Mankiewicz. The barge was there again, actually floating this time and it gave off pink smoke from petal-strewn fires on deck.

Unfortunately, one of the most spectacular scenes in the film, the queen's entry into Rome, with Cleopatra sitting with her little son Caesarion between the paws of a huge sphinx dragged by slaves, almost certainly never happened. Julius Caesar had *perhaps* met Cleopatra in Egypt (where she did *not* appear before him wrapped in a carpet, whatever Hollywood tells you) and she certainly had a son (Caesarion) by him. If she came to Rome at all, it was under the cover of darkness and she was secreted away in one of the general's villas. To Rome, she was the 'serpent of the Nile' and completely unwelcome.

The script was witty. When Richard Burton, playing Cleopatra's next lover, Marcus Antonius (Shakespeare's Mark Antony) says, 'I have a fondness for almost all things Greek,' the queen comes back with 'As an almost all Greek thing myself...' But the cost of the production, the tantrums of Taylor and the very public affair between her and Burton dwarfed everything else, some contending that these things alone spelt the end of the epic Hollywood film.

Other films about Caesar are almost all Shakespearean and, historically, can be ignored. Placed on a unique plinth by dramatists and literature experts, the poet from Stratford-upon-Avon was no historian, content to raid classical tittle-tattle and dream symbolism, with no concerns for accuracy.

Talking of which, *Carry On Cleo* (1964)! There were thirty-three *Carry On* films, of the dreadful, cliché-ridden 'so bad they're good' type that only the British film industry would have the brass neck to pull off. Even there, unpleasantness had to intrude. Spoof posters based on the Burton-Taylor film were used, but had to be withdrawn when 20th Century Fox objected. Amanda Barry was Cleopatra, Sid James was Marc Antony and Kenneth Williams was a camp Julius Caesar. None of it, of course, was meant to be taken seriously, but who can forget the murder of Caesar, when Williams rushes around with a dagger in his chest, shouting 'Infamy! Infamy! They've all got it infamy!' and the Roman army marching to the shouts of the drill sergeant, 'Sinister, dexter! Sinister, dexter! [left, right!]'?

All of which brings us full circle, in a way, to the Bible.

King of Kings

A colleague of mine once argued with me that there is more evidence for the existence of Jesus Christ than there is for the Roman invasion of Britain. In that, he was demonstrably wrong, in that Christ appears in one source only – the New Testament. The fact that there are four versions in that – Matthew, Mark, Luke and John – only muddies the waters further. Hollywood, however, has been remarkably consistent. In all versions dealing with the subject, Christ is 'King of kings and Lord of lords' and in nearly all versions he follows the Victorian artistic tradition of a tall, good-looking man with a beard, blond hair and blue eyes; everything, in fact, that a Galilean Jew of the first century was not.

George MacDonald Fraser recounts one of the problems with the life of Christ. Actor Alan Badel was due to star in a Biblical epic but was unhappy with the script relating to Christ. The producer, an unnamed Hollywood mogul, shuffled uncomfortably and said, 'Well, Alan, we thought Jesus sounded just a bit cocky in there.' There was a vague tradition, which may be no more than folklore, that it was a sort of sacrilege to show Christ's face. Jesus as background was the angle in *Ben-Hur* (see below). We see a vague figure wandering in the hills above Nazareth. We see him delivering the sermon on the mount, from behind. In one of the most memorable scenes in *any* historical film, a centurion taking Judah Ben-Hur to imprisonment in the galleys, is confronted by Jesus, offering the prisoner water. The expression on the centurion's face (there is no dialogue) has to be seen to be believed. He doesn't know what he's looking at; he only knows he cannot use his usual brutality here. And we see Christ again on his way to Calvary and on the cross. The hair is auburn; the face an enigma.

Earlier film-makers had no such qualms. We know that the earliest movies of the life of Christ were taken from the Oberammergau cycle of stage plays. The first was released in 1912, eclipsed by Griffith's *Intolerance* four years later. DeMille's *King of Kings* (1927) had H.B. Warner as Jesus, which was remade in 1961 with Jeffery Hunter in the title role, probably the most handsome actor to take on the part. Critics weren't generally impressed with *King of Kings*; it was known in the trade as 'I was a teenage Jesus' and the comeback by director Nicholas Ray probably made matters worse – '[critics] were not hip enough with the times of Christ.' Interestingly, the 1927 version was described by Mordaunt Hall of *The New York Times* as 'the most impressive of all motion pictures'. Clearly, audiences didn't get out much in the 1920s, despite being able to 'go to the pictures' on a regular basis. Whereas most Jesuses appear in a holy white robe, Hunter wore scarlet in some scenes. Hollywood has an obsession with red in ancient movies, especially for Roman tunics. Archaeologically, cloth doesn't survive well, but the few fragments we have of 2,000-year-old military uniforms imply that the usual colour was off-white.

Four years later, *The Greatest Story Ever Told* saw Max von Sydow as Christ, probably the least authentic-looking rendition of the son of God. Fine actor though von Sydow was, the black wig and beard did nothing for authenticity; neither did the location. Ignoring the Middle

East (for reasons of cost or politics?) director George Stevens filmed the whole thing in the American west on the grounds that Utah looked more like Palestine than Palestine! The script was dreadful, perhaps echoing Alan Badel's complaint. How much of the *real* Jesus is in the various versions of the Bible is highly debatable, yet movie-makers have been loath to tinker with 'God's spell' more than they have to. This was the film in which John Wayne played the centurion in charge of the crucifixion (a punishment usually reserved for slaves) and, according to cinema foaflore (urban legend) was told to improve his one line – 'Truly, he is the son of God' – by putting more awe into it. Consummate actor that Wayne was, he came back with, 'Aw, truly he is the son of God.' And if you believe that, you'll believe anything.

Critic John Simon went for the jugular. 'God is unlucky in *The Greatest Story Ever Told*. His only begotten son turns out to be a bore ... the photography is inspired mainly by Hallmark Cards ... As for pacing, the picture foes not let you forget a single second of its four hours.' Perhaps Mr Simon was lucky – the original ran for twenty minutes longer.

The Robe (1953) told the story from a different angle. There were authentic touches – the catacombs in Rome, the imperial villa, the slave-market, but the whole thing was arguably ruined by the now de rigueur celestial choirs (which is of course, Church music tradition and post-dates Christ by hundreds of years). The plotline is based on the effect that Christ's robe has on people around him (à la the Holy Grail). Richard Burton was the centurion hero (intended originally for Tyrone Power) and Victor Mature's Barabbas was to have been played by Burt Lancaster.

Probably the best film to be set in Christ's lifetime is *Ben-Hur* (1959) itself the third remake of the novel written in 1880 by Lew Wallace, New Mexico's state governor and American Civil War hero who had the unenviable task of coping with a tearaway called Henry McCarty, better known to Hollywood as Billy the Kid (see Chapter 8). Bearing in mind the obscene expenses – and profits – surrounding Biblical epics,

Wallace told his wife in 1880 that he hoped *Ben-Hur* might make him $35 a year! His descendants sold the film rights for millions. In 1926, MGM released the second movie version (the first was in 1907) and it cost an unprecedented $4 million and took nearly a year to shoot. Ramon Navarro, the up-and-coming heart-throb, was Judah, and doe-eyed May McAvoy was Esther, his love interest. The high spot (as in the remake) was the chariot race, filmed by forty cameras simultaneously, some mounted on cars that kept pace with the horses. There were accidents galore and at the end of the sequence, clearly dead horses lie among the wreckage of the chariots.

Charlton Heston, after his success as Moses three years earlier, was chosen for the 1959 remake of *Ben-Hur*. Others in the running were Rock Hudson, Marlon Brando and Burt Lancaster; any of them would have been terrible. His character, like his nemesis, Messala (Stephen Boyd), was fictional. In fact, apart from Quintus Arrius (Jack Hawkins) who may have been based by Wallace on Lucius Arruntius, naval commander in the years shortly before Christ, the only historical character other than Christ (apart from a brief appearance of Tiberius) is the Roman governor of Judea, Pontius Pilate (Frank Thring) and even he is dubious. He was certainly prefect in the area from 26 to 36 and put down various riots by force. His role in the trial of Jesus – 'and what is truth?' he asks – comes only from the Gospel of John. Thring plays him excellently as a world-weary politician, rather bored by the whole thing; he has seen dangerous, wandering Jews before.

It's not the film-makers' fault, but the whole premise of slaves being chained below decks as oarsmen is incorrect (Wallace gets it wrong). Oarsmen were highly trained members of a military team and would have been treated accordingly.

Heston's *Ben-Hur* was filmed in Italy and most of the leads were British actors. The dazzling chariot race (which still grips me after an estimated twenty-six viewings!) was done superbly under the direction of Second Unit leader Yakima Canutt. Heston had to do his own driving, as did Boyd and only in the *really* dangerous bits were stunt doubles used. Rome's real charioteers handled their four horses in the *quadriga* with eight reins; Canutt's version was cleverly reduced to two. Two teams of greys were used, one for the race itself, another to stand docilely in Sheik Ilderim's tent as Heston says goodnight to them. There were 15,000 extras watching the race and at the end, there was no direction; they all swarmed all over the place – their local hero had won. Next time you watch it, the Arab who picks up Messala's helmet is under no direction – it's entirely spontaneous.

In case director William Wyler was accused of religious bias, he had three historical research staff – a Protestant, a Catholic and a Hebrew scholar. Interestingly, bearing in mind earlier ancient world movies, there were no evil women in the story. Israeli actress Haya Harareet was lovely, but the critics didn't like her – 'Loved Ben, hated her.'

More recent 'tales of the Christ' haven't been that successful. Some audiences were outraged by Willem Dafoe's *The Last Temptation of Christ* (1988) because it showed Jesus as just a man, wanting more of a quiet, conventional life than the one God had mapped out for him. The oddest thing about this film was the casting of singer David Bowie as Pontius Pilate. Mel Gibson's ultra-violent *The Passion of Christ* (2004) seemed to serve no purpose at all, and yet, in true Hollywood tradition, there is a sequel in production, *The Passion of Christ – Resurrection*. By the time *Passion* came out, Gibson had blotted his copybook in Hollywood in a variety of ways and critics went for him. Richard Eyre of *The Guardian* wrote that the movie was 'made for zealots by a zealot; it's propaganda'. But it did well at the box office and was interesting in that part of the dialogue was in Aramaic, the language that Christ would have spoken.

Quo Vadis (1951) is rare among Hollywood films as the title is in Latin (it means, 'Where are you going?'). Rather pompously, the studio announced, 'In making this film, MGM feel privileged to add something of permanent value to the cultural treasure house of mankind.' Somebody else put it better – 'Ancient Rome is going to the dogs, Robert Taylor is going to the lions and Peter Ustinov is going crazy!' Patricia Laffan was the hapless Poppaea, mistress of the emperor

Nero (Ustinov), whom he eventually kicked to death. Leo Genn was a worldly-wise Gaius Petronius, saddled with the problem of the sadistic narcissist who ran Rome, murdered his own mother and eventually killed himself. Everybody else is fictional. Ustinov comes close to parody as the emperor, but as the historical record describes him as being so over-the-top, this was probably the right way to play him.

Salome may appear as a bit of an afterthought, but in fact there have been a number of films about her. As usual, she is portrayed as a femme fatale seductress (see Sheba, Cleopatra etc.) with various reincarnations pushing the censorship boundaries as far as they dared. She was the visceral opponent of John the Baptist, the precursor of Christ, famous for demanding his head on a platter. Whether she was a real character is open to serious doubt. Her first bizarre outing, *Salome*, was in 1923 from the play by Oscar Wilde and featuring the Bohemian artwork of Aubrey Beardsley. Most people were appalled by Wilde, Beardsley and Salome, so they made a great mix. Rita Hayworth played her in 1953, dancing to bring about the Baptist's downfall. Incidentally, the famous seven veils had by no means disappeared when the dance was over and the gorgeous Rita remained as fully clothed as ever. *Salome's Last Dance* (1987) – and let's hope it is – went back to the Wilde original, with the great Oscar watching his own play performed by prostitutes in a brothel. I can't help feeling that the historical dimension has been lost somehow, on more than one level.

The Light Goes Out – the end of Rome

After the Republic collapsed, Rome returned to its age of kings, except they were now called emperors. The problem with dictatorships, as we have seen in our times, is that they are wholly dependent on the personality of one man. If that man is Caligula or Nero, the system falls apart. Towards the end of the Roman empire, in the fifth century AD, the reigns of emperors could be measured in months, sometimes weeks. The reasons for the fall of Rome are complicated and are still being argued about by historians today, but the insanity and/or incompetence of the 'boss' has to feature somewhere.

Nero saw himself as an artist, writing dreadful music which he played on his lyre and was eventually forced to do what Romans considered fine and noble, that is commit suicide. Naturally, he has been played on the big screen by Charles Laughton as well as Peter Ustinov.

Before him chronologically came Gaius Julius Caesar Germanicus, better known to us as Caligula. The nickname means 'little boots' in reference to the fact that he reviewed troops who wore *caligae* when he was 5 years old. He hated the name. He was also bald as an adult, but with such a copious amount of body hair that he was referred to (behind his hairy back) as 'the goat'. The 'g' word (actually, the 'c' word as the Latin for goat is *caper*) was banned at court. Although accusations of his depravity have no doubt been exaggerated, he was a pretty nasty character and there were attempts to portray this in *Caligula* (1980). The film ran into censorship problems, leading to what Tom Dewe Mathews has called 'an historical mess ... reduced to ... a staccato farce'.

Caligula tries to follow the original account of the emperor's life as recorded by the Roman historian Suetonius. Financial backing came from the publishers of *Penthouse*, which probably says it all, and they insisted that Gore Vidal's rather tame script be embellished with gratuitous nudity and violent sex. Malcolm McDowell (who looks nothing like Suetonius' description of Caligula) spends the entire film looking rather bemused by it all. The removal of various scenes by the British Board of Film Censors (now the British Board of Film Classification) took place under strict secrecy and resulted in ten and a half minutes ending up on the cutting room floor, including a face wash in a bowl of semen, sex with a horse (the emperor's favourite grey, Cincinnatus, whom he made a consul) and toddlers sucking bottles in suggestive poses. None of this, by the way, is in Suetonius!

No doubt, Nero and Caligula were seen as role models by Commodus (technically Lucius Aelius Aurelius Commodus) played in the two films that feature him by Christopher Plummer and Joaquin

Phoenix. By now, it was the AD 80s (1964 and 2000 in Hollywood terms) and one of the best emperors of Rome, the philosopher Marcus Aurelius (Alec Guinness and Richard Harris respectively) is murdered by his psychopathic son. The vast set for Rome's forum was made in Spain and dwarfed anything that had gone before. The fortifications of Vindobona (today's Vienna) are good too. Guinness was excellent as Aurelius, full of commanding presence, but you just know the end is in sight because he is buried in a snowstorm (surely, it *never* snowed in ancient Rome) and the usually hardy Romans are wearing leggings, which no Hollywood extra would be seen dead in. Sophia Loren's Lucilla (Commodus' sister) is played as a radiant heroine, whereas she was every bit as nasty as the new emperor. The remake fails a little, not because Phoenix is less nasty than Plummer, but that Richard Harris just doesn't have Guinness' gravitas (itself a Latin word, of course).

The remake of *The Fall of the Roman Empire* is *Gladiator* (2000), grafting on the fictional General Maximus (there was one, but he lived two centuries later) played by Russell Crowe. 'So entertaining,' wrote Peter Bradshaw of *The Guardian*, 'and carried off with such chutzpah, you forgive the odd absurdity and wonder where this genre has been all your life.' For those of us of a certain age, the genre has never left us and we can see the cracks in the plaster. *Gladiator* was hugely overrated. Maximus' 'unleash hell' at the beginning of a battle against the beastly Hun (nineteen centuries before they became that!) has been lifted dozens of times since. Incidentally, the battle in the dark and impenetrable forests north of the Roman frontier was actually filmed in Surrey and the barbarians sounded like African tribesmen – their ominous chanting was pinched wholesale from the soundtrack of *Zulu* (see Chapter 7).

The makers of both versions of Rome's collapse were a little bit previous. Commodus was strangled in his bath ('Hooray' they would have cheered had either film been released to the old Saturday matinees for children) in 192 and Rome had another three centuries to die slowly. When it did, the light of civilization allegedly went out and the world – and Hollywood – were ready for the Dark Ages.

Chapter 2

The Dark Ages: From the Fall of Rome to Alfred the Great

With the fall of Rome's empire, sandals disappeared, but swords stayed. Most of them just got longer! No historian today uses the term Dark Ages (fifth to tenth centuries) because research over the last century has uncovered the richness and culture of various societies in that time frame. These are not inferior to those of Rome; they are merely different.

By the fourth century, the Roman empire was no longer what it had been. The late emperors are eminently forgettable, by and large, and the empire itself was split into two, with Rome as the western epicentre and Constantinople (today's Istanbul) as the eastern. Increasingly mobile nomadic peoples such as the Huns, the Vandals and the Goths had got the measure of the legions by now and were able to outmanoeuvre them. Unaccountably, an obscure Middle Eastern sect, Christianity, became the accepted religion of the dying empire, replacing the bewildering array of gods and goddesses that had characterized Rome in its heyday. The tribes who collectively destroyed Rome were outside of all this and the Romans dismissed them as barbarians (from the Latin *barbari*, the bearded ones).

The era has not been tackled extensively by Hollywood or any other film culture. The emperor who made Christianity acceptable was Constantine, elected *imperator* by the VI Legion at York, in Rome's Britannia province. His mother was a rabid Christian but the emperor was more ambivalent. Cornel Wilde played him in *Constantine and the Cross* (1961) and the audience was asked to believe that he really did see a flaming cross in the sky at the Battle of the Milvian Bridge – 'In this sign, conquer.' It wasn't until the fifth century, however, that the rot really set in. The Huns were a nomadic herding people but their cavalry was legendary. The first to use stirrups in battle, they literally rode rings around the Romans, still wobbling on their four-pronged saddles and hoping for the best.

The Sign of the Pagan (1954) is dismissed by Halliwell as an 'historic horse opera, rather cheaply done'. But then, Halliwell is dismissive of most films. In this case, however, he was probably right. The movie's central character is Attila, one of the many 'scourges of God' who didn't like Christians. The film's poster trumpeted, 'Against his ruthless pagan lusts – the power of a woman's love.' The love interest, provided by Ludmilla Tchérina as Honoria, the emperor's sister, is pure fiction, as is Attila's daughter's fling with a Roman general (Jeff Chandler). It came as no surprise to audiences at the time that Honoria was an expert exotic dancer (as you are, when you are the emperor's sister) who entertained the fur-clad Huns who clearly had never seen anything like it. Attila himself was Jack Palance, whose hard features had a vague oriental look about them. I sat transfixed as a 7-year-old watching him drinking wine from a goblet made from a human skull. Wow! How bad can a man get?

The real Attila, who may have been a dwarf, had extraordinary organizational powers, persuading other tribes to follow him west to the Rhine and east to China. The Huns were essentially a fast-moving cavalry army and couldn't handle sieges (which is where Jeff Chandler got the better of them). Despite that, Attila's army occupied much of northern Italy and were bought off from attacking Rome by Pope Leo I. The Hun leader died in 453, probably from a brain haemorrhage, amidst rumours of poison. Another stab at the scourge of God appeared the previous year with the equally savage-looking Anthony Quinn in *Attila the Hun* (1953), actually a dubbed Italian venture.

The trend among film-makers drifted, in the late 1950s, to those epic adventurers and marauders, the Vikings. The name means sea rovers and fits perfectly with a hardy northern people who sailed west as far as America and Canada, and east as far as Russia. Archaeologists have found the foundations of Viking long houses at Aisne-aux-Meadows in Newfoundland and the runic carvings of the Varangian Guard (the Viking bodyguard of the Byzantine emperor) can still be seen (in theory) in the mosque that used to be the church of Hagia Sophia in Istanbul.

As with the Bible, many of the characters who are Viking heroes are fictional and appear only in the sagas, yarns compiled largely by Greenlander Snorri Sturlusson in the thirteenth century. We know that Leif Erikson reached America. We know that Guthrum was defeated by Alfred, King of Wessex. After that, it gets a little hazy. Real Viking leaders, like Gorm and Erik Bloodaxe, even the very late Harald Hardrada (the harsh ruler) have been ignored entirely by Hollywood.

Enter Kirk Douglas. Two years before *Spartacus*, the cleft-chinned ragman's son christened Issur Demsky, morphed into the fictional Einar, complete with blond, spiky hair, one eye (eventually) and a lot of attitude, in *The Vikings* (1958). Einar's father in the film, however, was Ragnar (Ernest Borgnine) based on Ragnar Lothbrok (hairy breeches) who appears in the sagas with such authority that he probably was real (see Chapter 12). Asked why no one had made a film about the Vikings before, Douglas answered in two words – 'the weather'. Location shooting in the Norwegian fjords was a nightmare, with fog and driving rain. In fact, those two words might explain the famous Viking wanderlust in the first place. While Denmark is relatively warm, with flat country and good farming land, Norway and Sweden are craggy, soil-less and extremely cold.

The longships used in the film were so well made that they were actually sailed across the Atlantic after the wrap, just to prove that it could be done. There were only three of them, however, which made Douglas' full-scale invasion of England a little unlikely. Archaeologists now know that even the largest longships could carry only about 200 men. *The Vikings* had some nice touches – the drunken Valhalla-style feasts, Einar losing his eye to Tony Curtis' hawk, Ragnar leaping into a pit of starving wolves – but it is ruined by two things. Curtis has his hand cut off and walks around with a stump that is the least realistic piece of maiming in the history of cinema. And in the final assault, the Vikings attack a full-blown Medieval castle, with stone keep, ramparts and curtain walls, that would not be built until 300 years after the story is set. The only genuine historical character in the movie is Aelle, the king of Northumbria in the 860s, played by the perpetually slimy Frank Thring. In the sagas, Aelle has Ragnar thrown into a pit of snakes, whereas film-makers know that snarling wolves make for a far more exciting finish. Incidentally (spoiler alert) Tony Curtis kills Kirk Douglas, only for the ragman's son to retaliate two years later in *Spartacus*!

At first glance, *The Thirteenth Warrior* (1999) looks like pure Hollywood hokum and much of it is, a sort of *Magnificent Seven* meets *Godzilla*, but it could have been very different. The hero is Ahmed ibn Fadlan (Antonio Banderas) who was emissary to the khalif of Baghdad in 921. One of the most striking accounts of Viking ceremonial (other than the famous burial in a burning ship) comes from his account of his visit to the Vikings of Russia (the Rus themselves were invaders) in which a slave girl was strangled and stabbed so that her soul could accompany a chieftain to Valhalla. Cross-cultural examples like this in history are rare, but the moment vanishes in yet another 'sword and sorcery' movie.

Viking raids on Saxon England were aimed largely at defenceless monasteries and churches, the marauders vanishing into the sea-mist in their longships before help could arrive. 'There were immense flashes of lightning and fiery dragons were seen flying in the air,' wrote the Anglo-Saxon chronicler in 793, '... the raiding of the heathen men miserably devastated God's church in Lindisfarne through looting and slaughter ...' And by 980, they were back, in larger numbers than before and they weren't going away.

Saxon England was actually seven different kingdoms and the Vikings could pick them off one at a time. That was before Alfred the Great. The King of Wessex whose Victorian statue still stands in his capital at Winchester, reorganized the army, built a navy to fight the

Vikings at sea and stopped the entire country being overwhelmed by the Northmen. He defeated the Viking king Guthrum and forced him to become a Christian. He held the Vikings to a frontier across England beyond which was the Danelaw and there would be no more buying-off the enemy with the Danegeld, an annual cash tribute. He also defended the Church and his court became renowned for its learning and culture. A king like that deserved better than *Alfred the Great* (1969) in which a miscast David Hemmings played the hero. Michael York played a suitably surly Guthrum and Baird Searles excuses the flop that the film was by claiming that ninth-century England was small scale and had no fripperies, but that merely buys into the outdated notion that the 'Dark Ages' were drab and poverty stricken. Hemmings had a period face (he was excellent in *The Charge of the Light Brigade* (see Chapter 7) but not *this* period and he seemed a little lost in it all.

Before we leave scenes of Scandinavian slaughter, we should take a look at *The Viking Queen* (1966). The poster read 'See! Bladed chariots of death! Men roasted alive in the cages of Hell! Mighty legions of Rome! Barbarism of the mad emperor! Savage rites of the Iceni!' Confused by all this? I know I am. The film was about Boudicca, whose tribe the Iceni was, who rebelled against Rome in 60AD. She did not have knives on her chariot wheels, the mad emperor was Nero but he had nothing to do with Boudicca's revolt and the idea of roasting people in wicker cages comes from only one source and is probably not true. Incidentally, the Vikings would take another eight centuries to arrive in Britain.

The bottom line is that everybody was longing for the Middle Ages!

Chapter 3

The Middle Ages: From Hastings to Bosworth

'Yonder lies duh castle of my fodduh.'
The Black Shield of Falworth (1954)

'War, war; that's all you think about, Dick Plantagenet!'
King Richard and the Crusaders (1954)

'Let him be, you rattlepate!'
Knights of the Round Table (1953)

'Azim? What name is that? Irish?'
'Moorish!'
Robin Hood: Prince of Thieves (1991)

O f all the epochs in world history, Hollywood seems least comfortable with the Middle Ages. The *'Medium Aevum'* (Middle Age, note the singular) runs from the eleventh to the fifteenth century, although, inevitably, Medieval ideas continued in a variety of forms for much longer. All the quotations above, from the frankly awful to the just-about-acceptable, illustrate one of the problems of making historical movies – how to handle the dialogue.

Throwing in a smattering of 'thees' and 'thous' doesn't actually cut it. We have the problem of the written word versus the spoken. We know, for example, what Geoffrey Chaucer's poetry *said* when he wrote his *Canterbury Tales*; but how did it *sound*? Were the words he used in them the same as those he used when talking to his wife and children? To the man who stabled his horse? To the king he served as poet laureate? The answer is, we don't know. So a huge number of

Hollywood scriptwriters have had to leap virtually blindfolded into a world of which they know little, while at the same time telling a story that we can understand. The world of film ought to be universal, but it isn't for that reason. The one-reelers of the silent screen (especially slapstick comedies) worked because the gags were visual; you didn't need to read the cards to know what was going on. With the advent of sound, barriers went up.

My vision of the Middle Ages begins with one of the best films ever made – Samuel Bronston's *El Cid* (1961). The hero, Rodrigo Diaz of Bivar in Castile, was largely unknown outside Spain before Charlton Heston got caught up in Bronston's epic plans. The nickname comes from the Arabic *al-sayed*, the lord; fitting, in that in Rodrigo's eleventh century, two-thirds of Spain was Al-Andalus, under Muslim control. The Cid is part of the story of the *Reconquista*, the reconquest of the peninsula by the Christians, which took five centuries to complete. As always, Heston, in the title role, immersed himself in the background. 'There's a hell of a lot more in the man than is in the script,' he wrote in his journal for the end of July 1960, and as somebody who has done the same research (and then some!) I agree. Heston hit the nail on the head when he wrote, '[The Cid] seems to have been nearly as often a bad man as a good one.' He was right, but Hollywood, as we've noted, doesn't make movies about ambivalent people. El Cid had to wear a white hat. And if he couldn't do that because of the demands of eleventh-century costume, a white horse would do. The real Cid had such an animal – Babieca, the booby – and for the film, Heston rode two greys, both magnificent Barbs, the same breed that the Medieval original probably was.

Briefly told, Rodrigo Diaz was a minor *hidalgo* (nobleman) with estates near Burgos in northern Spain. In his day, the north was split into the individual kingdoms of Castile, Leon, Asturias and Aragon. He fought Christians as often as he fought Moors (hence Heston's good/bad comment above) and eventually took the city of Valencia (for himself or his king, Alfonso VI – experts argue), which he held for four years.

Nearly every character in the movie is real. The Cid's wife, Ximene (Sophia Loren), held on to Valencia as long as she could after his death before ending her days, allegedly, in a convent, standard practice at the time for widows. King Ferdinand (Ralph Truman) and his squabbling brood: Sancho (Gary Raymond); Alfonso (John Fraser); and Urraca (Geneviève Page) are more or less faithful to the historical record. The civilized emir Moutamin (Douglas Wilmer) who became the Cid's ally was a real-life character, as was the dodgy Al Kadir (played by – who better? – Frank Thring).

The problem for the film-makers is that the Cid's life is shrouded in legend dating from the twelfth century, much of it unsupported claptrap, and it is a credit to screenwriters Philip Yordan and Frederic Frank that they fell for none of it. Even so, Bronston's vision of 'a man's struggle for justice and peace' has more than a smidgeon of Hollywood hokum about it. Rodrigo Diaz was a man of war (he never lost a battle in his life) and his sense of justice would have very little to do with what we now think that means. Director Anthony Mann travelled all over Spain finding accurate location shots, but both Burgos cathedral and Medieval Valencia had to be studio-built because of the architectural progress of centuries. Valencia in particular is disappointing, as I discovered when I visited. There are still castles in Spain, but Valencia isn't one of them.

Seven thousand extras had to be clothed and armed for the battle sequences. The budget was $150,000 for set fittings such as tapestries and crucifixes. In the scene where Ximene and Rodrigo are reunited and find a mini-army of supporters waiting outside their barn, two of the extras had to be rushed to hospital with frostbite in the bitter cold of the Castilian high country.

The tournament between the Cid and Don Martin (Christopher Rhodes) the Aragonese champion, has rarely been equalled, but historically, it's a mess. The actual duel took place in the 1060s, but the horse bards (cloth coverings) are thirteenth century, the half-plate armour ditto and the murderous two-handed swords weren't invented for another 400 years! Even so, sit back and enjoy – you'll never see it bettered.

One thousand seven hundred horsemen from the Spanish army fought the battle on the beach under 'Valencia's' walls and huge mangonels (siege engines) were hauled into place. Leading the attack against them was Britain's Herbert Lom as the fanatical Berber chief Yussuf Ibn Teshufin (wrongly called Ben Yussuf in the credits). During rehearsals, an extraordinary thing happened. The work was underway early one morning and a shaft of sunlight broke over the shoulder of one of the Christian knights. This was exactly what Anthony Mann wanted. According to one of the Cid legends, Rodrigo was mortally wounded in this battle but left orders that his body should be mounted on horseback and should lead the attack the next day. The film follows this faithfully and the re-enacted scene, with the sun breaking over Heston's shoulder accompanied by the crash of an organ, is one of the best moments in any historical film.

In reality, of course, nothing like it ever happened. Spain's national hero, who today has statues erected to him as far away as New York, died of natural causes, peacefully in his bed.

We have to feel a little sorry for Macbeth. He is one of the real historical characters appropriated (and grossly distorted) by Shakespeare. The only portrayal of the Scots king of which I am aware is film versions of the Shakespeare play, which, as a study in the effects of murder and psychosis is brilliant, but he pinched the storyline from Hector Boethius and Ralph Holinshed and it has little bearing on history.

Macbeth Moray was a contemporary of the Cid, born in 1032. The man he allegedly killed, Duncan the Gracious, was nothing of the sort. He was heartless and incompetent and was killed in battle (at Pitgaeveny) against Macbeth who had been chosen by a council of Scottish nobles to replace him. For fourteen years, Macbeth ruled his country wisely, visiting Rome as all good Catholic Medieval kings did and dispensing justice. In 1064, Duncan's son Malcolm led an army against him and defeated Macbeth at Dunsinane. The Shakespearean notion about the moving wood at Birnham probably comes from the fact that Malcolm's army carried rowan sprigs in their helmets as a kind of uniform. Confusingly, both armies had foreign contingents – Englishmen, Vikings and even Normans. The battle was a draw but Macbeth was killed three years later after a guerrilla campaign. Revered and honoured, he was buried on the holy island of Iona.

Orson Welles produced a bizarre version of the Shakespeare play in 1948. He is universally regarded by almost everybody as a genius, but his various film performances are irritating (see Cesare Borgia in Chapter 4) and some of his direction is abysmal. The production was filmed in twenty-one days with papier mâché sets and incomprehensible Scottish accents. Move on quickly to a far better version (to which, predictably, Halliwell gives no stars), that starring Jon Finch in 1972. The now disgraced director Roman Polanski directed and tinkered with the script along with Kenneth Tynan and there is plenty of blood. But *Macbeth* is a bloody play; the word is used dozens of times by Shakespeare and the Japanese version is called *Throne of Blood* (to which Halliwell gives four stars!). *Hearing* soliloquies as narrative is far more effective than actors on stage speaking the lines and it works well. Francesca Annis was the deranged Lady Macbeth and Martin Shaw (never better) was Macbeth's lieutenant, Banquo.

'Will no one rid me of this troublesome priest?' Henry II is supposed to have asked in connection with his ex-friend turned pontificating pain, Thomas Becket. The position of the Catholic church in Europe in the Middle Ages was difficult. On the one hand, all churchmen and women, from cardinals downwards owed allegiance to the pope, God's vicar on earth. The fact that at various times there were two popes, one based in Rome, the other in Avignon, France, complicated matters still further. On the other hand, churchmen also owed allegiance to their king. As long as pope and king sang from the same hymn book, as it were, all was good. But when they didn't ... cue any number of Hollywood films based on the clash of ideologies.

It would be difficult to find two bigger egos than those of Henry II of England and Thomas Becket, Archbishop of Canterbury. Henry was the great-grandson of William the Conqueror, so he spoke no English and alienated himself still further from his people by marrying the feisty Eleanor of Aquitaine, thus holding estates in both England and France and contributing to the undying hatred between the two countries that lasted for centuries and hasn't quite gone away today.

Becket (1964) was based on Jean Anouilh's stage play, which makes for a lot of chat and not much action. Becket was Richard Burton, and the king Peter O'Toole. Too much is made of the Saxon-Norman thing (Becket was an Englishman) but the transformation of a hard-drinking, womanising and hard-hunting Becket into a holier-than-thou churchman is well done. The whole thing was hypocritical in the extreme. The Church was responsible for the moral tone of the country and Becket was letting his 'criminous clerks' get away, sometimes literally, with murder. As one of the greatest law-givers of the Middle Ages, Henry wasn't having any of that. There is no hard evidence that the king had Becket murdered, but he was certainly cut down by four knights whose names are recorded, while at prayer in his own cathedral. Guilty or not, Henry walked barefoot to Canterbury to be whipped by the monks as an act of penance. Becket went on to the almost predictable sainthood (his shrine became the most visited in England) and Henry went on (1968) to star in *The Lion in Winter*.

By now, it is 1183. The love affair between Henry and Eleanor is over but he keeps her walled up because he daren't let her go and the pair watch in horror over the brood of ghastly sons they have produced. Set in the breath-taking scenery around the castle of Chinon, the royals descend to spend a jolly Christmas together, along with the pushy young king of France (Timothy Dalton). The whole thing is about power politics, with everybody plotting against everyone else. They are literally at daggers drawn with Henry at one point preparing to execute his eldest son. The future Richard the Lionheart is played as a petulant bully – and homosexual – by Anthony Hopkins. Geoffrey – 'who mentions king and thinks of Geoffrey?' – is a snidely murderous John Castle, and John, gauche, useless and spotty, is Nigel Terry. Everybody was excellent in what was actually a twelfth-century soap and it was very funny. O'Toole growls his way through it, suitably padded to suggest late middle age and takes Katharine Hepburn's Eleanor off superbly with 'I taught you flute, lamb and lute, lamb.' She in turn tries to make light of what is a ghastly weekend with the priceless, 'What family doesn't have its little ups and downs?'

There are gaffes, of course – references to 'royal port', a kind of wine unknown at the time and an unlikely Christmas tree stands in the great hall. That said, *The Lion in Winter* is one of the best of the Medieval films.

Which brings us, chronologically, to the Crusades, which has produced more bad movies than good. The spread of militant Islam from the eighth century onwards, reaching southern France by 732 and dominating the whole of the Middle East and North Africa, was tolerated by the West for far too long. Not until the end of the eleventh century did open warfare break out. Christians like the Cid, had, it is true, been pushing back against the Islamic tide for years, but it was not until 1099, the year of the Cid's death, that a French knight, Godfrey de Bouillon, led an army to reconquer the holy city of Jerusalem from Islamic control. It was an insane situation, that three different faiths (Islam, Judaism and Christianity) should all regard Jerusalem as the holiest of places, but that city became the ultimate target of crusaders for centuries.

For film-makers, focus largely rests on the Third Crusade (1189–92) and its formidable English leader, Richard the Lionheart. Umpteen actors have played him: Henry Wilcoxson (*The Crusades* 1935); Ian Hunter (*The Adventures of Robin Hood* 1938); Anthony Hopkins (see above); George Sanders (*King Richard and the Crusaders* 1954); and Sean Connery (*Robin Hood: Prince of Thieves* 1991) to name the most obvious. In the Robin Hood sagas especially, 'good king Richard' usually turns up at the end (Connery got an alleged $1 million for three minutes' screen time) to knight the brave outlaw of Sherwood Forest and to get his throne back from the evil, snivelling Prince John. The real Richard was probably homosexual (made explicit in *The Lion in Winter*) and, although a better general than Saladin, his Syrian adversary, was ultimately unable to take Jerusalem and came back defeated. In the process, he had virtually bankrupted his country and of the ten years of his reign, spent only six months in England.

Wilcoxson's armour in DeMille's *The Crusades* is a *little* fantastical, though his men are more accurately portrayed in mail and surcoats. Far too many of them, however, especially in the siege of Acre, are carrying aluminium shields, a metal unknown at the time. The real crusaders had to make do with wood – iron is far too heavy. Loretta Young looked very pretty as Richard's marriage-of-convenience wife, Berengaria, but since history tells us so little about her, what else was there for her to do?

I have tried to ignore the Robin Hood sagas – and Walter Scott's *Ivanhoe* (1952) because Richard is virtually the only historical figure in them.

For me, the crusader genre was saved in 2005 in Ridley Scott's *Kingdom of Heaven*. The problem with de Bouillon taking Jerusalem in 1099 was that the Christians then had to hold on to it and that proved far more difficult. Two orders of knights – the Hospitallers and the Templars – were set up for this purpose, but spent most of their time bickering with each other, which explains, in international politics terms, why Richard's Third Crusade failed too. Heart-throb Orlando Bloom proved a gutsy hero in the figure of Balin, a French knight on the run for murder, and both Liam Neeson and Jeremy Irons are archetypally grizzled old crusaders who have been there, done that. Casting Gassan Massoud, a Syrian actor, to play Saladin was masterly. He is streets ahead of Rex Harrison, be-turbanned and 'browned up' in *King Richard and the Crusaders*, based on another Walter Scott novel, *The Talisman*.

There are some remarkable scenes in *Kingdom of Heaven* and realistic battles. Who can forget the crusader army, sun dazzling off helmets and a fierce wind blowing their banners almost horizontally, being led by the leper king of Jerusalem, Baldwin (Edward Norton), complete with silver mask to hide his disfiguring disease? In the Middle Ages, leprosy was thought to be highly contagious and panic would have spread throughout the army had Baldwin's condition become known.

When Hollywood strays out of Europe, it becomes more than a little unhinged. Chronologically, after the zenith of the crusades, comes Genghis Khan (universal ruler). His name was Temujin and he has a claim to be the first practitioner of both Blitzkrieg (lightning war) and total war. In his attacks, especially on China, he used his brilliant Mongol cavalry as Attila had with his Huns and burned hundreds of outlying peasant villages. When he reached China's Great Wall, he realized he had no siege engines to break it down, so he stole one, copied its technology and continued to wreak havoc inside China itself.

Temujin had been fighting for his role as Mongol chieftain from the age of 13 and, like all successful conquerors, had the wisdom to adapt the good policies of those he conquered. He pinched the alphabet and laws from the Uigurs and extended his empire as far as Tibet and India by 1225. His lieutenants went further into Russia and Crimea, where they were called Tartars. He died in August 1227, aged 75, of natural causes; allegedly, today, the paterfamilias of a third of the world (on account of his many wives).

Hollywood hasn't done him justice. First, in 1955, John Wayne played the great warlord, as one critic said, as part cavalry officer, part Indian chief. This was *The Conqueror* in which a very unconvincing Wayne wears a silly 'Chinese' moustache and spends far too much time wooing Susan Hayward. The film made history in its own right because it was filmed in Arizona at a time when atomic tests were being carried out and cast and crew were, allegedly, exposed to radiation. 'The Duke's' death in 1979 was not linked with this, as some claimed, but had far more to do with his sixty-a-day smoking habit. Eleven years later, they tried again, this time using a new, dynamic lead actor, the Egyptian Omar Sharif, fresh from his astonishing debut in *Lawrence of Arabia* (see Chapter 9) two years earlier. This time it was directly called *Genghis Khan* and Stephen Boyd was on hand to play Jamuga, Tenujin's rival (in historical reality, of course, one of many). Sharif's dad was Michael Hordern (he had been Charlton Heston's in *El Cid*), pulled apart (rather unrealistically) by four horses, and both James Mason and Robert Morley played Chinese mandarins. Morley recounted later that his Fu Manchu style fingernails gave him problems on set (sharp-eyed viewers have noticed that they are frequently missing) and his emperor character was finally blown up (at last, an historical fact insofar as the Chinese invented gunpowder). The 1960s was the epoch in which British actors were wheeled in to give a production more gravitas. Sadly, Sharif wasn't much better than Wayne, although his helmet was, and the still I have in front of me shows him sitting his grey horse looking rather embarrassed at having conquered a third of the known world.

For reasons I explained in the Overture, I haven't included many foreign films in this book. *Alexander Nevsky* is an exception, because stylistically, it is brilliant. Thirteenth-century Russia was not the superpower it became by the twentieth century but was divided into a number of minor kingdoms stretching from the Baltic to the Bering Sea. Perhaps the most powerful was Novgorod, whose prince in the 1240s was Alexander Nevsky (Alexander of the River Neva). Typical of the fragmentation of the west in this (as in any) period, Pope Gregory IX launched a crusade against the Greek Orthodox church of Mother Russia. The fact that both sides in this war were Christian was irrelevant – it was all about liturgy and ceremonial. The 'baddies' in Sergei Eisenstein's 1938 film were the German knights of the Teutonic Order, one of many such chivalric societies set up in the Middle Ages. Nevsky was played by Nikolai Cherkasov, Russia's answer to Charlton Heston when Charlton Heston was still only 15! His followers are hearty, jovial types, honest and courageous and the Germans are portrayed as faceless automatons. In fact, the knights' helmets, with their towering horn crests, are authentic; only the infantry in their Stahlhelms looked like the 1930s Wehrmacht.

The central part of the film is the famous battle on the ice, when the armies clashed on Lake Peipus in April 1242 and, given the black and white 'fuzz' of the time, has rarely been bettered on film. The music score was by Sergei Prokofiev, as much of a legend in his genre as the film's director was in his.

But there was a problem. Not for the first or last time, an historical movie got caught up in contemporary politics. Eisenstein's take on the Germans in 1938 was that they were the political enemy. Russia was now the USSR, a Communist state under Joseph Stalin (the fake surname could itself have been a Hollywood title – man of steel) while Germany was a Nazi state under Adolf Hitler. By the time the film was released, however, these two horrors, from diametrically opposite political standpoints, had buried the hatchet in the back of Poland, which they partitioned between them and Eisenstein's anti-German movie no longer fitted the playbill. It was banned, in true Communist style, and Eisenstein became a pariah.

Hollywood ventured again outside Medieval Europe in *The Adventures of Marco Polo* in 1938. Any movie with 'Adventures' in the title probably isn't meant to be taken too seriously and that shows in that stoic judge's son Gary Cooper is appallingly miscast as the Venetian adventurer with a yen (excuse the pun) for Eastern parts. Polo's family got as far as China (then known as Cathay) in the 1250s, where they were welcomed by Kublai Khan, descendant of Genghis. Young Marco accompanied his elders on another visit in 1271, having visited Baghdad and Yarkad on the way and crossing the Gobi Desert. He was sent by the khan as ambassador to what is today Myanmar and India. The notes he kept for those momentous years, which extended Europeans' knowledge of the world, were later written up as journals. It didn't help that a later 'travelogue', allegedly written by an English knight, John Mandeville (actually a Frenchman), was a fictional fabrication describing men with faces in their chests and women who urinated standing up. As a result, and by association, Polo's travels were disbelieved for centuries.

Baird Searles describes Cooper's Polo as 'a sort of "Aw-shucks" ... cowboy meets baker's daughter' sort of movie in which not even a suave and menacing villain like Basil Rathbone can save the whole thing.

Chronologically, this brings us back to Britain and *Braveheart* (see Overture). All that remains to be said about this is that William Wallace, the film's hero, was probably not Scots at all, but a Welshman (Wallace is a corruption of Wallensis, the Latinized version of Welsh, stranger). It is deeply ironic that Scottish independence activists today should claim as one of their heroes somebody from another country altogether, rather as the French claim that Napoleon was 'one of their own'. A number of things about *Braveheart* jar. The ludicrous 'war paint' of blue and white, which adorned fans' faces on the football and rugby terraces for years afterwards, isn't remotely historical. There are no recorded instances of it. Wallace and Edward I (Patrick McGoohan) did not die simultaneously, but two years apart. And the notion that the horse thief and murderer had a brief, dodgy affair with the queen of England is like something out of an adult-rated Harry Potter movie, were such a thing to exist.

By and large, Hollywood has ignored the 'hurling time' of the fourteenth century in which most of Europe seems to have been convulsed by the Black Death and subsequent peasant risings, focusing instead on the early fifteenth century, by which time the Hundred Years' War (actually 114 years) was coming to an end. Because of the doubling up of Normandy and England from 1066, kings of England laid claim to vast swathes of French territory and periodically fought with kings of France over it (one of the themes of *The Lion in Winter*, for example).

Film critic Mark Kermode condemns Ridley Scott's *The Last Duel* (2021) in these terms – '[It] plays like an armour-clad *Rashomon* crossed with a #MeToo-infected remake of *Straw Dogs*.' Both those movies were hugely influential in their day. *Rashomon* (1951) tells the story of a rape from four viewpoints and is set in Medieval Japan. *Straw Dogs* (1971) deals with rape too, when a mild American couple are attacked by oafs in a Cornish village. Both films are fiction, but *The Last Duel* is based on fact, its details mentioned in the fourteenth-century chronicles of Jean Froissart and the film itself is based on a factual account by Eric Jager in 2004.

The movie was delayed because of COVID but was filmed in gritty realism (like all Scott's work) in France and Ireland. For the uninitiated (and there is no attempt in the film to explain who is fighting who in the opening sequences) the action takes place in 1380s France during a relative lull in the Hundred Years' War with England. It was a time when the French were gaining the upper hand under the brilliant generalship of Bertrand du Guesclin who doesn't get so much as a mention in the script. The central characters are real, Jean de Carrouges (Matt Damon, with dreadful hair!) and Jacques le Gris (Adam Driver) are squires serving Pierre, Compte d'Alençon (Ben Affleck in a ludicrous blond goatee). Le Gris rapes de Carrouges' wife (played superbly by Jodie Comer) and de Carrouges demands satisfaction under the Medieval chivalric code of trial by combat. So far, so true, but seeing the same story three times from the points of view of the protagonists (à la *Rashomon*) is tedious. De Carrouges really did fight alongside the Scots in a failed campaign against England and he did die (as the end credits tell us) on crusade, specifically the Nicopolis campaign of 1396 against the Turks under Bayezid, the Thunderbolt.

We are reminded in the movie that decisions relating to sexual morality were in the hands of the Medieval church (who, in theory at least, understood nothing about such matters due to their vows of chastity). It was all about money and land, too, with marriage dowries, inheritance and the strict hierarchy of feudal France. If you've seen the film and thought the acting of the king, Charles VI, by Alex Lawther was poor, remember that he was barking, known as Charles the Mad and suffered from bouts of insanity all his life.

The movie flopped at the box office, Ridley Scott complaining about the naïve youth of cinema audiences – 'What we've got today [are] the audiences who were brought up on those f****** cell phones. The millennials do not ever want to be taught anything.' It did well on streaming, however. What was good about the film was that it exposed the yawning gap between the code of chivalry (largely a romantic, vellum exercise) and the misogynistic reality where women of all classes were treated like dirt. Where it fell down was in the script – who thought that Matt Damon and Ben Affleck could do that effectively?

Even though the details of the actual duel are accurate, according to Froissart, there is one glaring omission. Jacques le Gris was a squire; Jean de Carrouges was by then a knight. Under the laws of chivalry, only men of the same rank could fight each other in a legal trial. In reality, le Gris was knighted on the tournament ground before the duel started. This is not shown in *The Last Duel*.

Perhaps oddly, William Shakespeare didn't write plays about Edward III or the Black Prince, but he did about Henry V. For Hollywood, and even more so for us, Shakespeare is a problem. The man from Stratford-upon-Avon, the son of a glover, without a university background and unlikely ever to have left England, claims to know an awful lot about other cultures and other times. This he lifted from 'experts' who were nothing of the sort. The chroniclers who were Shakespeare's sources, like Holinshed and Hall, were not historians in the modern sense. They recorded any bit of superstitious twaddle as though it were fact and Shakespeare embellished various scenes to add to the drama. So when the young King Henry, formerly the drunken Jack-the-lad Prince Hal, is scornfully sent a set of tennis balls by the French king to mock his youth, we lap it up as genuine and are not at all surprised when the king launches a military campaign in 1415. It's simply payback time. The tennis story, by the way, is pure tosh.

For the record, Henry was a warrior king par excellence. He put down the Welsh rebellion of Owain Glyndŵr and was wounded in the face at the battle of Shrewsbury. The only portrait of him (a Tudor copy) shows him from the left; the wound was to the right. Both Laurence Olivier and Kenneth Branagh, who have played the king, are far too personable-looking. In 1414, he launched the French campaign, claiming a right to the French throne (which he essentially made up) and taking the port of Honfleur – 'Once more unto the breach, dear friends, once more ...' – before trouncing the flower of French chivalry at Agincourt in October 1415.

The first of the two films was made during the Second World War and its morale-boosting timing is obvious. Cleverly, it opens at London's Globe theatre in the early 1600s, takes us back through stylized Medieval interiors that are taken straight from fifteenth-century illuminated books of hours and then out into the open for the Agincourt battle itself. The image of the king's army, outnumbered four to one, half-starved and hit by dysentery, is clear from Shakespeare and Olivier's 1944 *Henry V* is faithful to all that. His archers, armed with 6-foot yew bows, stand stoically behind their sharpened stakes, even if they haven't got their hose rolled down to cope with the dysentery problem. William Walton's thundering score as the arrows hiss skyward thrills the blood even today. Even if you know nothing of history, you *know* it's not going to end well for the French.

Ignoring the lessons of the battles their fathers fought (and lost) like Crecy and Poitiers, the knights charge headlong in realistic plate armour, the camera, on a rail track gliding alongside them to increase the idea of speed. There were perhaps 6,000 such knights at Agincourt, each of them riding destriers that weighed up to a ton. The momentum of such a charge, delivered at 20 miles an hour, would have been horrendous.

Except that it wasn't. Olivier's thoroughbreds are too light and fast, the beautiful grasslands are in Ireland and nothing about this charge is right. Fast forward to Branagh's version (1989). 'The more I thought about it,' the director and actor wrote, 'the more convinced I became that here was a play to be relieved from jingoism and its World War Two associations.' It was panned at the time, largely because Branagh wanted to point up the 'pity of war' and to portray Henry as anything but a hero. In one important respect, however, he got Agincourt absolutely right, while Olivier didn't. The battle, fought on St Crispin's Day (21 October), took place in a narrow half valley between two woods (not the Irish open spaces) and the weather was appalling. Thousands of boots and hoofs had churned the ground to mud and the much-vaunted charge of the French cavalry was slowed to a walking pace. The English archers, who could release six arrows a minute, had ample time to mow the enemy down. In terms of visuals, however, Olivier wins hands down. His armour and his heraldry are spot on, whereas Branagh looks as though he was last in line at the costume tent. In Medieval battles, it was vitally important for a king commanding his army to be *seen* as a rallying point for his own side. Looking like just another sodden bloke, Branagh doesn't remotely convey this. Both films, brilliantly, made use of the haunting – and contemporary – Agincourt carol as part of the music score.

In one respect, one of Olivier's scenes put back historical understanding by centuries. Edward, Duke of York, was killed leading the vanguard (main battle) at Agincourt and Tudor chroniclers, a century and a half later, referred to him as fat, contending that he suffocated because of his size. There is no evidence for this, but Olivier goes a stage further, having the duke hoisted into his saddle with a winch, adding credence to the nonsense that an armoured knight, once unhorsed, was like a beetle on its back, unable to get up again without assistance.

Incidentally, *Henry V* (1944 version) is the first historical film that I am aware of which produced its own merchandise. The toy company Britains produced its metal 'knights of Agincourt' series complete with correct heraldry on shields and horse bards.

The end of the Hundred Years' War brings us to one of the most enigmatic personalities in history – La Pucelle, as the French called her, the Maid of Orleans, Jeanne d'Arc. Such an astonishing character, a woman pitched into a man's world, was filmed by Cecil B. DeMille as early as 1917. Cleverly using the situation as it was then, British Tommies in their trenches stumble upon Joan's sword and her story is told in flashback. The movie was called *Joan the Woman*, in an attempt to get behind the saint portrayed in so many statues all over France. She was played by internationally famous soprano Geraldine Farrar, ironic in that this was, of course, a silent film.

Fast forward to 1948. Ingrid Bergman was starring in a stage version of *Joan of Lorraine* on Broadway and RKO studios decided to put this version on to celluloid (as *Joan of Arc*). The result was a disaster. 'It is childishly oversimplified,' wrote critic Herman G. Weinberg, 'its battles papier mâché, its heroine far too worldly, its spiritual context that of a chromo art calendar.' The legend of Joan is that she began hearing the voices of angels from the age of 13. By the time she was 17, she was riding at the head of the French army, in full plate armour (approximate weight 40lb – that's twenty bags of sugar!) in a bid to kick the English out of France once and for all. Bergman looked too matronly for all this at 33. Her armour is plastic and her hair terrible. The 1999 remake, starring Milla Jovovich, is far better. Milla is nubile, passing easily for a teenager (although she was 24 at the time) and looks superb in fifteenth-century German armour (where all the best such 'harnesses' were made). To those purists who scoff and say that appearance doesn't matter when it comes to realism, we have to factor in the point that Frenchmen followed Joan because she was an icon. They *may* have believed she was sent by God to rid them of the cursed English, but it was her combination of little girl and sex object that drew them physically.

The historical record on Joan is flimsy and quickly descends into legend. She was a peasant girl from Domremy in Lorraine and, claiming to hear voices from Heaven, persuaded the local landowner, in 1426 or 1427, to take her to the (unstable) dauphin, the future Charles VII at Chinon (the setting for *The Lion in Winter*, incidentally). The dauphin accepted her, gave her a horse, armour and her own banner and she led the French army to victory in the siege of Orleans. She was eventually captured by the Burgundians (enemies of France) and sold to the English. A church court found her guilty of heresy and sorcery and she was burnt alive in the market place at Rouen on 30 May 1431 at the age of 19. She was canonized in 1920.

If Robert Morley wasn't great as the emperor of China (see above) he was rather more convincing as Louis XI of France. Continuing the old Hollywood tradition, rather than writing a screenplay from scratch based on the historical record, film-makers are all too happy to take fiction from the past and pretend it's accurate. One of the guiltiest parties here was Walter Scott. Throughout the 1820s, he wrote a series of historical novels which were enormously popular to a readership who knew no better. *Some* people saw through him – 'Though none by sabre or by shot, Fell half so flat as Walter Scott' (attributed to Lord Erskine) – but Hollywood was still raiding his backlist 130 years later. *The Talisman*, as we have seen, became *King Richard and the Crusaders* and *Ivanhoe* was set in Robin Hood country. Post Hundred Years' War it was the turn of *Quentin Durward* (1955) starring a rather ageing Robert Taylor. 'Theirs,' said the film posters, 'was a time of love and violence' – which probably covers every historical movie ever made. One of several 'baddies' pitting themselves against Durward/Taylor was the 'spider king', Louis XI. Morley looks nothing like contemporary sketches of the real man (Basil Rathbone played him too, in *If I Were King* in 1938) but he exudes duplicity and treachery under an exterior of typical Morley bonhomie. The king was probably as mad as a snake by the end of his life.

With the Hundred Years' War over – and won, against all the odds, by France – there was nothing for the English nobility to do but turn on each other. This was the Wars of the Roses, a power struggle between the squabbling families of Lancaster and York against the prolonged uselessness of Henry VI. In the days when kings actually ruled, a child king or a weak adult one (Henry had been both) was a disaster and usually paved the way for rebellion and chaos. Once again, Hollywood threw its lot in with Shakespeare. His three parts of *Henry VI* and

Richard III prepared the ground for the arrival of the rulers for whom he wrote, the Tudors (see next chapter) and, in the case of Richard in particular, it is a travesty of history.

There is no more contentious king in English history than Richard III, last of the Plantagenets. We are so imbued with Shakespeare's hunchbacked villain, with his bad wig, deformed hand and Machiavellian tendencies, that it came as something of a surprise to most people to find that the king's body, discovered by chance under a car park in Leicester, should have suffered from no more than mild scoliosis, a spinal curvature. The play itself, probably written in the mid-1590s, from sources written by the usual suspects, portrayed Richard as an almost pantomime villain, murdering his way through eleven people, including his own wife and two little nephews in order to get to the crown. Since his *Henry V* did so well at the box office, Laurence Olivier transferred the 'foul toad' to the big screen (a film I saw in an unwitting act of child abuse by my parents!) in the summer of its release in 1956.

Like *Henry V*, most of the scenes are studio-based until the final battle, Richard, whether Duke of Gloucester or king, heaving himself around the set with a malevolent smile on his face, casting huge deformed shadows on the stonework. He engineers his brother Clarence's death (untrue), has Lord Hastings executed for no reason (he was a traitor), hires a hit man (Patrick Troughton) to kill his nephews, the princes in the Tower (probably untrue and certainly not provable), hints that he has done away with his wife, Anne (tuberculosis actually did that), and all the time, the 'rightful' heir, Stanley Baker in a blond wig, is just itching to put everything right.

The Battle of Bosworth, the last in which a king of England was killed, was fought in open farmland near the village of Sutton Cheney in Leicestershire, but Olivier filmed it in Spain. The golden grass on screen more or less accords with a scorching August day when the battle was fought, but nothing else rings true. Olivier was famous for doing his own stunts and got an arrow in his leg during filming, but the cloud of arrows is generally well done. One sequence, when Richard and Richmond (Baker) briefly clash swords, was clearly done in the studio and it shows. The scene where the king is hacked to death by foot soldiers terrified me as a small child and, bearing in mind the head wounds found on the real king's body, is probably quite accurate.

It used to be accepted that 1485, the year of Bosworth, was the end of the Middle Ages and the modern age began neatly in 1486. Today, we are rather more flexible about such things. Kings like Richard routinely used firearms in battle. He personally backed the printing press that was to revolutionize communication. The government structures that the Tudors favoured were already in place under him. On the other hand, a lot of Medievalism, outdated concepts and the power of the Church, survived for decades after that time.

In 1956, few people had much of a grasp of all this. 'Now civil wounds are stopped,' the Earl of Richmond says at the end of *Richard III*, 'That she may long live here, God say Amen.'

Hooray, we all cheered. The Tudors are here!

P.S. Well, not just yet. Just as Kenneth Branagh had resurrected Henry V, so Ian McKellen brought Richard III back from the dead in 1995. This was more than a remake in modern dress because it transferred Richard's world to the Fascist dictatorship of the 1930s and it worked extremely well. Richard's boar badge is a kind of swastika hung on giant banners. Fifty years on, the world was now aware of the dangers of smoking and what a disgusting habit it was, so you know the Duke of Gloucester is a baddie because he smokes like a chimney. The upstart Wyville family, the queen's brood and Richard's in-laws, are played by brash Americans and don't fit right in. The Duke of Buckingham (Jim Broadbent) is a rather malevolent prime minister figure. Bosworth takes place in a war-torn city setting and when I saw this in the cinema I was intrigued to know how McKellen would handle the famous (and unhistorical) line, 'A horse! A horse! My kingdom for a horse!' The place erupted with laughter and applause when the king's jeep broke down and he is forced to ask for a four-legged friend instead!

Chapter 4

The Renaissance: From Bluff King Hal to Gloriana

It's interesting how film-makers have concertinaed time. In Chapter 1, the ancient world covered many centuries, the earliest of which are lost in the cliched mists of time. The Dark Ages of Chapter 2 spanned only 400 years and have not spawned many movies. Chapter 3's Middle Ages chronicled another 400, this time more star-studded. But this chapter, in terms of English history, covers less than 100 years and only charts two generations – Bluff King Hal was Henry VIII; Gloriana was his daughter, Elizabeth. Even so, there have been some excellent films made about this period, all of which are worth seeing. How many of them come close to historical reality is another matter entirely.

Nobody really wants to know about the first Tudor, Henry VII. The man became king because he got lucky at Bosworth and he has few qualities to recommend him. The filmic story really starts with his eldest surviving son, who became Henry VIII.

The Tudors were the first monarchs to have reasonably accurate portraits painted of themselves. You will look in vain for such things in the early fifteenth century and before; king's heads on Medieval coins are symbolic generalizations – hair, a beard, two eyes, nose and mouth – that's your lot. The important piece of art on a coin was the crown – *that* was the symbol of power and greatness. Easily the best, and best known, court artist of the early sixteenth century was Hans Holbein. Born in Augsburg, Austria and the son of a painter, he visited England several times and painted the great and good before appointment to Henry VIII's court in 1536. He died of the plague seven years later.

Virtually everybody who has played the larger-than-life monarch (and there have been several) have adapted the 'Holbein' pose at some time or other, either in their films or as part of the PR for them. And that study is a masterpiece in macho. Henry's country was among the poorest in Europe at the time and he had to impress, trying to compete with richer, more powerful rulers like Francois I of France and Maximilians I and II of the Holy Roman Empire. His sumptuous clothes say it all. Under the Tudors (and their increasingly neurotic and paranoid governments) there were strict rules as to what various social classes could wear; you could be imprisoned for the wrong type of fur or coloured ribbon. We know from the king's suits of armour (he was a keen jouster) that in 1509 his waist measurement was 31 inches. By 1546, the year before his death, it had ballooned to 54 inches. Holbein's portrait shows all of this – the huge shoulders and the padded sleeves, the paunch heavily decorated with bling. Even – and perhaps especially – the codpiece over his genitals; Henry boasting again. The irony is that, although he had, famously, six wives, he wasn't all that energetic in bed.

Look at Holbein. And now look at Charles Laughton, who played him in *The Private Life of Henry VIII*, directed by Alexander Korda in 1933. It was played for laughs with the tag line 'the things I do for England!' but Laughton's costume is *way* below Holbein's. The studio has skimped on the bling (this was the unemployed, depressed 1930s after all) and his codpiece is almost invisible.

Henry has captured the imagination of film-makers because of the extraordinary events of his reign. Married to his dead brother's wife (Katherine of Aragon) the pair failed to produce that essential commodity, a son and heir. The Tudors had taken the throne by force and their position was tenuous at best. They had no police force and no standing army and there was danger everywhere. Henry added to all that by trying to divorce Katherine and install wife number two, the not-as-gorgeous-as-she'd-have-you-believe Anne Boleyn. He sent Thomas Wolsey (either Orson Welles or Anthony Quayle, take your pick) to the pope who was the only man legally able to arrange this. The pope refused (his city was under attack by Katherine's uncle at the time) so, in a fit of pique, Henry set up his own church and granted himself a divorce. This has confused the hell out of everybody (especially schoolchildren who have to learn it) ever since. Henry's church was still Catholic; it was just no longer run by the pope. Think of it as the Church *in* England (the Church *of* England followed a few years later). This gave Henry the chance to make a lot of cash on the side. He dissolved the obscenely rich monasteries and sold off the plate, the jewelled shrines and the land (keeping the money for himself) and wiped out most of the papal support at one stroke. He then married Anne Boleyn, but, ironically, she could only provide another daughter, Elizabeth. Since the king already had one girl – Mary, by Katherine of Aragon – he was no further forward.

This, the king's 'great matter' as it was called in the 1530s, forms the central storyline to all the movies made about Henry VIII. As George MacDonald Fraser says, 'Medieval historians still disagree about what killed Henry VIII. Was it cardio-renal failure, chronic sinusitis, syphilis, brain damage caused originally by jousting, or just plain obesity? Whatever the cause, the ultimate death blow was dealt by Charles Laughton.' The real Henry was a scholar, musician, sportsman, effective politician. Laughton played him as a buffoon, for ever throwing chicken legs over his shoulder at banquets. All that said, the public loved it and the image of the king spread around a world that had never heard of him.

The best lookalike for Henry was probably Montague Love in Mark Twain's *The Prince and the Pauper* (filmed in 1957); the least convincing, as we might expect, was a leering (when did he not?) Sid James in *Carry on Henry* (1971). Becoming ever more outrageous, the tag line to this one was 'A Great Guy with His Chopper'. It was a parody of real events – 'Marie of Normandy' is removed for eating too much garlic. The love-hate relationship of the British public with these films is best summed up by Kenneth Williams, who played Thomas Cromwell. In 1970, he wrote, 'I read the script ... and I think it's abysmal.' Nine years later, he had softened – '... amazing how well this was made! Everyone in it was competent ...' but he'd changed his mind again by 1988. 'Oh, dear! It was so bad in places ... truly chronic dialogue ... dreadful acting. Sid James had never been quite as bad as this. A collection of such rubbish you're amazed it could ever had been stuck together. Only an audience of illiterates could ever have found this tripe amusing.' Film critic Peter Buckley was perhaps more informed. 'There is a delicious send-up of that most boring and perennial line of cinematic yawns, the historical romance.'

Of the serious films of the king, however, a lot of talented people tried to lay the ghost of Charles Laughton to rest. One of the most interesting versions is *Anne of the Thousand Days* (1969), directed by Hal Wallis. Predictably, the ever-curmudgeonly Halliwell gives it only one star, perhaps because Richard Burton, as the king, isn't very good. To begin with his hair, contrary to history and nearly everybody who has played him, was dark, as was his beard. The cruelty of the man was well brought out by Burton, but he clearly hasn't got the pizzazz of the real Henry. All right, handling the divorce, excommunication from the pope, sniffiness from the Church etc. can't have been a bundle of laughs, but Burton looks as if his fee has just been cut. Geneviève Bujold as Anne is excellent – she's little and vulnerable, but her dark eyes flash and you just know she's a handful who is about to morph into a stoical heroine.

Critics didn't like the costumes, complaining that they looked as if they'd come from Nathan's (costumiers) racks. They had, as had all historical films at the time (see *Peterloo* in Chapter 7), so that was a daft comment to make. John Colicos is a slimy Thomas Cromwell (long before Hilary Mantel unaccountably tried to make a hero of him) and Anthony Quayle still moves my wife to tears with his portrayal of the broken Thomas Wolsey, having failed to get the king the divorce he so desperately needs.

My favourite scene is the last one. Henry is out hunting when Anne's head is lopped off by the headsman. He doesn't care. A cannon booms out to signal the death. A little girl, perhaps 5, is learning to walk in her court dress in a garden. She has long auburn hair and as the gun roars, she turns to the sound. She is the future Elizabeth, the greatest of the Tudors. And her father has just had her mother executed.

Just as *Anne of the Thousand Days* is really about the queen, not the king, so Robert Bolt's *A Man For All Seasons* (1966) is about Thomas More, another victim of Henry VIII's obsession. More is a fascinating character, a man of courage and convictions, but I cannot warm to him. Famously painted by Holbein along with his entire family at their home in Chelsea (then reached by boat along the Thames) he is swarthier than anyone who has played him and looks less than the saint the Catholic church made him in the 1930s. Everything about the film is superb – the thumping Tudor music score, the gilded barges on the river, the costumes, the performances (by everybody) – it's all excellent. Orson Welles is an unsympathetic, reptilian Wolsey, sitting like Jabba the Hutt in his cardinal's robes. Cromwell is Leo McKern, little, strutting, the typical nasty piece of work that the Tudors hired to do their dirty work for them. A lackey prepared to sell his soul for promotion, Richard Rich was played by newcomer John Hurt, reminding us all that the only way to get to the top in the sixteenth century was to spend hours hanging about outside famous people's houses. The king was Robert Shaw. He not only looked like Henry, laughing, bullying, loud, he showed the inner steel that the man must have possessed. He'd like everything to be sweetness and light, but it must be strictly on his terms.

Towering above everybody, though, is Paul Schofield as More. Calm, quiet, honest as the day is long in a vengeful, wicked world, he refuses to bow to Henry's demands of support, loses his position at court and finally his life as a result. The women around him – Wendy Hiller his (illiterate) wife, Alice; Susannah York his (incredibly literate) daughter, Margaret – are quite brilliant. The final scene where they say their farewells is heartbreaking. More was executed on Tower Green in 1535, four centuries before his canonization.

Charlton Heston was desperate to play Schofield's part and did, in his own version of the Bolt play, four years later. Good though Heston is, it was a word-for-word remake of the original and seemed rather pointless. He redeemed himself however in his version of Henry in *The Prince and the Pauper* (1977), lurching on his bad leg, growling at everybody and delivering what were allegedly his last words with his jester, Will Somers, crying at his bedside – 'Monks, monks, monks!'

Henry's wives appeared from time to time in various films. Vanessa Redgrave (blink and you'll miss her) was Anne Boleyn in *A Man For All Seasons*. Irene Papas was downtrodden and wronged as Katherine of Aragon in *Anne of the Thousand Days*. In *The Private Life of Henry VIII* we sail through most of them – Merle Oberon was Anne Boleyn; Wendy Barrie, Jane Seymour; Elsa Lanchester (then Laughton's wife) was his 'Flanders Mare', Anne of Cleves; Binnie Barnes was Catherine Howard.

In what may be a unique female focus, Glynis Johns played Mary Tudor in *The Sword and the Rose* (1952). This is not Henry's eldest daughter, who became known to later generations as 'Bloody Mary' but the king's sister, who was briefly queen of France before marrying the Duke of Suffolk, Charles Brandon. The Brandons were typical nouveaux riches ennobled from nothing by the Tudors, determined as they were to curb the power of the aristocracy which had caused the Wars of the Roses. Brandon was played by Richard Todd and there is some good rapier-play between him and perennial 'baddie' Michael Gough. For those who are weaponry-minded, swords were now thinner-bladed, sharper and longer. In fact, one of the laws of Queen Elizabeth was to limit their length to avoid fatalities.

Another 'Tudor' lady who hit the headlines for all the wrong reasons was Jane Grey. When Henry's only son, Edward VI, died (probably of tuberculosis) at 15, the crown should have slid sideways to his oldest sister, Mary. The problem, in what was now a Protestant country, was that Mary was a devout Catholic, daughter, as she was, of Katherine of Aragon. Jane was the daughter of the Marquess of Dorset and was forced into a lightning marriage of convenience to Lord Guildford Dudley, son of the Protector who actually governed England. She ruled for nine days before Mary asserted herself, and she was executed on Tower Hill in February 1554. Neither Helena Bonham Carter nor Carey Elwes look very happy in stills from *Lady Jane* (1985), either because they fear their fate or because they know what a stinker they are starring in. Guardsmen attending Helena's execution look as if they've stepped off a Spanish galleon forty years later!

In this unhappy period for the English monarchy, Jean Simmons starred in *Young Bess* (1953). 'Wildly reliable as to fact,' says Halliwell (and for once, he's not wrong). Elizabeth's childhood, spent largely in Hatfield House, was notoriously troubled. Having disappointed her obnoxious father by being female, she was in and out of prison, declared illegitimate and feared for her life against the wrath of her 'driven' half-sister Mary. In the film, she is protected by the handsome swashbuckler Stewart Granger as Thomas Seymour, while in reality there is more than a hint that he was sexually abusing her from the age of 13. The costumes were good, and grizzled John Carradine made an effective Protector Somerset. Everything else was below par (pun intended).

It is difficult to believe the adulation that surrounded Elizabeth as queen and she loved every minute of it. Her first film appearance was probably *La Reine Elizabeth* in 1912 when the 'immortal' stage actress Sarah Bernhardt played her. As ever, Sarah managed to wear her favourite art nouveau gowns, still 300 years in the future in Elizabeth's reign.

In the year after Laughton's much-vaunted triumph as Henry VIII, his youngest child made another appearance in *The Private Lives of Elizabeth and Essex* (1939). This time the queen was Bette Davis and her courtier/rival the Earl of Essex a rather gloomy-looking Errol Flynn. In most of their scenes together, it looks as though Flynn is thinking, 'Remember the money, remember the money,' although the tempestuous chemistry between them works well. By the 1590s, when the film is set, Essex was the queen's favourite and a rising star. At 35 he was a successful soldier and diplomat. She was thirty years his senior (there was only one-year difference between Davis and Flynn) and it showed. Despite the glorious red wig and sumptuous clothes, Elizabeth had lost most of her teeth and her scrawny chest embarrassed most of her courtiers. She had reigned, by 1598, for forty years and to many people that seemed a day too much. Essex tried to overthrow other members of the Privy Council and lead a rising in London. It failed and he was executed for high treason in February 1601.

There are some nice touches in the film – he turning his back on her (tick the factual box); she boxing his ears (ditto, but on the wrong occasion). There was no last-minute meeting. Records show that the queen was playing the virginals when a messenger brought the news of Essex's death and she missed a couple of chords – that was all.

Interestingly, sometimes, they come back. Just as Laughton played Henry VIII several times, so Bette Davis took on the Elizabeth role sixteen years later. This time, the would-be lover was Walter Ralegh (Richard Todd) and the film was called *The Virgin Queen* (1955), which raises all sorts of questions. The question of the queen's marriage was central to her reign. The unstable Tudor regime could only continue if Elizabeth married and produced an heir. Several European princes lined up as suitors and she turned them all down, declaring that she wouldn't allow any man to be her master. Such was the animosity against female rulers in Britain (especially after the unpopularity of sister Mary) that a royal husband would grab power and she would end up as a mere consort.

It is highly implausible that the queen was technically a virgin. Her affairs with the Earl of Leicester in the 1570s, Walter Ralegh slightly later and Essex towards the end of her reign made this unlikely, but certainly it was a central tenet of her PR persona. The sets are good, the goblet-work excellent, the costumes just right. And nobody does frosty better than Bette Davis. When she discovered that Ralegh had made Bess Throckmorton, one of her ladies-in-waiting, pregnant (he'd actually married her in secret) she flew into one of her monumental rages and had them both imprisoned in the Tower. Whether the queen and Ralegh's relationship was actually sexual or not, *no one* was allowed to be any courtier's focus of attention other than Elizabeth herself.

Elizabeth created the Church *of* England in 1558, providing a compromise (*via media* in Latin) between the extremes of Catholicism and Puritanism. It didn't quite come off, through no fault of the queen's, but tied up with religious issues was the thorny question of that other icon of female power, Mary, Queen of Scots. She first appeared in a full length film in 1936 (in *Mary of Scotland*), using the Broadway play script of Maxwell Anderson. Katharine Hepburn played the queen and it was not her finest hour.

The real Mary was queen of Scotland at the age of 1 week (such were the vagaries of inheritance and life expectancy in the sixteenth century). At 17, she was queen of France, having been out of Scotland for fourteen years. Her husband's sudden death saw her return to a country bitterly divided over religion, not to mention the centuries-old feuding of the Highland clans. She was, to all intents and purposes, a Frenchwoman, but, by being a cousin of the heirless Elizabeth, was next in line for the throne of England.

She married the bisexual Lord Darnley, who was an inveterate plotter who became jealous of his wife's secretary, David Rizzio, and had him murdered. Darnley too died when his house at Kirk o' Field in Edinburgh was blown up. The Calvinist clan chiefs, aided and abetted by the probably deranged zealot John Knox, forced her to abdicate in favour of her infant son, James, and Mary herself fled to England where she spent the next nineteen years as a prisoner of Elizabeth. *Mary, Queen of Scots* (1971) was an altogether better film, with Vanessa Redgrave in the title role. To those who complained that she was far too tall (at 5ft 11in) for Mary, they were actually the same height, which is astonishing in a sixteenth-century woman, especially when her death mask shows a little, elfin face. Timothy Dalton (a sometime James Bond) was a suitably effete Darnley, complete with blond wig and Nigel Davenport was Mary's duplicitous love interest, the Earl of

Bothwell. Patrick McGoohan was chilling as the Earl of Moray, Ian Holm pathetic as Mary's secretary, David Rizzio and the Scottish clan leaders were portrayed as the thugs they undoubtedly were. Where the movie got it wrong, because Hollywood can't resist a face-to-face confrontation (see *Cromwell* etc.) was in the woodland meeting of Mary and her cousin Elizabeth. The English queen was played with relish by future MP Glenda Jackson, who had already made the role her own on television. Most of us felt like thrashing the annoying Mary with a riding crop (as Elizabeth did in the film) but, in fact, the two never met in their lives.

One of the many contemporary portraits of Elizabeth is the Armada Portrait, commemorating the defeat of the Spanish fleet on its way to invade England in 1588. This remarkable success, which had far more to do with bad weather in the Channel than superior English seamanship, was depicted in *Fire Over England* (1937) and again in *Elizabeth: The Golden Age* (2007). In the first, black and white, version, Flora Robson was a regal Elizabeth, even though the battle scenes were made from bad models in a studio water tank. At the time, critic Graham Greene wrote, '[The producers] have done one remarkable thing; they have caught the very spirit of an English public schoolmistress' vision of history.' But, unless you were Spanish, there was no other way at looking at it and since Spain was in the throes of a civil war at the time, I very much doubt whether anybody cared.

Cate Blanchett's two excursions into Elizabethan England (1998 and 2007) have both been excellent, although I preferred the first. The young princess coping with the Catholic viciousness of sister Mary, her frustration at the religious bigotry of most of her subjects and her dalliance with her Master of Horse, Robert Dudley (Joseph Fiennes), are all admirably handled. Too many shots are filmed from the roofs of cathedrals (most Tudor rooms had low ceilings) and Elizabeth's conscious decision to stay the virgin queen for the sake of England is completely unhistorical, but everybody in the cast is good, particularly Richard Attenborough as Lord Burghley, Elizabeth's chancellor, trying to guide the young queen in the right direction. The Catholic plotters in the rebellion of the North (1569) are ably led by a dastardly Christopher Eccleston. The second, Armada-based, film is not as good. Clive Owen doesn't convince as Ralegh and it doesn't help that, although the queen did indeed wear armour and ride a white horse to encourage her troops at Tilbury, we know now (as those troops didn't) that the Armada had already been dispersed by storms at sea and the whole thing was a masterly PR stunt.

I cannot leave the Tudors without the P.S. of *Shakespeare in Love* (1998). Written by Tom Stoppard and Marc Norman, this is where the sixteenth century is played for laughs, but it is littered with real characters and is hugely entertaining. Having been a spoiled and over-indulged fop as Dudley in *Elizabeth*, Joseph Fiennes makes amends as Shakespeare (with a *little* too much hair, perhaps). The love story, with Gwyneth Paltrow (before she began selling 'products') is pure fiction, although it is at least likely that the Stratford man was indeed playing away from home (Stratford to London was two days' ride in those days). Actors Ned Alleyn (Ben Affleck) and Richard Burbage (Martin Clunes) vie with each other to make a dishonest buck, watched over by the official censor, Master of the Revels Edmund Tilney (Simon Callow). Enigmatically, an uncredited Rupert Everett plays Kit Marlowe, the playwright who is Shakespeare's (and everyone else's) literary hero. And Geoffrey Rush, a sinister Francis Walsingham the spymaster in *Elizabeth* is a harassed and tortured (literally) Philip Henslowe in *Shakespeare in Love*.

But there is far more to this period than Hollywood's endless love affair with the Tudors, which has carried over into television in the age of streaming (see Chapter 12). The term Renaissance means rebirth – in this case, of culture – in a conscious attempt to revisit the glory that was Greece and the grandeur that was Rome, both of which had been minimized, but not eradicated, during the Middle Ages (there was, after all, a twelfth-century renaissance before the famous one).

In trying to recreate the past, artists, architects, poets, explorers and 'scientists' actually moved forward, creating the world we know today.

Discovery – and exploitation – of the New World we will look at in a later chapter, but there was plenty of excitement, not to mention skulduggery, going on in Europe to launch a thousand films.

Enter the Borgias. The late fifteenth and early sixteenth century served to produce a number of vicious, twisted rulers whose cruelty has become legendary. Much of this is anecdotal and exaggerated, but historical truth has never stood much in the way of Hollywood. Richard III in England (Shakespeare says) murdered eleven people to become king; Cesare Borgia in Italy was a mass murderer; his sister Lucrezia a serial poisoner. In Russia, Ivan IV was not called 'the Terrible' for nothing. He killed his own son and employed a secret police who butchered whole villages for laughs. How could Hollywood resist?

Bride of Vengeance (1944) starred Paulette Goddard as Lucrezia Borgia, which accidentally got the story more or less right by portraying her as a nice (as opposed to murderous) person. In the 1940s, heroines like Goddard could never play 'baddies', so the star's own persona saved Lucrezia from the usual treatment we might expect. It was studio-bound and badly acted, despite looking good. Macdonald Carey was a reasonable lookalike for Cesare, even though in the 1940s, any man with a goatee beard was suspect.

Prince of Foxes, released in the same year, was far better, if only because Orson Welles, then striking-looking and scary, was Cesare. The hero was the ever-bland Tyrone Power but Welles acted him off the set. The plot is too simplistic for the real story. Cesare was the illegitimate son of Pope Alexander VI, which is probably all you need to know about the Catholic church at the time and was Captain-General of the Papal army (ditto the last comment). Patron of the arts and model for Nicollo Machiavelli's *The Prince* (1513) Cesare remains one of history's villains, despite worthy attempts to rehabilitate him. Lucrezia was another illegitimate child of Pope Alexander and was forced into marriage three times to further her father's ambitions. Like most women at the centre of politics in the past (Cleopatra, Catherine the Great, Marie Antoinette) she has been vilified for very little reason, with claims of her murderous tendencies and incest with her brother and her father.

Talking of which ... Julius II. He was the pontiff who commissioned Michelangelo to paint the ceiling in the Sistine Chapel, even though the artist warned him that he was a sculptor, not a painter. In *The Agony and the Ecstasy* (1965), Julius was played by Rex Harrison, and Michelangelo was Charlton Heston. Harrison is always Harrison, but we have to feel sympathy for him, when the artist was taking *so* long to finish the work. 'When will you make an end?' is his perennial question throughout the film. The painting is of course a masterpiece, created in extraordinarily difficult conditions – if you have ever painted a ceiling in a conventional house at the top of a ladder, you'll know what I mean. Multiply that by the height of Pope Sixtus' church and factor in the Italian temperatures and it must have been unbearable – but the film is deeply flawed. Heston *looks* like Michelangelo but is too tall – as he is for virtually everybody – and the hints at the actor's homosexuality are as vague as you might expect, given the time it was made. In Britain, the law regarding homosexual acts was not changed until 1967. In various states in America, such changes took much longer. For good measure, therefore, Diane Cilento wafts through the movie in gorgeous Renaissance gowns.

The other Renaissance family to dominate, apart from the Borgias, is the Medici. The fact that both originated from Italy is no coincidence – that was where (to quote Peter O'Toole as Henry II in *The Lion in Winter*) 'they keep the pope'. It was also where the Renaissance began, producing a whole crop of talented artists whose names are almost legendary today. Despite the fact that Catherine de Medici was one of the most formidable women in history, the only English language film to feature her focuses instead on a royal mistress, Diane of Poitiers – in *Diane* (1956) – in which a very young Roger Moore (pre-*The Saint* and James Bond) is taught to fence by the dazzling femme fatale. All power to Lana Turner as Diane – handling a rapier in a Renaissance gown is no mean feat.

Ivan the Terrible (in two parts, 1944 and 1958) was another of those foreign films (see *Alexander Nevsky*) that deserves inclusion here because of its compelling and dramatic content. It too was made by Sergei Eisenstein and, like *Nevsky*, suffered the effects of censorship from Stalin's despotism. Even though 'Uncle Joe' had commissioned the film, when he saw it, he realized how like Ivan IV, an early Romanov ruler, he was. Outside the USSR (and, secretly, inside it) he was known as 'the Red Tsar'. The second part of the film, in which Ivan descends into madness, was not shown in Russia until five years after both Stalin and Eisenstein were dead. A third section was never filmed at all.

To western audiences, *Ivan the Terrible* is an art-house film, in black and white (except for two colour sequences) and full of static scenes, giant shadows on walls and oblique, Russian symbolism. You have to blink to realise that Ivan is played by Nikolai Cherkasov, who was the Heston lookalike in *Alexander Nevsky*. Ivan's long, lank hair, his pointy head and dangling beard are designed to put the fear of God into boyars, peasants and cinema audiences alike. Since the film was released, research has been carried out on the tsar's skeleton and we know that he suffered from osteophytes, bone spurs in the feet, which must have caused him constant pain and may have contributed to his temper and the more barbaric acts of his reign. Stalin had no such excuse.

Chapter 5

The Swashbucklers: From the Musketeers to the Pirates

According to the Oxford Concise Dictionary, a swashbuckler was a boastful, swaggering oaf – history is full of these; so were Hollywood films. The buckler itself was a small circular shield carried throughout the Middle Ages and I can't help feeling that the 'swash' is the onomatopoeic sound of a sword slicing through the air.

We find the first of these in Elizabethan days, as in Errol Flynn's *The Sea Hawk* (1940) in which he plays a fictional 'sea-dog'. Traditionally, these men came from West Country sea ports such as Plymouth and included men like Francis Drake and Walter Ralegh. At least one, Martin Frobisher, was a Yorkshireman. As Elizabeth's campaign got under way, first to support the Protestant Dutch in their revolt against Spain and then in direct conflict with Spain itself, she appointed such men as privateers, unofficially sanctioned to raid Spanish ships on the high seas and to damage Spanish settlements in the Americas. A considerable amount of economic damage was done to Spain, then Europe's richest country, as a result. In *The Sea Hawk*, Flora Robson reprised her role as Elizabeth from *Fire Over England* (1937).

No sooner are we in the seventeenth century than the French take over. Just as Spain had her *sieclo d'oro* (golden century – the sixteenth) so France had the next 100 years in which the French empire, clothes, manners, wine, food, even the language, became the apogee (see – I told you!) at which everybody else aimed, but we have to turn to the nineteenth century to see French swashbuckling at its best.

Alexandre Dumas was a prolific writer, both of novels and plays and the storyline of his musketeer series *screamed* swashbuckling. Set in the reign of the feckless Louis XIII and the Machiavellian Cardinal

Richelieu, there was never a time when plotting and counter-plotting were more pernicious in French history.

The central characters of the *Musketeers* were fictional, although the Musketeer-wannabe, D'Artagnan, *may* be based on Charles de Batz who commanded the 1st Company, the King's Mousquetaires in the 1620s. Those at the top, however, were real enough. Louis XIII was one of a long line of kings whose political posturing and *huge* personal expenditure led ultimately to the French Revolution (see Chapter 7). He was almost certainly bisexual, but nothing is made of this in any of the many (at least twelve) movies made about the Musketeers. Richelieu was the power behind the throne, a churchman (with nothing remotely Christian about him) who became adviser to the king in 1624. He arranged an alliance with England by marrying the French princess Henrietta Maria to Charles I (leading to the English Civil War and the movie *Cromwell*) and destroyed La Rochelle, the Huguenot (Protestant) centre in France, which led to thousands of Huguenots running to England for safety. From 1629 onwards, he was effectively the ruler of France. He founded the Academie Français in 1634, but the plays he wrote were unreadable and unactable.

There have been at least six 'talkie' Musketeers movies (including a musical with the Ritz brothers!) but the best of these along the way was the 1949 version with the acrobatic Gene Kelly as D'Artagnan. The ever-dodgy Vincent Price was Richelieu, Angela Lansbury (in her pre-*Murder She Wrote* days) such a gorgeous Queen Anne that you wonder why the real Louis XIII had other interests. John Sutton was the English Duke of Buckingham, who *may* have had a romantic interest in the queen, but there is virtually no evidence for it.

In the 1973 version, the screenplay was by George MacDonald Fraser, who played it for laughs. Even so, the settings, of Versailles and the slums of Paris, are superbly and authentically done. The siege of La Rochelle shows realistic cannon and breastworks and the fights are dazzlingly true to life. There *were* orders of fencing – France and Italy had different schools – but Dumas' Musketeers are men who want to stay alive. They use feet, furniture, clubs, fists, even laundry to that end and although slapstick, I suspect this was exactly how swordplay was *really* handled in the seventeenth century. Richard Lester was the director and real-life Frenchman Jean-Pierre Cassel was the king, Geraldine Chaplin the queen. The Duke of Buckingham was played by Simon Ward and his servant, Felton, who murdered him in 1629, was played in curmudgeonly Puritan style by Michael Gothard. Nearly stealing the show as Richelieu was Charlton Heston, slightly stooped and limping, conniving behind the scenes like the duplicitous slime he was. I noticed only one slip in the writing – the Duke of Buckingham is referred to as prime minister, 120 years before that title was used and 150 years before it was official. A remake in 1993 by the 'brat pack' led by Kiefer Sutherland was appalling. 'A half-hearted romp,' wrote Halliwell, 'by a group of actors to whom swashbuckling is a lost art, this is simply *Young Guns* [see Chapter 8] with swords …' It does, however, contain one of my favourite (unhistorical) lines. Rattling around France in a coach, Porthos (Oliver Platt) breaks open the wine. 'Here we are,' Kiefer Sutherland's D'Artagnan upbraids him, 'chasing the villains and you're drinking champagne!' 'You're right,' says Platt, discarding his bottle and opening another one. 'Something red.'

Perhaps the greatest swashbuckler of them all – and a genuine historical character – is Cyrano de Bergerac. He was the hero of an 1890s play by Edmond Rostand (the second largest role after Hamlet in any stage production) and was based on Savinien de Cyrano de Bergerac, born in Paris in 1619. He is reported to have fought over 1,000 duels, largely because his large nose became the subject of ridicule from men who quickly regretted it. He was also a playwright and amateur astrologer. José Ferrer played him in the black and white 1950 version and the French remake in 1990 won a number of awards. I found it dreadful because of its subtitles and the fact that Gerard Depardieu is far too big and lumpy to make a convincing swordsman.

When we turn to England, the swashbuckling becomes deadly serious, without the panache of Cyrano and the Musketeers. It also created one of the worst historical films ever made – *Cromwell* (1970). Critic Brenda Dains wrote, 'It tries to combine serious intentions with the widest kind of popular appeal and falls unhappily between the two. It will offend the purists and bore the kiddies.' The film's souvenir brochure boasted all sorts of historical pedigree. Its narrative was written by Maurice Ashley, then perhaps *the* expert on seventeenth-century England who in turn acknowledges his indebtedness to two earlier 'greats', Charles Firth and C.V. Wedgwood. Sadly, historical interpretation marches on faster than the pikemen of the New Model and Firth is woefully out of date today. The brochure makes much of the fact that *Cromwell* 'must be historically accurate', which is deeply ironic because much of it wasn't. As all too often, the battle sequences, Edgehill (1642) and Naseby (1645) were filmed in Spain simply because the Spanish army could still provide cavalry. Whitehall – the king's palace and the Houses of Parliament – were rebuilt 1640s style on the Shepperton lot because the real buildings there today didn't exist at the time. Today's Houses of Parliament even have a statue of Oliver Cromwell outside them! There were 15,986 props and 3,851 costumes. The film *looks* gorgeous and authentic, the acting is fine but there is sometimes a problem when the writer and director are the same person; who reined in Ken Hughes?

Historically, it is the storyline that is weak. Oliver Cromwell comes across as a man of the people, which he certainly never was (see *Winstanley* below) and his closing speech in the film, promising to make Britain great, full of justice, progress and education reads like something out of a political manifesto. The *real* Cromwell was a landowner and it showed. Only in the flashes of anger against Catholicism does the film's character get it right. In 1649, the Lord Protector put the men, women and children of Drogheda to the sword because he believed, as did most Puritans, that Irish Papists were sub-human. Richard Harris is a poor Cromwell, partly because he doesn't look like him and because the real man had far more layers than Harris can reveal. Alec Guinness as Charles I is, by contrast, superb. Visually right, his Lowland Scots delivery, complete with stammer, is spot on. And audiences can't believe the king can be so stubborn and stupid.

The battle scenes are good, but the premise is wrong. Cromwell never commanded the army (that was General 'Black Tom' Fairfax, played by Douglas Wilmer with his usual dignity, but no stammer – yes, he had one too!) and he certainly wouldn't have ordered his cavalry to attack at the gallop. The New Model 'ironsider' advanced at 'a pretty round trot', far more sensible an approach than the hell-for-leather cavaliers who followed Prince Rupert. The prince is a caricature in *Cromwell*. Played with panache by Timothy Dalton, he rides a grey (Black Barbarie was … er … black) and carries a little poodle in the crook of his arm. Boye was actually a hunting poodle, about the size of an Alsatian, and ran alongside Barbarie in battle. In the film he is still there at Naseby, whereas, in fact, the dog was killed at Marston Moor the previous year. Incidentally, since Rupert was considered to be a witch, if not the devil himself, Boye was assumed to be his familiar, carrying out his master's evil deeds. Unsurprisingly, none of this is in the film.

Most appalling of all however is the date structure. We are told on screen the date of the Battle of Naseby – 14 June 1645 – and we see Cromwell's son, also Oliver, killed in that fight. When we see the lad's headstone however, it clearly reads 1644, which may well confuse anyone watching who has been taking note of dates, because they clearly can't both be right. They're not – the gravestone has it right, because Oliver junior died of typhoid fever, not in battle.

For all its faults, *Cromwell* is superb by comparison with *To Kill a King* (2003) which changes emphasis to Fairfax played with wooden dullness by Dougray Scott. Cromwell in this version is Tim Roth, usually excellent but this time defeated by a bad script, which gives him no presence at all. Someone like Roth couldn't possibly have ruled England as a virtual dictator for ten years. Both actors deserved far better. At the time, Philip French in the *Observer* wrote, 'A decent and honourable film' focusing on ideas, which he admits is 'unfashionable in contemporary cinema'.

Another 'ideas' film is *Winstanley* (1975), an art-house movie whose theme was probably too complicated and off-beat to make it a box office success. Released only five years after *Cromwell*, it deals with the real revolutionaries of the Civil War era (of which Cromwell was not one), the Diggers. They and the Levellers were crypto-communists who wanted to level the hedgerows that were symbolic of land ownership. In a series of strong verbal clashes in the church at Putney in 1647, Cromwell himself (who does not appear in the film) destroyed their anarchic arguments and the movement failed. Kevin Brownlow directed a cast, largely of unknowns, and also wrote the screenplay; I think we have met this problem before!

Witchfinder General (1968) was on a different plane altogether, set in the closing years of the Civil War. The psychology of civil war is still not fully understood. Contemporaries referred to 'this war without an enemy' and 'the world turned upside down' in attempts to explain it. And in the chaotic topsy-turvy atmosphere at the end of the war, greedy malevolents like Matthew Hopkins saw a means to make money. Cashing in on the witch-craze, which had been prevalent for at least sixty years by this time, the East Anglian lawyer offered his services to eradicate witchcraft in communities who were irrationally afraid of it. In two years, using torture and hysteria, he was responsible for the deaths by hanging of over 200 people, all of it for hard cash. The title of the film comes from the honorary title he gave himself. The movie is outside the scope of historical films and is usually classed as horror, especially as Hopkins was played by Vincent Price, the prince of schlock at the time. In the United States, it had the inexplicable title of *The Conqueror Worm* and was filmed in grim black and white, complete with gnarled, creepy trees and the sound of creaking ropes. The director was Michael Reeves who died young without repeating his success. Apart from Hopkins and his sidekick, John Stearne, and one of their victims, John Lowes (Rupert Davies), the only other real character in the movie is Oliver Cromwell, played by Patrick Wymark, who is a very good Lord Protector lookalike.

Then, 'saints be praised', as Barry Fitzgerald constantly said on the big screen, Oliver Cromwell died (1658). His son Richard ('tumbledown Dick') was a disaster, the country saw sense and they brought back the king. The Restoration in 1660 saw the reopening of theatres, the return of the phallic maypole, gaiety (in every sense) at the licentious court of Charles II. Puritanism was dead. This, at least, is the Sellar and Yeatman version of history in their hilarious 1936 parody *1066 And All That* and Hollywood lapped it up!

Forever Amber (1947) was a smash hit bodice-ripper of a novel and an average film. Visually, however, it's good. The refugees getting out of London as it burns (1666) look real and the outrageous fashions at the royal court even suit George Sanders as the king. For those of you who felt sorry for Charles I in *Cromwell*, by the way, most of the regicides who signed his death warrant were executed. Where they had already died, as with Cromwell and his son-in-law Henry Ireton, they dug up their bodies and dragged them round the London streets. People knew how to take revenge in the seventeenth century!

The most famous – and interesting – thing about Charles II is his succession of mistresses and he wasn't remotely class-conscious about it. Eleanor Gwynne was the best known. She was a country girl who went to London to find the bright lights in the early 1660s, sold oranges on street corners and got comedy roles, then called 'breeches parts', in plays on Drury Lane, the heart of the capital's theatreland. 'Pretty, witty Nell' had a son by the king (the boy became the Duke of St Albans) but Nell herself only appears in *Hudson's Bay* (1940), which is covered in a later chapter.

Before we know it, Hollywood takes us out of Restoration England, by way of Execution Dock, where felons' bodies bobbed on the tidal Thames, to the ever-wackier shores of the Caribbean, where they kept pirates. So much tosh has been filmed – and written – about these people that it is now nearly impossible to assess their real place in history. Long before Johnny Depp camped it up mercilessly in the

Pirates of the Caribbean series, Hollywood had been serving up decades of hokum to provide entertainment. Clashing swords, dodgy model ships, gorgeous heroines and sumptuous sandy settings all added to the magic. Unfortunately, very little of it is true and you could argue that the pirates really belong in the Crime section of this book.

Chronologically, the earliest of these (discounting Elizabeth's seadogs who were pirates in all but name) takes place in the 1680s and the grim days of Judge Jeffreys, the 'hanging judge'. The movie was *Captain Blood* (1935) in which Errol Flynn played a fictional Irish doctor accused of treason for helping a wounded supporter of Monmouth's rebellion. In a nutshell, when Charles II died in 1685, his successor was his kid brother, James, Duke of York. Unfortunately, in a staunchly Protestant country, James was Catholic, so Charles' illegitimate son (also James, just to confuse the cinema-going public further), the Duke of Monmouth, made a bid for the throne. It didn't work – he was defeated at Sedgemoor, the last battle on English soil – and his followers, who mostly came from the West Country, were rounded up and either hanged or deported.

The man responsible for much of this was George Jeffreys, who was Chief Justice in 1683. He was a political intriguer, perfectly happy to carry out judicial execution of any of the king's enemies and his handling of the 'Bloody Assize' was one of the worst examples of legal excess in history. When James II fell in the Glorious Revolution of 1688, Jeffreys fell with him and died in the Tower the following year. None of this is in the movie, of course, which follows a different piratical course, providing some excellent swordplay between Flynn and the dastardly Basil Rathbone, both of whom look marvellous in lawn sleeves!

Ten years later, another Captain flashed across the screen. This one was real but he was no *beau sabreur* like Flynn, largely because he was played by Charles Laughton. William Kidd was a Scots privateer, given a reward by New York City (then still a colonial settlement) for protecting their trading interests against the French. Nominally working for the British government off Madagascar by 1697, he attacked anything afloat. Two years later, he was brought to book and hanged in London. *Captain Kidd* (1945) was below par on any level, but it didn't help that the period is not well known historically and, for British audiences at the time, Madagascar might as well have been on the far side of the moon.

The Black Swan (1942) was much better, 'performed', as *The Times* said, 'by actors as though to the hokum born'. The hero is the ever-bland Tyrone Power, but the character interest lies in the always watchable Laird Cregar as the poacher-turned-gamekeeper, Henry Morgan. The overweight Cregar has such panache that he gets away with a dreadful Welsh accent and makes the buccaneer all the more believable by scratching his head under the silly wig at times of stress. The real Morgan came from a family of Glamorgan gentry, was kidnapped in Bristol and shipped to Barbados in the West Indies. He ended up, despite countless acts of piracy in Porto Bello ad Maracaibo, as lieutenant governor of Jamaica, which probably tells you all you need to know about the government of the colonies.

One of the 'baddies' Morgan was tasked to catch in his gubernatorial role was Edward Teach, known as Blackbeard. *Blackbeard the Pirate* (1952) purported to tell the story. Unfortunately, an over-the-top character like Teach, usually shown in prints of his time with candles burning from his dreadlocks, could only be played by an over-the-top actor. Enter Robert Newton, who had played Robert Louis Stevenson's Long John Silver in *Treasure Island* two years earlier, complete with beetling brows, rolling eyes and lots of 'Ar, Jim, lad' in the dialogue. MacDonald Fraser thinks the real Teach may have been quite like him, which strains credulity every which way. He was certainly a hell-raiser, with seven wives, a tendency to shoot people under tables and was killed in a duel. The rest is Disney.

Moving forward only a few years in history and virtual millennia in terms of Hollywood, Liam Neeson gave us *Rob Roy* in 1995. Since *Braveheart*, the Scots had lost out big time. When Elizabeth I died in 1603, her nearest successor was the unlovely James Stuart, the VI of

Scotland, who became the I of England. Just over a century later, the 1707 Act of Union dismantled the Edinburgh parliament and brought a surly band of Lowland Scots to Westminster. Despite providing a great deal of talent via the engineers and entrepreneurs of the Industrial Revolution, no one in England really appreciated the Scots. When Dr Samuel Johnson, he of the Dictionary, visited the Highlands, he was appalled by them. He might have echoed Edward I/Patrick McGoohan's line in *Braveheart* – 'The trouble with Scotland is that it is full of Scots.'

Rob Roy (Red Robert) MacGregor was a clan chief at a time, the early eighteenth century, when tribal warfare was a constant in Scotland (it always had been). In modern times, we can equate it with gang warfare, petty squabbles over nothing which turn violent nonetheless.

History intervened in the case of Rob Roy because the supporters of the exiled James II were bad losers. Calling themselves Jacobites (James in Latin is Jacobus) they twice invaded Scotland to get 'their' throne back. The first effort was in 1715 ('the Fifteen' as Scots call it) and his involvement in this gave Roy the reputation of a Robin Hood, escaping from impossible prisons and giving to the poor. It was this fake heroism that Walter Scott built up in his 1818 novel and which Hollywood reprised in 1995. Richard Todd had played him in the 1953 version. In the Neeson version, Scottish stalwart actors Brian Cox and Andrew Keir provide realism, but for me, Tim Roth as Cunningham was the standout character. He is the 'baddie' of course, but his swordsmanship far exceeds Neeson's, which is how it would have been, given the two men's training. Although MacGregor himself was pardoned rather than face transportation, two of his sons were hanged as common criminals, which is exactly what they were.

The Scottish saga continued with the second attempt of the Jacobites to win the throne back in 'the 45' (1745), an even more romantic adventure than that thirty years earlier. By this time the claimant was James II's grandson, the 'Young Pretender', 'Bonnie Prince Charlie'. Just how 'bonnie' Charles Stuart was lay very much in the eye of the beholder and the *Skye Boat Song* and the prince's rescue by Flora MacDonald was the stuff of balladeers, bodice-ripper novels and, of course, Hollywood. That said, the movie of the same name, *Bonnie Prince Charlie* (1948) was a disaster movie worse than the Battle of Culloden, which finished off Charlie's hopes once and for all. The director was Alexander Korda, the Hungarian who was more British than the British (and certainly more British than Charlie, who spent most of his life in France) but this was not his finest hour and the critics roasted him.

The film's running time was dramatically cut and David Niven was seriously miscast as the reckless Stuart prince. 'Time,' wrote Gerald Garnett in 1975, 'has made it the film industry's biggest joke.' It flopped at the box office, with serious losses in a film industry struggling to make a comeback after the lean war years. The *New Yorker* complained that Niven rallying his Highlanders sounded as if he was summoning a waiter. George MacDonald Fraser points out how nearly the '45 rebellion succeeded – a victory at Prestonpans, the invasion of England and panic in London – but this overplays reality. The clans were never fully behind Charlie – he was a Frenchman in a kilt – and ordinary, unpaid soldiers were essentially farm labourers with a harvest to worry about. Contrast that with the Duke of Cumberland's professional redcoats, armed to the teeth with artillery and cavalry (the rebels had neither) and Culloden, April 1746, was a foregone conclusion. The English named a flower, Sweet William, after Cumberland; the Scots called a weed Stinking Billy. The prince, rather less bonnie than he used to be, died a hopeless drunk in France in 1788, an anachronism and embarrassment to all who knew him.

There is one last gasp of the swashbuckler films, though it's tempting to put those three (two remakes and an original) in the Age of Empire chapter. *Mutiny on the Bounty* (1935 and 1962) and *The Bounty* (1984) are not only studies of claustrophobia in history and the effect it has on otherwise rational men, they are a developing thesis in how Hollywood works over time. MacDonald Fraser devotes five pages in his *Hollywood History of the World* to these films, which is probably four too many. The ship HMS *Bounty* was sent to Tahiti in 1787 to pick up breadfruit plants (then regarded as an actual alternative to bread) to be taken to the West Indies. Its commander was William Bligh, a brilliant navigator and, by the standards of the day, a humane captain. His Number Two (as they always said in Second World War films) was his friend Fletcher Christian. The man was only 22, inexperienced and possibly unstable. On Tahiti, everybody had a whale of a time with the bare-breasted, grass-skirt-wearing native girls. As the 1935 movie poster said, 'They'll take this town by storm ... fighting, laughing, loving, breaking every law of the seven seas!'

On the outward voyage, however, disgruntled seamen complained to Christian, who led a mutiny in which Bligh and his supporters were cast adrift in an open rowing boat, 3,000 miles from land. Thanks to Bligh's navigational skills, he reached Timor without the loss of a single life and got back to London. His court martial acquitted him of blame and he went on to become an admiral, highly praised by Horatio Nelson himself (see Chapter 7). Christian and his mutineers reached Pitcairn Island (then off the map) where their descendants live to this day. It was nineteen years before they were found, by which time Christian was dead and the *Bounty* burned.

In the 1935 version, Charles Laughton was an insufferable William Bligh, spitting venom at everybody and threatening keel-hauling (dragging men by ropes under the barnacle-encrusted hull of the ship), which had been outlawed years before, and reminding us all that midshipmen (junior officers) like Franchot Tone were 'the lowest form of animal life in the British navy'. Clark Gable was the heroic Fletcher, standing up to his boss' vicious regime. The 1962 remake starred Trevor Howard as Bligh and Marlon Brando was an appalling Christian, complete with dreadful 'upper class British' accent and a silly half ponytail. The word 'bastard' had been heard in British films before (for example *The Blue Lamp* in 1950) but never with such venom as in the 1962 *Mutiny*; there were mixed howls of laughter and outrage when I watched it in the cinema as a 14-year-old.

In *The Bounty*, Hollywood tried to make amends for the absurdity of the first two efforts. Anthony Hopkins was perhaps *too* restrained as Bligh and Mel Gibson, Hollywood's perennial rebel, showed signs of insanity as Christian (nobody's eyes flash berserker like Gibson's). The tale was told in flashback at Bligh's court martial, which was probably a mistake, because we know from the beginning how it ended, at least for one of the central characters.

The Bounty sailed into history and legend two years before the French Revolution. That in turn upset Europe's *ancien régime* and ushered in the Age of Empire. But before that, ships had other missions. And many of them were sailing west.

Chapter 6

The New World: From the Halls of Montezuma to Uncle Sam

'In fourteen hundred and ninety-two, Columbus sailed the ocean blue' British (and probably American) schoolchildren were once taught. Thanks to today's rewriting – and refilming – of history it's unlikely that there will be any more films about the man. He was by no means the first European to reach Terra Nova (the New World) but his name stuck and Lief Erikson's Vikings, the Irish Brendan and the Welsh Madoc, other, earlier explorers, have either been forgotten or dismissed as fiction. Even the man who gave the new country its name – Amerigo Vespucci – lies on the cutting room floor of history.

Before he was outed as a racist explorer, Cristoforo Colon, the Venetian who sold a mad idea (that the world was round) to Ferdinand and Isabella, rulers of Spain, was hailed as a hero and a brilliant navigator. He was neither, maintaining to his dying day that he had found not a new world but an old one – Cathay (China) or the Spice Islands nearby.

Stills from *Christopher Columbus* (1949) show sumptuous costumes at the court of Ferdinand and Isabella, among the most authentic of any Renaissance movie and Fredric March as the adventurer looks good. It didn't do well at the box office, however, *Time* magazine commenting 'Even ten-year-olds will find it about as thrilling as an afternoon spent looking at Christmas cards.'

Later attempts to cash in on anniversaries fared no better. In 1992, *Christopher Columbus: The Discovery* had Marlon Brando in the title role. 'Dead meat,' said *The Guardian*. 'It's the sort of film that makes you worry not about the characters but the actors playing them …'

The same year *1492: Conquest of Paradise* had Gerard Depardieu as the explorer and was directed by Ridley Scott, who is usually better than this. The film cost $47 million and grossed $7 million worldwide. Columbus' ships, the *Nina*, the *Pinta* and the *Santa Maria* were well-enough made to make the transatlantic crossing and are still on display in Spain.

Not to be outdone, the *Carry On* team were at it again! *Carry On Columbus* (1992) got in on the centenary act. It was one of the worst of a tired old series, 'with' as one critic said, 'a succession of single entendres'. Jim Dale was a lacklustre Columbus and most of the other stalwarts were dead or retired.

Today, the exploitation of indigenous people like the Aztecs and the Incas is not only well known but widely acknowledged. That was not, of course, how Hollywood reviewed it in the past, when explorers from the Old World were *Boys' Own* heroes and the Indians were all 'baddies'. *Captain from Castile* (1947) is one such adventure. Tyrone Power was bland again as the eponymous hero, but his boss, Hernán Cortés, is played with believability by Cesar Romero. The Aztec temples are good, based on contemporary conquistador sketches, as are the plumed costumes of the royal court. It was filmed on location and Alfred Nevin's music score is excellent. The real Cortes was a piece of work. In his late teens, he explored/exploited Cuba and with 550 men and 17 horses (the names of which we still know) he invaded what is today Mexico. Although he was seriously outnumbered by King Montezuma's troops, the Aztecs had never seen either horses or firearms before and were very rattled by the experience. Mexico essentially became New Spain, the settlers appalled by the violence of the Aztecs, especially their slaughter of their own people in huge numbers for religious sacrifice. This wasn't merely Christian/European hyperbole; archaeology has revealed thousands of bones in and around temples.

While Cortes was busy destroying the Aztec civilization, Francisco Pizarro was doing much the same to the Incas. In *Royal Hunt of the Sun* (1969), Robert Shaw is a blond, hard-eyed nut in thigh boots and lawn sleeves (a swashbuckler to the last) as the conquistador and the Incan king, Atahualpa, is a bronzed Christopher Plummer. Like Cortes, Pizarro had a background in exploration/invasion before he ever saw Peru. Harder even than Cortés, the Spaniard tricked Atahualpa and made him his prisoner. Having secured the equivalent of £3.5 million in ransom, he had the king murdered anyway. For those who believe in kismet (fate) the conquistadors fell out among themselves and Pizarro was murdered in 1541. As proof that native rulers behaved exactly like their European invaders, Atahualpa had overthrown his brother before the Spaniards arrived in order to seize the throne, so in Hollywood terms, what we have are two 'baddies' contending for the same territory. The problem with *Royal Hunt of the Sun* is that it was based on a stage play by Peter Shaffer, using trendy sets and performances then in vogue in London and on Broadway. Plummer had played the king on stage and did so again, with a body language and high, piping voice that created the idea of an alien culture very well, but left audiences more than a little mystified.

While Pizarro was being courtly (if devious) with Atahualpa, one of his minions, Lope de Aguirre, was unleashing hell and noisily going mad in the jungles of Peru. *Aguirre, the Wrath of God* (1972) was pretty bad as far as film titles go, but it is a haunting movie, more about man's fight with nature than with other men. The director was Werner Hertzog and it was made in Germany with Peruvian and Mexican location shots. Aguirre is the ever-fascinating Klaus Kinski whose long blond hair and rolling eyes merely underline the fact that he is as mad as a snake. The conquistador's exploits purport to come from the chronicles of Bernal Díaz del Castillo, one of several monks from Columbus onwards who kept 'records' of expeditions to the Americas. The details are as vague and unverifiable as any in history and we should, of course, be wary of one man's account as the basis for *anything* historical. They are all looking for El Dorado, the legendary city of gold (Columbus was too) but they won't find it up the deadly Amazon. What they do find is illness, insanity and death. It ends (spoiler alert) with Aguirre dying on a raft floating on the river with corpses and squabbling monkeys scampering over them. According to Herzog, Kinski was just as barking on set as Aguirre was supposed to be.

Some people still think that the exploration of America began in 1620 when the Pilgrim Fathers sailed westward from Plymouth on board *The Mayflower*. 'Pilgrim' was a dead word by that time in the sense of Catholics visiting saints' shrines all over Europe, but it was made popular again by John Bunyan, born in that extraordinarily confused period of the Civil War when the world was 'turned upside down'. Bunyan was a member of a Puritan sect that spent most of its time arguing with other Puritan sects and he spent a great deal of time in Bedford Gaol. His *Pilgrim's Progress* was written in 1672, with subsequent additions, by which time England was trying to forget all about the 'Godly' who had caused so much havoc (including witch-persecution) over the previous century.

The Pilgrim Fathers were a bunch of misfits unable to live with the reasonable and rational ideas of the Church of England and they first tried to set up a fundamentalist society in the Netherlands. The Dutch (rightly) laughed at them and they set off for the New World where there were no laws to impede their hysterical nonsense. Landing on the American coast, they called it Providence (praise be to God!) and New England, by definition bringing all their prejudices with them. The natives they found there taught them how to clear forests and plant corn, literally keeping them alive, and a few years later, they repaid them by 'buying' Manhattan for the equivalent of 24 dollars! They also laid the ground for the Second Amendment to the Constitution by carrying their guns to church, in case the Indians got testy (which they eventually did).

None of this duplicity is shown in *Plymouth Adventure* (1952) in which the usually dependable Spencer Tracy captains the ship. Reviewing the movie in 1973, Judith Crist wrote, 'It demonstrates how Hollywood can dull down as well as jazz up history.' Everybody looks groomed and clean after weeks at sea and the sets are risible. The film is a reminder, however, that it was not just Spain who was interested in colonization (poor old Portugal barely gets a mention from Hollywood). In the northern area of what would become the United States and Canada, the British and the French squeezed out the Dutch (New York was once New Amsterdam) and fought with each other over territory for 160 years. Some of the explorers here were convinced that there was a north-west passage south of the Arctic; others saw the fortune to be made by hunting animals and providing furs for the European fashion market. One of these was the Frenchman Pierre Esprit Radisson, played by Paul Muni in *Hudson's Bay* (1940). This is the movie in which Vincent Price is a throwback to the swashbuckling days playing Charles II and the film itself isn't bad at all. Virginia Field is Nell Gwynne, complete with a hairstyle that perfectly blends 1940s fashion with those of the 1670s. Radisson's foil in the film was his real-life friend Groisallers (Gooseberry) played by Laird Cregar (who somehow manages to get into a canoe). Unaccountably spurned by the French government of Louis XIV, Radisson sold his wares to the British and made a fortune. It was from this alliance that Canada came about.

Interestingly, *Hudson's Bay* belongs in a way in this book's last chapter (The One-Eyed Monster) because it backs capitalism ('greed is good') and the fur trade (shock! horror!) yet believes in the preservation of the great forest and is nice to Indians (at a time when Hollywood Westerns were not). Slightly bizarre was the casting of Nigel Bruce – Sherlock Holmes' Dr Watson in the Rathbone version – as Prince Rupert of the Rhine who had interests in Canada; eat your heart out, Timothy Dalton!

Before 1776, the year that the colonists declared their independence from Britain, it was all about the thirteen colonies, especially in the north, trying to cope with increasingly awkward natives, whose land, of course, they had pinched, and the French, who had also been there from the beginning of European exploration. It's very telling that to Britain, the clash of arms between them and the French in 1756–63 is called the Seven Years' War (one of dozens since 1066) but to the

Americans, it is the French and Indian war. In physical appearance, Hollywood largely got these years right. Heroes like the fictional Natty Bumpo (who, thank God, had a sensible nickname – Hawkeye) wore caps of racoon fur and fringed buckskin jackets and leggings, and the forest Indians – the Iroquois, the Mohicans, the Seminoles and the Creeks – wore loin cloths and had shaven heads, apart from a central scalp lock. This was superficial – purists would argue that there were many cultural differences between the tribes. By and large, however, the costume departments followed the superb artwork of explorers like John White who drew the natives they saw in Virginia and elsewhere from the 1570s.

The problem was that, just as Walter Scott was making history up for his hugely popular Medieval novels of the 1820s, James Fenimore Cooper was doing much the same in the newly created United States. *The Last of the Mohicans* (1826), *The Deerslayer* (1841) and *The Pathfinder* of the previous year, all told derring-do tales of the eighteenth century, which were very approximate historically.

The first *Last of the Mohicans* (1936) was a trashy Western starring Randolph Scott, but the 1992 remake pulled out all the stops to make everything believable. Hawkeye was played by Daniel Day-Lewis who looks as though he really knows how to handle a flintlock musket (the first of the 'long rifles') at speed, spitting out cartridge paper as he runs through the everglades. What was particularly striking (apart from the brilliant music score) was the honourable appearance of both British and French commanders. The British surrender a fort and the French stand to attention with their flags lowered as it happens. If it didn't *really* happen quite like that, it should have done. Maurice Roëves was a brilliant Colonel Munro looking as if he had worn a horsehair wig and cocked hat all his life and Patrice Chéreau was excellent as General de Montcalm, accepting victory without a hint of snidery.

This was 1757 and the fort was Fort William Henry in New York State. Over 12,000 French and Indian troops besieged Munro and with over 300 dead and an outbreak of smallpox (disease was always a worse killer than shot and shell on historical campaigns) the English felt compelled to surrender. At least fifty of Munro's men, women and children were butchered hours after the surrender, not by the French, who remained true to their commander's word, but by the Indians, who didn't share the same sense of honour (even in 1992, you couldn't say that openly).

Louis Joseph, Marquis de Montcalm Crezan de Saint Vivien, crossed swords with General Wolfe on the Heights of Abraham at Quebec two years later and this time was not so lucky. His army was defeated and he was killed in the rout. That was the month (September 1759) when Major Robert Rogers (he of the Rangers) mounted a commando raid against the Abenaki Indians who had been attacking white settlements for seventy years. *Northwest Passage* (1940) is one of the best movies on eighteenth-century America ever made. Spencer Tracy doesn't only *look* like Rogers, his quiet, commanding presence assures you that his men will follow him anywhere. The film's posters were a *little* over the top – 'Half men, half demons, warriors such as the world had never known ... they lived with death and danger for the women who hungered for their love!' As a child, when I first saw this film, I must have missed the hungry women bit, but the sight of Tracy and co. up to their waists in foaming rapids, muskets kept high out of the water, was sterling stuff. And how creepy was the deranged Ranger who marched on with a sack containing the head of an Abenaki Indian! There was to have been a second part to the film, but the original novel was never completed and neither was the movie.

With the French threat to North America effectively ended (they were later allowed to keep Quebec as a consolation prize) the thirteen British colonies began to flex their muscles in defiance of edicts from London, common sense and the fact that *none* of North America actually belonged to them and spread west, crossing the Allegheny mountains despite the 1763 proclamation that told them not to. It should not have come as a surprise to the colonists (but it did) when the Ottowa chief, Pontiac, went on the warpath to stop them. With hindsight, this was probably the last opportunity the natives would have to halt the westward advance, when settler numbers were still relatively small, but inter-tribal rivalries never went away and Pontiac was murdered by an Illinois. It says everything when you remember what Ecuyer, commanding Fort Pitt (Pittsburgh) said when called upon by the natives to surrender, 'This is our home.' A Swiss mercenary making such a statement to men whose home it *actually* was defies belief.

Cecil B. DeMille's answer to it all was *Unconquered* (1947). 'Plunging over the falls – lashed at the stake – trapped by savages in the mightiest love-spectacle DeMille ever filmed' said the press handouts, but this was DeMille *way* below his best. Gary Cooper fails to convince (as he often did) as a British officer. Paulette Goddard made an unlikely convict sentenced to transportation and don't get me started on Boris Karloff as a Seneca chief! The history was terrible but it looked good and the public saw it in droves.

Umpteen movies were made by Hollywood throughout the history of cinema with the same theme. The pre-1776 colonist was honest, brave, ready for a fight and always falling in love with gorgeously unlikely heroines. The 'baddie' was either an unscrupulous white trader (usually played by Brian Donlevy, whose little moustache gave away his treacherous tendencies) or a pompous snob of a British officer who was so stuck in the bad old ways of the *ancien régime* it was laughable. Unbelievably, they were still using these stereotypes into the 1980s.

Oddly, bearing in mind how important it was to America, Hollywood has made few films about the War of Independence and they have all been bad. There were no real characters in *Drums Along the Mohawk* (1939) but it looked like a pre-cowboy and Indian Western despite being set in New York during the war. The same was true of the *Howards of Virginia* (called *The Tree of Liberty* in Britain) with Cary Grant as the lead (putting a lightweight romantic lead, however charming, into an historical film is always a mistake).

John Paul Jones (1959) threw in a whole galaxy of historical characters in what ought to have been a straightforward tale. The cast list reads like a who's who of the late eighteenth century. For the record, John Paul (the Jones bit was added later) was a Scots sailor who owned a slave ship and inherited land in Virginia. He served in the new American navy in 1776 and fought a couple of engagements on board his frigate *Le Bonhom Richard*. Flying the American flag and commanding a French squadron made him a double-dyed traitor as far as the British were concerned. His famous 'I have not yet begun to fight' as his ship was crippled and on fire has become one of the iconic statements of independence. Robert Stack played Jones in the movie but others wandering in and out of shot included: Louis XVI of France and his wife, the Austrian woman, Marie Antoinette; Catherine the Great of Russia; George III of Britain and his nemesis, the pamphleteer John Wilkes; American founding fathers Ben Franklin, Patrick Henry, John Hancock and John Adams; oh, and George Washington. Even if Jones met all these people – and it seems unlikely – putting them all in one movie would seem to be historical overkill.

A much better – and rather underrated – film is *Die Schlacht am Delaware* 'The Crossing' in England and the US (2000), a German production with American actors (see Overture). It's not clear why Hollywood has largely kept away from George Washington. He was, after all, America's first president and one of the best. He wasn't a great soldier but he was a great leader of men, as this film, about the Continental Army's attack on the Prussians at Trenton, New Jersey, shows. The cold, the exhaustion, the determination of a handful of amateurs against one of the best organized armies in the world, is beautifully made.

By the time we come to *Revolution* (1985) a silent revolution of a different kind had happened. The simplistic good versus bad of Hollywood had been replaced by balanced, nuanced movies that were as near to historical accuracy as film-makers could get, given the codes and restrictions outlined in Overture. Ever since 1776, generations of American schoolchildren had been force-fed the one-dimensional view – the colonists were good, honest folk who just wanted to get on with their lives and the British, arrogant and aloof, not only wouldn't let them, but taxed them to the hilt. By the 1980s, *real* history was kicking in and with it the realization that the colonies were far freer before 1776 than the States of the Union have ever been since. Colonial self-government was a reality – a right granted to them by the British.

Hollywood should have treated the War of Independence as it did America's own Civil War, with sweeping battles and real heroism, both available in the historical record. Instead, it got bogged down in minutiae. '[Director Hugh] Hudson,' critic David Eisenstein wrote, 'has thrown what doubtless started as a perfectly straightforward script to the winds and marched off in search of images that would somehow galvanize the whole show into life. But as his camera stumbles through the smoke, fire and mobs of expensively costumed extras, it's clear he's not going to find them.' The war is focused on two enemies – the colonist Al Pacino and the infantry sergeant Donald Sutherland – making the whole thing low-key and ridiculously claustrophobic. Pacino can be very good, but he's no eighteenth-century revolutionary.

Neither is Mel Gibson. In 2000, he played another in a long line of his anti-the-system heroes in *The Patriot*. As Jonathan Foreman wrote, 'If the Nazis had won the war in Europe and their propaganda machine had decided to make a film about the American revolution, *The Patriot* is the sort of movie you could expect to see.' The acting was average (Mad Max in lawn sleeves and an open waistcoat) and the history lamentable. What rightly annoyed the critics was the character of Colonel Banastre (his name was changed to let the movie get away with murder) Tarleton, the British cavalry commander. In the movie, sadistic Tarleton hacks a woman to death with his sabre, something that the real man never did and, given the mores of the time, wouldn't even have contemplated. This was crude propaganda of the worst sort, unforgiveable considering when it was made.

Hollywood didn't make much of the next (and last) war between America and Britain either. Having established the United States, with

The New World: From the Halls of Montezuma to Uncle Sam

its federal system and written constitution (both alien concepts to the British) the new country was allying itself as far as trade went with the French and by 1812, Britain had been fighting France for nearly twenty years. When the Royal Navy began searching American ships, the president, James Madison, declared war. The conflict was short lived and resulted in the burning of most of Washington DC, including the White House, and the British defeat at New Orleans.

Ironically, this was a battle that need never have been fought – terms had been agreed between the governments days earlier. *The Buccaneer* (1938 and 1958) sounds like a return to swashbuckling days, but it's a true(ish) story of Jean Lafitte, a French pirate who attacked anybody's shipping at the mouth of the Mississippi. General Andrew Jackson (Charlton Heston in the later version) persuades Lafitte (Akim Tamaroff and then Yul Brynner – with hair!) to defend New Orleans against the woefully incompetent General Pakenham. DeMille's 1958 version was a disappointing affair with a studio-bound battle and little to recommend it. Heston, as always, looks like 'Old Hickory' (Jackson) but is surely much too gentlemanly for him. The general who went on to become president may have been a lawyer, but he was also something of an oaf. He did his best to wipe out the Cree nation in his war with them and his inauguration in 1829 saw an unruly mob of supporters trash the White House nearly as badly as the British had in 1812.

Fast forward to 1836 as the United States, along with nearly every country in Europe, was racing to grab somebody else's territory. Texas had belonged to Spain, but there was a growing movement towards independence in the 1830s to create the Republic of Texas. It was considered large enough to become a country in its own right. Mexico, the rightful owner, had other ideas and war broke out. For Americans, the holy of holies became the Alamo, a broken-down Catholic mission church in San Antonio de Bexar. Today a hugely popular tourist centre, the exact events of the thirteen-day siege there (February–March 1836) are disputed by historians. There have been a number of films with 'Alamo' in the title, but only two which depict the siege itself. *The Alamo* of 1960 is streets ahead of the remake (2004); even the tag lines are worlds apart. In 1960 – 'The Mission that became a Fortress ... The Fortress that became a Shrine'. In 2004 – 'Stand Your Ground'. Hmm.

Under the command of William Travis (Laurence Harvey in the 1960 version) a ragtag group of volunteers (fewer than 200) under James Bowie (Richard Widmark) and David Crockett (John Wayne) holds out against the 2,500 of General Santa Ana, the governor. With epic odds like that, what can go wrong? Well, the 2004 remake for a start! There are a lot of mistakes in the John Wayne version. Harvey and Widmark spend most of the movie bickering, whereas their real characters worked well together. Bowie had been sent by General Sam Houston (Richard Boone) not to defend the Alamo as the film insists, but to evacuate it and blow it up (see *Khartoum*, Chapter 7). The characterization of the leads is open to debate. Bowie, inventor of the famous hunting knife, was a Mexican citizen and major landowner. For much of the siege he was ill in bed, not hurt in the action as the film implies. The enigmatic Davy Crockett was the hero of little boys of my age, watching television in the 1950s. He was a Tennessean frontiersman, complete with coonskin cap and fringed buckskin (Wayne wore his usual bib-fronted shirt and waistcoat *far* too often for us purists!) but he had served as a congressman, which makes him a cut above his moronic but loveable Tennesseans in the movie – 'Do this mean what I think it do?' 'It do.'

In the 1960 film, Crockett dies in the fighting, but there is a school of thought that he and a small group surrendered, were put on trial by Santa Ana and shot by firing squad.

Of the remake, with a very dull Billy Bob Thornton as Crockett, Desson Thomson of *The Washington Post* wrote, 'Those 13 days feel like the Hundred Years' War.'

As the nineteenth century wore on, a major problem was growing in American politics, one that has never gone away; the problem of the 'peculiar institution', as it was called – slavery.

In 1619, twenty men were brought from West Africa in a Dutch trader to work as unpaid labour in the colonies. Slavery was standard in the African states and black slaves in the colonies and emergent states were treated no worse than they had been at home. By today's standards, of course, the conditions of the slaves on the transatlantic crossing were appalling, with as many as 25 per cent of them dying long before they reached America. Families were broken up as men, women and children were sold indiscriminately especially in the plantations of the 'South'. By the 1850s, as the number of states grew and society became more aware of the moral questions involved, debates took place in Congress and elsewhere, in which abolitionists tried to end the evil trade and slave owners pressured to keep their 'property'.

One man in the thick of these debates was the Congressman from Illinois (although he was born in Kentucky), Abraham Lincoln. *Young Mr Lincoln* (1938) is singled out by George MacDonald Fraser as Henry Fonda's best performance and he cannot understand why he didn't even get an Oscar nomination for it. The movie was a success, largely because it looked at the sixteenth president before he became old and furrowed by the wrong of it all. As president, Lincoln presided over a civil war which cost well over half a million lives, more than in all America's other wars put together. According to legend, when he met Harriet Beecher Stowe, author of the seminal *Uncle Tom's Cabin*, he said, 'So you're the little woman who caused this great war of ours.' But it's more likely that he carried the bulk of the guilt himself.

Other actors had played Lincoln already – Frank McGlynn in a series of cameos in the 1930s, Walter Huston and Raymond Massey, all of whom focused on the pivotal period of the war itself. One of these, Huston's version in 1930, is regarded by Harry Medved as one of the worst fifty movies of all time. Its director was D.W. Griffith, who, as we shall see below, had a very chequered Hollywood career, today more so than ever. The promotional leaflet read 'The Wonder Film of the Century ['Talkies' were only 3 years old] about the Most Romantic Figure who ever lived.' Hagiography on celluloid is as bad as hagiography in print (probably worse because it reaches larger audiences) and it always leads to a fall. 'Totally dull,' said the critics, 'the results were waxworks.'

Lincoln's rise from log cabin to White House is a gift for filmmakers, but Griffith blows it. We have a verbatim record of the Lincoln–Douglas debates of the 1850s but the screenplay waters it down to basics and we sit wondering what all the fuss was about. At Ford's Theatre in April 1865, we see Huston/Lincoln arriving in his box and giving part of his inaugural address to the theatre-goers who actually just want to get on with enjoying the farce *Our American Cousin*. In reality, of course, Lincoln made no such speech, although the audience was probably a little miffed when the president arrived late and the show had to halt. 'Mr Lincoln has been shot!' shouts one member of the audience, after we've just seen Mr Lincoln being shot and another one says, 'Now he belongs to the ages.' At that point, Lincoln was still alive and the quotation comes hours later from Secretary of War Edwin Stanton, who may (he was understandably upset at the time) have said 'angels', not 'ages'. We have all the tunes of the period – the South's *Dixie* (actually written by a Northerner) and the North's *Battle Hymn of the Republic*. Appropriately, the production manager, according to the film's credits, was O.O. Dull!

Young Mr Lincoln sought to improve on Griffith's nonsense and it did well. Fonda *looked* like Lincoln, albeit a far more handsome version. The real 'honest Abe' was arguably the least photogenic president America has ever had. One 'fan' (a little girl) suggested he grow a beard to hide his scrawny neck.

In 1940, the Warner Studios produced 'the thundering story that challenges all filmdom to watch its excitement' (which is a little over the top if you've ever seen it). It was called *Santa Fe Trail* and dealt with one of the most enigmatic characters in American history – John Brown of Osawatomie. The film's title is irrelevant, but the characters are real. Brown himself was an Abolitionist, albeit a deranged one, who wanted to end slavery by raising a slave rebellion. It didn't work. Despite months of planning and spreading the word, of the 4.5 million slaves in the South, only five turned up at the appointed place of insurrection, Harper's Ferry in Virginia, in 1859. Raymond Massey, gaunt-cheeked, wild-haired and bearded, was an impressive John Brown. Erroll Flynn was Erroll Flynn, playing the future Confederate cavalry commander J.E.B. Stuart. His sidekick in the movie was George Armstrong Custer, played by future president Ronald Reagan, which is odd because Custer didn't attend West Point until 1861 by which time John Brown's body was 'a moulderin' in the grave'.

But Lincoln's early years are merely a taster of the cataclysm of the Civil War. Historians are still divided over the causes of this. Was it about slavery, which is the simplistic 'woke' view of the world, or was it about state rights versus the federal system, which had been brewing since the United/Disunited States came into being?

The granddaddy of all Civil War films, however, was D.W. Griffith's *Birth of a Nation* (1915), famously described by President Woodrow Wilson as being 'like history written with lightning'. It wasn't history at all, seen from the biased viewpoint of the South, but it did contain actual characters Ulysses S. Grant, Lincoln and his assassin, John Wilkes Booth. As a piece of cinema, *Birth of a Nation* (originally called *The Clansman*) was revolutionary, with panoramic camera sweeps for the battle scenes that we now take for granted. There were riots in some movie theatres where the film was shown and the real 'baddies' in the story are clearly white actors in black-face, to try to minimize the racial threat. Since the storyline goes on to cover the North's barbaric treatment of the South in the Reconstruction era (1866 onwards) it also covered the rise of the Ku Klux Klan under General Nathan Forrest. Wearing white hoods and burning crosses, Klansmen went on the rampage, lynching the (now free) blacks with impunity. Many believed that the movie's impact led to a revival of the KKK which led, in turn, to yet more lynchings in the 1920s. 'Forget it, Louis,' Irving Thalberg said to producer Louis B. Mayer in 1936. 'No Civil War picture ever made a nickel.'

Three films stand out about the Civil War. Chronologically the first of these was *Glory* (1989) about one of the first black regiments raised by the American government, the 54th Massachusetts Infantry. There had been much hand-wringing about this since the war started – the risk of arming ex-slaves was considered by many to be too great and of course there was no question of officers being black. Accordingly, the 54th were led by Robert Gould Shaw, a Harvard graduate whose name is still on the college's In Memoriam wall. Matthew Broderick played him superbly, using authentic-sounding 1860s dialogue and he is ably supported by a fine cast. Carey Elwes is Broderick's less altruistic Number Two and Morgan Freeman is excellent as the grave-digger promoted to sergeant. As a white soldier in another unit says of him, 'Stripes on a n****r? That's like tits on a bull,' proving that the average Joe north of the Mason–Dixon line was every bit as racist as he was south of it.

The 'uppity n****r' was Denzel Washington, cast against type as a surly rebel resenting just about everything. The 54th's baptism of fire was actually a suicide mission, to take Fort Wagner, one of many Southern-held citadels on the coast. The attack was a disaster and the casualty rate appalling. Gould Shaw was buried in a common grave along with his men. When his father heard of his death, he said he was proud that his son could have no finer companions in the hereafter. Those sad people who look for tiny gaffes in historical movies will point out that as the 54th march through the plantations bringing freedom to people who were actually freed nearly two years earlier, one of the extras is still wearing his wristwatch. By that time, engrossed in *Glory*, nobody cares. For me, one small, electrifying role is that of the ex-slave Frederick Douglass. With his wild white hair and beard, he is the picture of dignity and an extraordinarily accurate lookalike.

Gods and Generals (2003) and *Gettysburg* (1993) appear as a boxed set of DVDs today, although chronologically, they were released the wrong way round. The director was Ronald Maxwell and, as with *Glory*, the look and feel of both movies is absolutely right. Seeing the recruits of both sides stumbling across the actual fields where the battles were fought, we get the sense of the amateur military engagements of both armies. The officers may have graduated from West Point, the military academy on the Hudson, but the rank and file were farm boys and mill hands. Most of them could shoot tolerably well, but they had no idea of discipline. Many were illiterate and the war saw them leave home for the first time in their lives. My one gripe about both movies is that 'Johnny Reb' and 'Billy Yank' are too old; the average age of the Civil War soldier was 19.

Gods and Generals focuses on the campaigns of Fredericksburg and Chancellorsville, when the South still had the upper hand. Robert Duvall makes an impressive Robert E. Lee, the Rebel commander, complete with grey horse Traveller. We see the war from both sides, with Jeff Daniels as Colonel Lawrence Chamberlain, the same role he played in *Gettysburg*, but the main focus is on Stephen Lang as General Thomas 'Stonewall' Jackson. When he is mortally wounded by his own trigger-happy pickets on a night of dark confusion, Lee said, 'Jackson has lost his left arm and I've lost my right.' It is faithfully reproduced in the film without the melodrama and violins that Hollywood would have given it in decades gone by. What is also clear from both movies is the ragtag appearance of the men involved. To refer to the respective armies as 'the Blue and the Grey' is a serious over-simplification. Take any ten extras standing side by side at, say, Chancellorsville, and you have at least three different shades of those colours.

Gettysburg was described in the film's publicity as the 'bloodiest battle fought on American soil' but that was actually Antietam, in 1862. Martin Sheen was an excellent Robert E. Lee and Tom Berenger, almost unrecognizable under the huge beard, was General James Longstreet. As with *Gods and Generals*, the military history has been immaculately researched, with the action in the woods around Little Round Top faithfully photographed. Depicting Pickett's Charge shows superbly the tactical problem in the 1860s. Firearms' technology had improved apace; battlefield formations hadn't. So the Charge was actually a long, uphill slog by infantrymen into a wall of cannon and rifle fire that brought the South's men down in their hundreds. As commanders said glumly in the First World War, 'ground gained; nil'. Encouragingly, the

DVD boxed set contains a section on *The Authentication of the Film*, covering the lengths to which film-makers go these days to get it right. This should be compulsory viewing for every producer, director, actor, designer and cameraman in the film business.

And so we come back to Abraham Lincoln. Steven Spielberg directed Daniel Day-Lewis in *Lincoln* in 2012. Contrary to what most people believe, the president was not a committed Abolitionist until the war was well under way and this movie is about his momentous decision to push the Emancipation Proclamation through Congress. The House of Representatives is shown in the film as the chaotic rough-house it was (and still is, at times!) with everybody shouting the odds and convinced they are right. Bruce McGill is an impressive Edwin Stanton lookalike, even if Sally Field is a little too likeable as the unstable Mary Todd, the president's wife.

In the previous year, *The Conspirator* had been directed by Robert Redford. It dealt with the trial of Mary Surratt, the only woman convicted of the assassination conspiracy against Lincoln. In April 1865, four days after Robert E. Lee surrendered at Appomattox Court House, Virginia, Lincoln and his wife attended Ford's Theatre in Washington DC. There he was shot in the back of the head by a deranged Southerner, the actor John Wilkes Booth, and the search was on for his accomplices. Mary Surratt kept a boarding house where several of the conspirators stayed in the days prior to the assassination. Robin Wright was excellent as the enigmatic Mary; we are still not sure of her guilt by the time the film ends. James McAvoy is superb as her reluctant defence counsel and the court is exposed for all the bias and manipulation of justice that it actually showed at the time. Because, like *Lincoln*, it is very wordy and slow-moving, *Conspirator* sank without trace at the box office.

La Amistad was a Spanish slave trade ship, one of hundreds carrying slaves on the notorious triangle between West Africa, Britain and the Americas. In 1839, it became the centre of an international legal battle when slaves from the Mende tribe took control of the ship from the traders off Cuba and reached the United States. There, a legal case before the Supreme Court dragged on until 1841 when it was decided that the slaves should be freed.

Today, slavery has become *the* issue in history to a new generation who have little or no knowledge of the institution. Several of the movies above have slavery as their backdrop, but *Amistad* (1997) confronted the issue head-on. Based on a factual account, the film starred the impressive Dijmon Hounsou as Sengbe Pieh (Cinqué in the film), the leader of the revolt. He speaks no English; in fact, the first word he is able to say is 'free' and it makes the heart glow. Matthew McConaughey is the idealistic defence lawyer Roger Baldwin, but dwarfing them all (as ever) is Anthony Hopkins as the grouchy old Congressman (and former president) John Quincy Adams. With his bald head and fierce eyes, Hopkins is perfect.

There are lovely touches – President Martin Van Buren (Nigel Hawthorne) flits in and out; Isabella II of Spain (Anna Paquin) is a 9-year-old bouncing on her bed in a sumptuous court dress. And then there is that surreal moment when the *Amistad*, stolen by its slaves, glides silently past another ship at night, where the white guests are all on deck, enjoying a party. Director Steven Spielberg insisted that the Pieh character be able to learn the Mende language (Hounsou had ten days in which to this) and turned down at least two high-profile black actors because they were not right for the part. Hopkins and Hounsou became so involved in their parts that it was all they could do in their scene together not to cry.

There was, as there is all too often in Hollywood movies, an unseemly row between Spielberg's Dreamworks studio and an author who claimed that her novel on the theme had been plagiarized. Historical critics played the movie down. The *Amistad* case, said Eric Toner of Columbia University, was not a 'turning point' in the slavery issue as the slave trade had been outlawed in 1840. Since that was the date in which the film was set, that seems rather a 'beside the point' argument. Perhaps inevitably, in these days when everybody, it seems, is more than prepared to rubbish the past, one critic called it a 'white saviour narrative' and 'sanctimonious drivel'. Given the fact that it was whites who owned slaves and whites who made up 100 per cent of American courts and government, how could it be anything else?

In 1853, *Twelve Years A Slave* was written by Solomon Northup about his kidnapping in Washington DC in 1841 and being sold into slavery. The same criticism of the movie – of a white saviour mentality – was levelled at this film too (in 2013). The attitudes of slave owners, as Christians defending slavery, are incomprehensible and unacceptable today, but Northup himself accepted their position. 'Stark, visceral and unrelenting,' wrote Paul MacInnes in *The Guardian*, '[the movie] is not just a great film but a necessary one.' Another critic talked about the insuperable 'hero problem' – 'We can handle 12 Years a Slave. But don't expect 60 Years a Slave any time soon. And 200 Years, Millions of Slaves? Forget about it.'

There can't be much 'white saviourism' in *Harriet* (2019) because the saviour (of other slaves) was a black woman, Araminta Ross, better known to us as Harriet Tubman. The extraordinary woman, born a slave in 1822, was played by Cynthia Erivo and, inevitably, eyebrows were raised because Ms Erivo is British (a kind of racism in reverse). The movie faithfully charts Tubman's work as organizer and runner of the Underground Railroad, whereby escaping slaves followed the North Star ('follow the drinking gourd' as the spiritual said) via friendly farmsteads, to the North and freedom. Many reviewers found *Harriet* formulaic, saved only by Erivo's fine performance, but it was a film that was long overdue in terms of a salutation to the independence of black Americans and women in general.

The relevance of the end of slavery will hardly be noticed in the chapter on further western expansion, but it was because it came to an end (bloodily and belatedly) that one in five cowboys 'West of the Pecos' was black.

America – and Hollywood – were ready for the greatest adventure story in the country's history; the Wild West. But outside America, there were other adventures and other stories – and Hollywood was up for that, too.

Chapter 7

The Age of Empire: From Bonaparte to Ekaterinburg

Out of the chaos of the late eighteenth century, with revolution in the American colonies and France, emerged, eventually, democracy in the West, but it was by no means a steady process and, ironically, the only way for society to cope with the collapse of the *ancien régime* was to recreate it, stronger and more pushy than ever. Guiltiest of all the countries involved was France and in that context, the focus of early nineteenth-century history – and of the Hollywood movies devoted to that period – was Napoleon. He has appeared in more films than any other historical figure, perhaps because it took the combined weight of most of Europe and nearly twenty years to defeat him.

'The little Corsican' was born to a family of minor gentry in Ajaccio – the house is still there, open to visitors except on Mondays – in 1769 when Corsica was effectively French territory. He attended a military academy at Brienne and was commissioned in the artillery. Always a political soldier, Napoleone Buonaparte as he was then, associated with the revolutionaries in Paris and emerged in 1796 as 'the sword of the revolution'. He even helped himself to Josephine de Beauharnais, mistress of the politician Paul Barras and dropped the Corsican spelling of his name.

A grateful revolutionary government gave Lieutenant Bonaparte command of the Army of Italy, suitably promoted him to general and let him get on with it. Taking on the Austrians and the Piedmontese simultaneously, he thrashed them both and returned in triumph to Paris. Still more grateful, the government gave him his head to campaign anywhere in the world. He invaded Egypt, easily defeating the locals but his fleet was destroyed by Horatio Nelson at Aboukir Bay in 1798.

Establishing himself at the heart of a political triumvirate and referring to the executed Louis XVI as 'my poor uncle' (they weren't remotely related) he embarked on a whirlwind series of campaigns to defeat every European army sent against him. In 1804, having overthrown his political rivals in a coup, he declared himself emperor of the French and crowned himself in Rheims cathedral (the pope was there, but did not officiate). By 1807, he was master of Europe. The only country that held out against him was Britain, Napoleon's planned invasion thwarted by another fleet annihilation by Nelson at Trafalgar.

His invasion of Russia in 1812 was a step too far, his supply lines over-extended against an enemy who did what the Russians always do, let their appalling weather do their fighting for them. Of the 600,000 men of the Grande Armée, only 40,000 came back from the snows of Moscow. A coalition army defeated him at Leipzig the following year and the emperor was exiled to Elba while Europe paused for breath and old boundaries were re-established. In that hiatus, Bonaparte escaped and mounted the hundred days' campaign, culminating in his ultimate defeat at Waterloo at the hands of Wellington's British and Blucher's Prussian forces. 'La Gloire', after which the French still hankered a century later, was over.

Just as a military genius like Alexander the Great or Genghis Khan is difficult to portray in film, Napoleon presented the same challenges to film-makers. Abel Gance opted in 1927, the year of sound, for *Napoleon*, which used a triptych screen effect (pre-Cinerama) to create sweeping scenes, concentrating on the soldier's early career. Gance intended to make later films covering all the years to 1815 but he never finished the project. Albert Dieudonné played the Corsican, impoverished and gaunt (as portraits show he was at the time) from the legendary – and apocryphal – snowball fight at Brienne to his triumph at the head of the army of Italy.

The movie premiered at the Paris Opera House and lasted for an astonishing six hours. Its re-release by MGM in 1981 had reduced it to a single screen and a humble seventy-eight minutes. Gance pulls no punches. From Cadet Buonaparte, with his stained and holey socks and scruffy hair in the 'mode à la guillotine' to the ragged, half-starved and mutinous army of Italy, every scene is a faithful recreation of how it probably was. He meets Josephine at a 'victims' ball' (only for those who had been imprisoned during The Terror of the revolutionary government in the 1790s). There are clichés everywhere, even if in 1927 no one had seen them before. The young Napoleon almost certainly didn't own a pet eagle (symbol, of course of the French, like the Roman, army); neither did a fortune teller tell Josephine that she would one day be empress of the French. The problem with this movie, riveting as it is, is that it has so often been edited and re-edited that the impact of the original has been lost.

From the sublime to the ridiculous – *Desirée* (1954). Halliwell's verdict is the right one – 'Heavy-going costume piece, with all contributors distinctly uncomfortable'. Michael Rennie emerges with some dignity as Bernadotte (although he looks nothing like him) the French general who ended up, in those improbable days, as king of Sweden. Jean Simmons played the lead, the daughter of a wealthy silk merchant (not a shopkeeper as the film's blurb contends) who was possibly Bonaparte's first love. Climbing the political ladder as he was, Desirée was not the catch he needed and so he dropped her, although her sister Julie did go on to marry Bernadotte and so become queen of Sweden. In the film, of course, it is Jean Simmons who ties that particular knot. Marlon Brando is woeful as Napoleon, brooding as Brando always does whatever role he is playing. The whole thing seems to have been made on a shoestring, the epic campaigns shown by a montage of banners against a black background. For the 1812 Moscow campaign, the banners are covered with fake snow! The only scene worthy of an historic accolade is the recreation of David's famous painting of the 1804 coronation, with Josephine (Merle Oberon) being crowned by her over-the-top husband. As in the original painting, the pope looks less than happy to be there. As Baird Searles says in *Epic*, '*Desirée* is hardly history, but it's a lot of fun.'

Charles Boyer was a far better Napoleon in *Marie Walewska* (1937) released in Britain and the United States as *Conquest*. Marie was the emperor's second wife, the result of a political marriage, which only achieved a weak, ineffectual son who died from pneumonia after reviewing some troops in 1832. Halliwell calls the movie 'measured and dignified' but George MacDonald Fraser rightly praises Boyer's performance. 'He epitomised the man ... the quick, abrupt manner, the restless energy, the direct stare, the sudden passions ... but always the impatient dynamo underneath.' Greta Garbo was a bit gooey as Marie, but the Polish princess really *did* have a crush on 'the bête noire' before she even met him. There are mistakes in the film – Napoleon *had* met his little son before his exile to Elba and Marie was not there when he surrendered to the British on the *Bellerophon* – but these things are the constant irritations of historical recreations.

The Russians have cashed in hugely on this period of their history. Before Napoleon was a twinkling in the eye of the revolution, they offered the world Catherine the Great. No one who has played the empress looks remotely like her, which is a pity because the contemporary portraits make some of her more strenuous sexual excesses (involving chains and horses etc.) rather unlikely. She was a German princess, born in Stettin in 1729 and married the heir to the Russian throne in 1745. She was notoriously promiscuous but only two lovers have emerged in the historical record. For this, Tsar Peter exiled her but he himself was overthrown in a palace coup and she was made empress. This says far more about the flakiness of the Russian boyars than the ability of Catherine herself, although she would prove to be the energetic and enlightened ruler that hidebound, backward Russia desperately needed. A mistress (pun intended) of court intrigues, she was undoubtedly a very clever woman and under her, Russia expanded into Polish, Turkish and Swedish territory.

Peter was a half-wit, played by Sam Jaffe in *The Scarlet Empress* (1934). Catherine 'is photographed from behind veils,' wrote *The New Yorker* reviewing the movie forty years later, 'while dwarfs dither about and bells ring and everybody tries to look degenerate.' Remember that this was the decade of Eisenstein's *Alexander Nevsky* and *Ivan the Terrible* (see chapters 3 and 4) when such things were expected of Russian court life. The empress herself was portrayed by Marlene Dietrich, sultry enough but far too thin for the real woman. She wears a gorgeous but historically incorrect French hussar uniform – in white, no less – to a crescendo of the 1812 Overture, that particular piece of music lying nearly fifty years in the future.

The Rise of Catherine the Great appeared almost simultaneously with *The Scarlet Empress*. This was a British effort directed by Alexander Korda, famous for his depictions of empires generally and worth watching for the superior cast. Although the lead, Elisabeth Bergner, sank more or less without trace with only a couple of dozen minor roles in the next forty years, everybody else is excellent, especially Flora Robson as a stuffy royal matriarch and Douglas Fairbanks Jnr, playing against type as mad Tsar Peter. He ponders whimsically about the average Russian soldier, Ivan Ivanovitch, and sums up his views on his pushy wife with the immortal line, 'If she wasn't on the throne, she'd be on the street.'

By the time Napoleon arrived on the scene, Catherine had been dead for sixteen years and 1812 gave the Russians an epic experience to prove their often-expressed patriotism. During the 1860s, Leo Tolstoy, himself an ex-artillery officer, wrote *War and Peace* relating to the 1812 campaign. It took him six years to write and is one of the longest novels in any language. It's essentially a soap, about a Russian family caught up in the Napoleonic invasion. There have been a number of films based on this, most of them excellent. The first of the standouts was the American-Italian version of 1956, produced by Carlo Ponti. The battle scenes were directed by King Vidor and photographed by Jack Cardiff, both superb practitioners in the field. In those pre-CGI days, the Grande Armee and its Russian equivalent were composed of actual extras, even if the numbers inevitably fell short of the almost 1 million men who clashed, for example, at Borodino. Henry Fonda, who played the lead male role, thought that Vidor destroyed the film by endless rewriting of Irving Shaw's/Tolstoy's original.

The uniforms are fine and the sense of hopelessness as Napoleon's freezing troops struggle through the snow is well brought out. Napoleon himself was played by Herbert Lom, probably the best version of the emperor on celluloid. We see him at Austerlitz, victorious and in Moscow, on his way to being defeated. He is excellent on both occasions. Out-growling everybody is veteran actor Oscar Homolka as the one-eyed General Kutuzov, luring the French ever deeper into the death-trap of the Russian winter.

The film took four years to make, almost exactly a century after Tolstoy wrote the book and cost an extraordinary $100 million! The American release appeared in two halves, with bad dubbing (there were Italians, Czechs, Austrians, Americans, British, Belgians and Swedes in the cast). This was the first film in which battle scenes were filmed from overhead by helicopter, showing the infantry squares and cavalry charges in all their sweeping grandeur.

The second *War and Peace* was Sergei Bondarchuk's 1967 version, with some of the most spectacular battle scenes ever made. It took five years to make, but the bill came in at a mere $70 million. It followed Tolstoy's novel very closely and Napoleon (Vladislav Strzhelchik) looks every inch the finest general in Europe.

The last appearance of the emperor in the cinema to date, if we exclude the brilliant but rather unhistorical *Time Bandits*, was *Waterloo* (1971) produced by Dino De Laurentiis and directed (again) by Bondarchuk. The cast and crew were multinational, as with *War and Peace*, but this was the first time that the Duke of Wellington achieved a starring role, played (perhaps too jokily) by Christopher Plummer. The Russian involvement, apart from Bondarchuk, was huge. They ploughed £4 million into production, provided nearly 20,000 Red Army soldiers, a brigade of cavalry and the location, near Uzhgorod in Ukraine. The layout of the battlefield, with its ripening corn, the woods that hid the Prussians and the farmhouse of La Haye Sainte, were all excellent. The film cost over £12 million, but would have been three times that without Russian help. Five miles of '1815' roads were created, as well as 5,000 trees planted and two hills bulldozed to create the Belgian countryside fifteen years before Belgium came into existence.

We see Napoleon (Rod Steiger) abdicating in front of his tearful *grognards* (grumblers) before his exile to Elba. We see the fat and crippled Louis XVIII (Orson Welles) carried on a litter back to his throne. Marshal Ney (a fiery, red-headed Dan O'Herlihy) is sent to take the emperor prisoner when he returns from exile and, far from bringing him back in a cage, hands him his sword in obedience. The scene where Steiger says to a would-be firing squad, 'If you want to kill your emperor, here I am,' is superbly done.

Arthur Wellesley, the Duke of Wellington, is at the Duchess of Richmond's ball in Brussels when news arrives that Napoleon is on the march again. The weather was awful and since the whole battle was filmed in sweltering heat in August, artificially produced rain had to be poured on to the 'scum of the earth enlisted for drink' who were the downtrodden infantry.

The horses sink in the mud and the whispered narrative over the scenes – 'This mud will kill us' – are particularly effective. Neither Steiger nor Plummer were accomplished horsemen (the real Napoleon wasn't much of a rider either) and it shows in a number of shots. General William Picton (Jack Hawkins) is shown correctly in his civilian dress. His top hat, blown off his head by the musket-ball that killed him, can still be seen in Chelsea's National Army Museum today.

But it wasn't all accuracy and light. The celebrated charge of the Scots Greys – 'those men on grey horses are terrifying,' as Napoleon said – is ludicrously done. Almost half of the regiment carry curved, as opposed to straight, bladed swords and, unforgivably, half way through, the film turns to slow motion, which not only exposes uniform gaffes but negates the point of a hell-for-leather charge. Similarly, when we see the aerial shots of the British squares, facing the French cavalry, several of them have broken, with extras scattering. In reality, not a single square broke and the cavalry were wasting their time.

The silliest – and least historical – moment in the film comes when a young British soldier breaks out from the ranks shouting 'Why? Why are we killing each other? Why?' As an attempt to show the traumatic effects of a black-powder battle on mere boys, it's just about feasible. But *no one* in the British army of 1815 would query why he should be killing Frenchmen; his ancestors had been doing it for 800 years!

Towards the end, as Lord Uxbridge has his leg blown off and darkness descends, the British call on the French infantry to surrender. General Cambronne, although he denied it later, shouted back 'Merde!' (Shit!) Nearly 60,000 men were killed or wounded at Waterloo, Napoleon's tyranny ended forever.

The period of Napoleon's greatness produced enemies as well as friends and none greater than in Britain. Two of them stand out as examples of their (very different) personalities and tendencies. The first was the prime minister, William Pitt. He was the son of the Earl of Chatham, a politician of the mid-eighteenth century who had helped to build the British Empire in parts of the world as far apart as Canada, North America, the West Indies and India. The younger Pitt was a brilliant economist who understood the needs of a burgeoning Industrial Revolution, but he was only 24 when George III chose him as prime minister and no one expected him to last. When the French Revolution broke out in July 1789, Pitt opposed it, especially as it went on to produce ever more extremism, including the execution of the king and queen, Louis XVI and 'the Austrian woman', Marie Antoinette and oversaw republican kangaroo courts that threatened dissidents with the guillotine.

Pitt was played by Julian Wadham in *The Madness of King George* (1994) in which Nigel Hawthorne was superb as the deranged king. The script was an excellent mix of humour and pathos by Alan Bennett, adapted from his stage play. The events of this episode in George's life took place in 1788–89 *before* the Revolution, but Wadham's performance is excellent as the prime minister who owes his position to a man who is now as mad as a snake. The later, larger picture was provided by Robert Donat in *The Young Mr Pitt* (1942). This was a very different portrayal, if only because Britain was at war at the time and the movie is, essentially, propaganda; for Revolutionary and Napoleonic France, read Nazi Germany. Robert Morley *is* Charles James Fox, the pro-French leader of the Whig opposition to Pitt's Tories and we have a sense of the prime minister's vulnerability when, in the final scene, he opts for a glass of port rather than the medicine that might save his life. He died, largely of exhaustion, in January 1806.

The much more up-front hero against Napoleon is Horatio Nelson. Unlike Wellington, who had a different kind of arrogance, Nelson was an unrepentant exhibitionist, adoring the adulation with which he was surrounded for most of his career. As such, he is a legend, complete with falsehoods and exaggerations. In the odd little museum to him in Monmouth (it is there on the rather thin pretext that he went there once to select timber for his warships from the Forest of Dean nearby) there are no less than four glass eyes which he used during his colourful career. Which is odd, because he didn't lose an eye! He lost the sight in one, not as a result of action but because sand blew into his face off the ramparts of a fort at Calvi and infection set in. The loss of the arm was genuine and no doubt caused headaches for the actors who played him on the big screen.

Nelson was born in Burnham Thorpe, Norfolk, the son of a vicar, in 1758. He joined the navy as a midshipman at the age of 12 (standard then) and saw service in the West Indies. He married the widow Frances Nisbet and semi-retired before the outbreak of war against Revolutionary France. As commander of the *Agamemnon* (many British ships of the line had classical Greek names), he found himself in Naples and met Emma Hamilton, the wife of the British Ambassador there. Their relationship, which caused a scandal at the time, is the very stuff of Hollywood biopics.

Astonishing victories followed as the promoted admiral used the 'Nelson touch' to smash the French off Cape St Vincent and Aboukir Bay (the Battle of the Nile). He was now Baron Nelson with a pension of £2,000 a year (£2.8 million today) and was made Duke of Bronté by a grateful king of Naples. Back home, Napoleon divorced his wife and Emma produced a baby, Horatia. He disobeyed orders so that he could destroy the Franco-Danish fleet at Copenhagen in 1801, allegedly not seeing a signal to break off action because he put his telescope to his blind eye! The end came at Trafalgar in October 1805 when Nelson broke the French fleet line in two places and destroyed forever any hopes that Napoleon had had of invading Britain. Wearing his decorations on deck made him a target and he was shot by a sniper in the rigging of the *Redoubtable*. Even his death-bed scene was shrouded in mystery. Did he say to Thomas Hardy, captain of the *Victory*, 'kiss me,' as he died? Or was it the Persian word 'Kismet' (fate)?

That Hamilton Woman (1941) was, like *The Young Mr Pitt*, a propaganda piece. The British title was *Lady Hamilton*, but the American version rings truer for the mood of the public in Nelson's own day; officers of His Majesty's Royal Navy just didn't behave like that. Critic C.A. Lejeune was very dismissive of the movie:

> the film would have been a better job if had stuck more to this man Nelson and bothered less about that woman Hamilton. These are not days [1941] when we have much patience for looking at history through the eyes of a trollop. And I am not at all sure that English people, who have been fighting for two years for something they like to call an ideal, will very much care for the implication that the future died with Nelson.

The Age of Empire: From Bonaparte to Ekaterinburg 109

The admiral was played by Laurence Olivier, to George MacDonald Fraser the definitive Nelson, even if he was 7 inches too tall for the real man – next time you're looking over the *Victory* in Portsmouth harbour, check out the size of Nelson's 'cot'. Vivien Leigh was Emma, looking gorgeous in a variety of hats and frilly gowns. Her own shady past (Emma's, not Vivien's) as barmaid, ladies' maid and stripper, is ignored entirely. Olivier and Leigh were what Burton and Taylor were in *Cleopatra* (see Chapter 1) – famous lovers and luvvies on an international scale and the chemistry between them is excellent. The story is about a love affair, however, not a war and, given the technical and financial constraints of the time, it is not too surprising that the ships at Trafalgar are models on a pond. Inevitably, the ever-present Henry Wilcoxon as Captain Hardy is *far* too large to serve in a ship of the line. The remake of the Hamilton story, with Glenda Jackson as Emma and Peter Finch as Nelson was disappointing and audiences could not help noticing that Finch had, after all, two arms!

Two oddities emerge from the Regency period (1810–20) while the war against Napoleon still raged. The first was *Beau Brummel* (1954), the story of a dandy whose exaggerated fashion sense popularized dark clothing and trousers (as opposed to the eighteenth-century obsession with breeches). Stewart Granger at his most gorgeous was Brummel, but the scene is stolen by Peter Ustinov as a petulant Prince Regent and Robert Morley as George III descending into senility.

Lady Caroline Lamb (1972) was altogether darker, if only because the heroine was borderline insane herself. Caroline Ponsonby married the politician William Lamb, later Lord Melbourne and prime minister, in the year of Trafalgar and outraged London society by her whacky behaviour thereafter. Sarah Miles was Caroline, appearing in a range of skimpy outfits designed to appal the great and good and she set her cap at Lord Byron, 'mad, bad and dangerous to know', played by Richard Chamberlain, at the time the heart-throb *du jour*. He got Byron's gammy leg right (he had a club foot) but looked nothing like the maverick poet. Jon Finch was handsome enough for Lamb, but rather too bland and everybody else was miscast. Olivier wasn't convincing as Wellington; neither was the fact that one scene featured Lady Butler's famous painting *Scotland Forever!*, the charge of the Scots Greys at Waterloo. There were two things wrong with this; Wellington, constantly complained that his cavalry 'got him into scrapes' and the charge, gutsy though it was, was largely a failure. He'd hardly hang the picture in pride of place in his Horse Guards office. Secondly, and far more obviously, Lady Butler didn't paint the picture until 1881, nearly thirty years after Wellington's death! Ralph Richardson didn't shine as George III and John Mills was far too hirsute for the bald foreign minister, George Canning.

The 'long peace' between 1815 and 1854 hasn't interested Hollywood much and Mike Leigh's *Peterloo* (2018) is one of the few movies on the period. Partly as a result of the long war against Napoleon, Britain was broke by 1815 and ordinary working-class folk were suffering as a result. Machinery and factories were the way forward, but they caused dislocation among, for example, the handloom weavers of Manchester. When a huge crowd descended on the city in August 1819 to listen to the rabble-rouser Henry Hunt, the magistrates panicked and ordered in the army to make arrests. The result was eleven deaths and over 400 injuries, among them children. It should have made a riveting film, but under Mike Leigh, it didn't. The uniforms (of the Manchester and Salford Yeomanry and the 15th Hussars) looked far too new and clean, even if the grime of the people was well done. There were a couple of accurate moments – the officer of the 15th berating his men for over-use of their swords and the old lady coming face to face with a yeoman she knew – 'Nay, Tom Shelmerdine, tha' shan't ride over me' – but generally, it was stodgy stuff. *Everybody* in government, from the Prince Regent (Tim McInnerny) down was played as a caricature, which may have been Leigh's point, but it's woeful history.

It was not until 1854 that the cameras rolled for the various versions of the Charge of the Light Brigade. By the 1850s, the camera itself had come into its own and Roger Fenton, among others, produced photographs of locations and personalities rather as Matthew Brady would do, rather more dramatically, in the American Civil War of the next decade.

The object of the Crimean War (1853–56) from the British point of view was to stop the Russian 'bear' from overwhelming Turkey and challenging British geographical links with India (see below). Bizarrely, after eight centuries of warfare and mutual suspicion, France and Britain found themselves on the same side supporting Turkey. The idea was to give the bear a bloody nose by taking the naval base of Sebastopol in Crimea (which was largely Turkish and Muslim in those days).

First into the fray was a silent short about the Light Brigade, filmed on location in California with lots of heroic riding about and not much history. It did at least feature Captain Louis Nolan who carried the fatal order that led to the Light Brigade's near-destruction; the actor playing him dislocated his shoulder during filming, but carried on regardless in true British tradition. Next came Errol Flynn. 'The reckless lancers sweep on and on,' said the film's publicity posters, 'so that a woman's heart might not be broken! You're not fighting a single legion – you're fighting the entire British army, Surat Khan!'

In two sentences, every single fact is wrong. Nobody cared, because the 1936 *The Charge of the Light Brigade*, directed by Michael Curtiz, was a runaway success. For the record, the Lancers may have been reckless, but the 17th were only one of five regiments – there were Hussars and Light Dragoons too. The charge had absolutely nothing to do with a woman, even if that woman was Olivia de Havilland. The British army was never divided into legions (that was Roman organization) and who, we may ask, was Surat Khan? The simple answer is that, in 1936, he was C. Henry Gordon, suitably 'browned up', and totally fictional, but the film's plotline was not simple at all.

Inverting actual events, Surat Khan is a supposed Indian prince who pretends friendship with the British, including the upright Captain Vickers (Flynn) while planning to attack them when their backs are turned. This is more or less what happened at Meerut and Cawnpore in the Indian Mutiny of 1857 – three years *after* the Light Brigade charged. In the Flynn version, Surat Khan has sneakily teamed up with the Russians (why isn't explained) and the whole charge happens as an act of revenge. Flynn, at the head of his fictional 27th Lancers (a regiment not created until the Second World War) disobeys orders and leads the suicidal attack which culminates in his death and that of the evil prince. It's pure hokum and all the more astonishing that Halliwell gives it three stars. None of the characters is real, except a virtual extra who is clearly supposed to be Lord Cardigan (who actually led the charge, not Captain Vickers). C.A. Lejeune sums up the reason for the film's success. 'When the noble six hundred, lances level and stirrups touching, pace, canter and finally charge down the mile-long valley, with the enemy guns tearing great holes in their ranks, you are a dead stock if your pulses don't thunder and your heart quicken perceptibly.' He's right, of course – I can conjure up twenty plus movies featuring cavalry charges and they *all* have that effect. But Lejeune goes on – 'this scene may be villainous history' – and he's right again. He also points out that in most scenes, the Union Jack is flying upside down!

The 1936 *Charge* went down in history for its cruelty to horses. Tripwires were hidden under the sand so that the galloping animals fell headlong, many breaking limbs and necks. There were complaints to the American Society for the Protection of Animals, including one from Flynn himself. And the whole thing was made worse when a stuntman was killed doubling for Flynn, leaping from horse to horse.

Fast forward to 1968 with a very different version of the Charge. Tony Richardson directed what was seen at the time as an anti-war movie (Vietnam was at its height) and it probably tried too hard to hit the right note. It was filmed in London and Turkey (Cold War Russia was hardly going to make the real locations available to restage a war they lost) with 5,000 extras, 1,000 horses, 6,000lb of TNT and 3,000 cannon balls. The uniforms were brilliantly accurate reconstructions created by the Mollo brothers, experts in the field, and the actors were encouraged to live in them to give the appearance of an army roughing it on campaign, with every extreme of weather possible. Having stood overlooking the 'Valley of Death' where the real charge happened, I can confirm that Captain Nolan's last ride, with the fatally vague order, was *nothing like* as steep as the scarp slope in the film.

David Hemmings played Nolan, a young, fanatical cavalry officer with nothing but contempt for the high command. That command was spearheaded by John Gielgud as the one-armed Waterloo veteran, Lord Raglan, and the cavalry was led with irascible bickering by Lord Lucan (Harry Andrews) and Lord Cardigan (Trevor Howard). For reasons of simplicity and to give the events cohesion, Nolan appears in Cardigan's 11th Hussars (whereas he actually served in the 15th) and the incident of the 'black bottle' when Cardigan threatened an officer with a court martial over a mess dinner misunderstanding, happened not to Nolan but to Captain Reynolds (not in the movie at all).

Two sub-plots stand out that have no historical veracity whatever. The first is the illicit romance between Nolan and Clarissa Morris (Vanessa Redgrave), the wife of Nolan's friend William Morris of the 17th Lancers (Mark Burns). Her actual name was Amelia and there is absolutely no hint of any hanky-panky on that score. The next is the hilarious scene when Lord Cardigan seduces Fanny Duberly on board his yacht, the *Dryad*. Cardigan did indeed sail for the Crimea on the boat and he regularly entertained officers and their wives below deck. Fanny was one of the few army wives present and her journals provide a fascinating glimpse of army life on campaign at the time. Jill Bennett played her as a rather silly nymphomaniac (she was certainly a flirt but probably nothing more) and her husband Henry (Peter Bowles) is a wholly innocent dupe. Incidentally, he wasn't in the 11th Hussars either, but paymaster to the 8th.

For reasons of his own, Richardson elected not to use the footage he had taken showing the charge of the Heavy Brigade, perhaps because that (successful) engagement contrasted too well with the failure of the Light Brigade that followed it. Probably for reasons of cost, he equipped the entire Light Brigade and not just the 11th Hussars in crimson overalls (trousers) thereby negating at least some of the Mollo brothers' work. Brilliant animation by Richard Williams taken from the contemporary satirical magazine *Punch* was scattered throughout. Halliwell gave the 1968 version only one star, but today it is regarded as a classic.

India was regarded as 'the brightest jewel in the imperial crown' but British involvement in the sub-continent was haphazard and in some ways, accidental. It used to be said that 'trade follows the flag' but in fact the reverse is usually true and it certainly was in India. Britain and France were vying with each other from the early eighteenth century to capture lucrative Indian markets. Accordingly, the British East India Company and the French Compagnie des Indes literally fought for possession of those markets and the territory that went with them. To that end, they both needed armies and fought each other – and the native princes – until the 1820s, by which time the French threat and presence had largely evaporated and Britain's 'John Company' had the field all to itself.

One of the heroes of the early years was Robert Clive, an unpredictable soldier who today would probably be diagnosed as bipolar. He attempted suicide in his twenties but survived and went on to claim victories over the French in India culminating in 1758. The 'Heaven-born general' as prime minister William Pitt called him, was sent out to restore order again in Bengal in 1764, but was accused by Parliament, where he had made enemies, of corruption. His next suicide attempt, in 1774, was successful.

Movies on this period in Indian history are exceptionally thin on the ground, although 'Bollywood' has made a few. *Clive of India* (1934) has the impeccably suave Ronald Colman as the general/

Above left: Alexander the Great was the most formidable general in the ancient world and had conquered a third of it by the time of his death, perhaps by poisoning, at the age of 33. He has been played by Richard Burton (1956) and Colin Farrell (2004). For once, the actors were the right age – unfortunately, neither of them had blond hair!

Above right: The emperor wannabe, murdered by his own followers in the Senate in March 44 BC. He has been played by, among others, Claude Rains, Rex Harrison and Kenneth Williams! Ironically, the name Caesar means 'curly', presumably a joke at the expense of a man renowned for sensitivity about his baldness. Only one portrayal, Harrison's in *Cleopatra* (1962), referred to his epilepsy, known in his own time as the falling sickness.

The Romans hated her because she was a powerful woman opposed to a state run entirely by men. Sixteen hundred years after her time, William Shakespeare took the same line. By the twentieth century she had become a femme fatale who used sex to achieve her goals. The furore on set involving the affair between Richard Burton and Elizabeth Taylor was nearly as frenetic as the real Cleopatra's links with both Julius Caesar and Mark Antony. Her coins do not show her to be a beauty, but she was undoubtedly an intellectual, which the various movies about her have ignored.

The conqueror of China, supposedly the progenitor of over 1.5million Chinese alive today. Of the two actors who have played him, one was American (John Wayne in *The Conqueror*, 1956) and the other Egyptian (Omar Sharif *Genghis Khan*, 1965) – both portrayals were dreadful.

The only contemporary portrait of Joan of Arc is this sketch from her trial for heresy in 1431. The portrayal of her by Ingrid Bergman (1948) when the actress was 33 did not impress and although Milla Jovovich was better in the 1999 production, she was still six years too old for the part. Joan was 19 when she died.

Henry VIII fills the screen as a larger-than-life monarch who changed the course of religion in sixteenth-century England. He has been played on the screen by such heavyweights as Richard Burton, Robert Shaw, Keith Michell, Charles Lawton, Charlton Heston and … Sid James! Although all these men brought something unique to the role, only Lawton was the right build for the middle-aged monarch whose waist measurement grew from 31 inches when he was 19 to 54 inches shortly before his death.

Above left: Elizabeth I refused to marry on the grounds that she would have 'no man as her master'. Famous for her temper and even her right hook, she has been played on screen by Flora Robson, Bette Davis, Glenda Jackson, Cate Blanchett and Judi Dench. Of all of them, only Judi is close to the right height, with Flora Robson being a whole 10 inches too tall.

Above right: One of France's pantomime villains, Cardinal Richelieu was the power behind the throne of Louis XIV. As such, he is the sinister presence in the many movies involving the three musketeers. He has been played by Hollywood greats George Arliss, Raymond Massey and Charlton Heston, none of them bad lookalikes.

Charles I's enemies maintained that he had two faces; the artist Vandyke went for three. In *Cromwell* (1970), he was played by Alec Guinness who was superb in the role, even down to the slight stammer and Lowland Scots accent. He is also an astonishing lookalike ...

... unlike Richard Harris, who played Oliver Cromwell in the same film. The film itself was riddled with inaccuracies and Harris failed to convince as the enigmatic Lord Protector.

Above left: Like many great women in history, Catherine's reputation rests on sexual rumour in which she seduced half her court and much of her army! In fact, she was a brilliant ruler at a time when Russia was attempting to Westernise. The two actresses who stand out as having played her are Helen Mirren and Marlene Dietrich. They were both the wrong shape, the wrong size and wore the wrong uniform, but at least Dietrich was the right nationality!

Above right: Napoleon was the greatest general in the modern world and he was also brilliant at PR. He crossed the Alps, not on a spirited charger, but on a mule *and* he was a bad rider. He is the most filmed historical figure of all and it's not over yet – Ridley Scott's *Napoleon* (starring Joaquin Phoenix) hit the cinemas in 2023.

A colonel at 24, Robert Gould Shaw, a Harvard scholar, was one of the first to command a black regiment in action for the American army. The 54th Massachusetts Infantry were sent on what amounted to a suicide mission to capture Fort Wagner during the Civil War. Matthew Broderick was superb in the role in *Glory* (1990).

Above: One of the unsung heroines of the American Civil War, Harriet Tubman ran the Underground Railroad, a relay system which enabled slaves to escape to the North, where there was no slavery. The casting of the British actress Cynthia Erivo in *Harriet* in 2019 raised some eyebrows because she was not American.

Left: Thousands of schoolboys (and even more men) fell in love with Doris Day in *Calamity Jane* (1953). I doubt they would have been so enamoured with the real 'Calam', Martha Cannary, who claimed to have been a scout for the army and a buffalo hunter. She also claimed to have had an affair with Wild Bill Hickok and the fact that none of this is true makes her all the more enigmatic.

The left-handed gun who wasn't. The best-known photograph of William Bonney, known as Billy the Kid was reversed in the earliest books – he was in fact right-handed. Those early books will also tell you that he killed twenty-one men by the time he was 21 years old. In fact, he may have killed four. Paul Newman, he was not!

The second-longest reigning monarch in British history, Victoria has been played by a number of actresses from Anna Neagle to Judi Dench. No one who has played the queen in her later years has come even close to her build or height.

Above left: As Governor of the Sudan, Charles Gordon tried to defend Khartoum in 1885 but was killed when the followers of the Mahdi overran the city. Charlton Heston played him in *Khartoum* (1966) but was too stately for the bustling little general and almost a foot too tall.

Above right: T.E. Lawrence, the British officer who led the Arabs in a revolt against the Turks during the First World War, was an enigma; a confused individual who shunned the limelight, he nevertheless had a huge ego. At 5ft 5in, however, it is difficult to imagine him leading his troops with the panache of Peter O'Toole (6ft 2in) in *Lawrence of Arabia* (1962).

Two of the most notorious villains of the 1930s, Bonnie Parker and Clyde Barrow were homicidal misfits who died in a hail of bullets. There was outrage in 1967 when the film *Bonnie and Clyde* had Faye Dunaway and Warren Beatty as two 'beautiful people' almost as the victims of the system.

governor (who looks nothing like the real man). We have to have, in the 1930s, the overarching love interest; the publicity says, 'Six words from a woman changed the map of Asia!' The woman in question was Margaret Maskelyne, Clive's wife whom he married in 1753. As with the Hamilton/Nelson relationship, the movie is more about the romance than the building of an empire and this is a pity because it leaves something of a hole in our history-cinematic experience. As J.B. Parish wrote, 'Patriotic pageantry, undistorted by facts'.

And that's where, until *The Man Who Would Be King* (1975) the Indian story ends. We have already seen a distorted view of the Mutiny in Errol Flynn's *Charge* version, but most of the Raj films of Alexander Korda – *Kim*, *The Drum* and so on – are based on the fiction of Rudyard Kipling and feature no real characters at all. So, it's fitting, perhaps, that the only real character in *The Man Who Would be King* is Kipling himself! The future 'poet laureate of Empire' was born in Bombay (today's Mumbai) in 1865 and, like many children of the Raj employees, was sent to boarding school in England. Back in India by 1880, he worked as a journalist on a number of newspapers and produced short stories with an Indian flavour that proved very popular. His romantic grasp of British history and his affection towards India and its people have all but disappeared today under fatuous accusations of racism. He was awarded the Nobel prize for literature in 1907 and his son Jack was killed on the Somme with the Irish Guards in 1915. The heroes of *The Man Who Would be King* are Sean Connery and Michael Caine, looking very period in their topees and side-whiskers but they are fiction. Kipling was played by Christopher Plummer, complete with heavy moustache and thick glasses, but as he is only essentially the film's narrator, his character is never fully fleshed out.

In the nineteenth century, Africa was the 'dark continent', a place of legends such as King Solomon's mines and Prester John, the mythical Christian king of Ethiopia. The Dutch and the British squabbled over territory in the far south and the driving force further north was to find the heart of the continent and the source of the Nile. The motto and raison d'être of the Spanish conquistadors (see Chapter 6) in sixteenth-century America was 'Gold, God and Glory' and the same applies to Africa 300 years later. Gold was realized in the mines of Kimberley and elsewhere, making men like Cecil Rhodes very rich indeed. God was the presence of the missionaries, men like David Livingstone who believed that illiterate black tribesmen needed muscular Christianity in their lives. Glory was what the army was all about, but the military history of the later century is peppered with mistakes, reversals and disasters.

David Livingstone was an extraordinary mix of committed Christian and explorer. From 1840 onwards, he ventured into 'darkest Africa', finding rivers and lakes that no white man had seen before. He even took his long-suffering wife with him. Long before Burton, Speke and Baker made their reputations, Livingstone was publishing travelogues that earned him membership of the prestigious Royal Geographical Society. In a country where roads were non-existent and communication slow and difficult, the Scotsman virtually disappeared in the late 1860s and the journalist Henry Morton Stanley was sent by *The New York Herald* to find him. This is the storyline of *Stanley and Livingstone* (1938), which divided critics. *Punch* described it as 'sound, worthy, interesting', whereas Graham Greene wrote, 'Most of the film consists of long shots of stand-ins moving across undistinguished scenery ... Mr [Spencer] Tracy [Stanley] is always a human being but Sir Cedric [Hardwicke] [Livingstone] is an elocution lesson, a handclasp.'

African history really came alive to western audiences in the 1960s and 1970s when Cy Endfield made two films covering the same conflict, the Anglo-Zulu War of 1879. The events – the Battle of Isandlwana and the defence of Rorke's Drift happened in that chronological order, only hours apart, but Endfield's films were made the other way around, separated in real film time by fifteen years, by which time a mini revolution had occurred in film-making. The first effort, *Zulu* (1964) was breath-taking, so inevitably Halliwell gives it one star and calls it 'standard period heroics', whereas it was anything but. The screenplay was written by historian John Prebble and although characterization is wrong in some instances, the essence of the film is very close to the truth.

The background to the Anglo-Zulu War (which hardly anyone in 1964 either knew or cared about) was that it was a war manufactured by a rogue diplomat, Sir Bartle Frere, who without his government's permission, sent an army under Lord Chelmsford into Zulu territory in Natal. At the time, the Zulu were the largest and most militaristic force in Africa and only a blockhead like Chelmsford could have assumed that he could beat them. A large part of his force, the 24th Foot, was wiped out at Isandlwana in January 1879, the worst single defeat ever inflicted on a British army. The next day, the triumphant warriors of the *impis* (regiments) of King Cetshwayo attacked the mission station at nearby Rorke's Drift. It is this action that is recorded in *Zulu*.

The mission station, barely defendable in military terms, was run by a Swedish missionary, Otto Witt. In the film he is played by Jack Hawkins as a drunk and his daughter, Margaretta (Ulla Jacobson) has been put there, one feels, to provide the essential 1960s arm candy. Witt cracks in the film under the strain of it all and has to be taken away, whereas the real man not only stayed but advocated taking on the Zulus in the first place – so much for the missionary spirit!

The station is commanded by Lieutenant John Chard of the Royal Engineers (Stanley Baker, who co-produced with Endfield). Baker didn't have Chard's magnificent moustache and it was never explained why he was wearing his elaborate full-dress uniform, but apart from that, his performance was superb. His Number Two was Lieutenant Gonville Bromhead of the 24th, played by Michael Caine, ridiculously blond for a dark-haired man, in his debut. Caine had auditioned for the part of a Cockney private, but Endfield turned him into a toff on the other side of a commission. Like Baker, he appears in full dress and doesn't seem at all bothered that both he and Baker are carrying Webley revolvers that weren't in use until the First World War.

The Zulu are magnificent, line after line of plumed warriors with deadly spears and zebra-skin shields, chanting and crashing into the British mealy-bags with no regard for their own lives. Cetshwayo was played by the actual chief of the tribe in 1964, Buthelezi. Individual character parts are wonderfully acted, but three stand out. The first is Corporal Schiess (Dickie Owen), a Swiss member of the Natal Carabiniers, who everybody thought was Dutch. Despite a crippled leg, he hacks his way through the Zulu lines with ease, survived and was decorated. Private Henry Hook (James Booth) is a dissolute, drunken rebel, always in hot water with the regiment at home. That was an unfortunate choice because the real Hook was a teetotaller and his family complained to Endfield, who apologized. The third was Colour Sergeant Frank Bourne (Nigel Greene), one of those timeless heroes who were the backbone of the British army. Greene was superb as the oasis of calm in a sea of trouble, but the real Bourne was known (behind his back) as 'the kid' – he was the youngest colour sergeant in the army at 24. One hundred and thirty soldiers, most of them from South Wales and Warwickshire, held off 4,000 Zulus for a day and a night before the attackers withdrew. The result was eleven Victoria Crosses, still the highest number awarded for a single action despite two world wars since then.

Zulu Dawn (1979) was Endfield's second bash at the story, this time focusing on the build-up to Chelmsford's invasion and Isandlwana itself. The film failed by comparison with *Zulu* because it tried to see the conflict from both sides, which hardly ever works. When the Zulu were distant, then terrifying warriors, we, the audience, were horrified by them. When we saw them as ordinary individuals (running rings around the British) they lost that edge and the defeat at Isandlwana makes little sense. Bartle Frere was suitably devious as played by John Mills; Bishop Colenso (after whom a town was named) was portrayed by Freddie Jones and the one-armed Colonel Durnford of the Natal Light Horse Brigade was Burt Lancaster, doing his best at an Irish accent. The high command was led by Peter O'Toole as Chelmsford, cold arrogance written all over him and a series of officer cameos – Simon Ward, Christopher Cazenove, Ronald Pickup, Michael Jayston among them – were excellent. Norris Newman (Noggs), the press reporter (Ronald Lacey), jarred a little, as though he were a 1970s observer, highly critical of Chelmsford who, had that actually happened, would have had the man arrested.

There have been all sorts of theories put forward to explain the defeat at Isandlwana, from rifle-smoke screening the enemy to cartridge cases that wouldn't open, to Zulus off their faces on hallucinatory drugs. None of this is realistic. Chelmsford should not have split his command. Colonel Pulleine (Denholm Elliott) should have laagered his camp. But the bottom line was that the 24th Regiment of Foot were outnumbered at least five to one and even with their superior fire-power could not have survived Cetshwayo's onslaught.

Cy Endfield never made the third of what should have been a trilogy on the defeat of the Zulu at Ulundi, their capital, later in the year. He probably never intended to. Ulundi was a massacre, where Chelmsford brought his artillery and his cavalry into play against an army that had neither. I doubt whether the average British film-going audience would have stomached that. Chelmsford, of course, received little in the way of retribution for a disastrous campaign. Cetshwayo was brought in chains to Britain, where many saw him as a fine example of 'the noble savage' and he became something of a celebrity.

A few miles to the north and a few years later, hostility against the British, indeed Europeans generally, erupted in the Sudan. The ex-civil servant, ex-slave trader Mohammed Ahmed claimed to be the Mahdi, the messiah prophesied in various versions of the Koran. He wiped out an Anglo-Egyptian army under General William Hicks and attacked the Sudanese capital Khartoum. Since the area was under British protection, the prime minister, William Gladstone, sent General Charles Gordon to organize the evacuation of Europeans in the city. He chose the wrong man. Gordon was, in his far less over-the-top way, as much of a religious fanatic as the Mahdi. He defended Khartoum, excellent engineer that he was and made a fight of it. By the time a relief column arrived, Gordon was dead and Khartoum had fallen.

I believe *Khartoum* (1966) is the only movie to feature Gladstone, the infuriating Scotsman who partially created modern Britain. He was played by Ralph Richardson with more cynicism than the real man possessed. Charlton Heston was Gordon, with a very good English accent but nearly a foot too tall for the real man and too stately. Gordon scuttled everywhere, nattering about this and that; perhaps 'Mr Epic' couldn't play a busybody. The Mahdi was an over-the-top Laurence Olivier, suitable 'browned up' in the days before anybody cared about cultural appropriation. The two never met of course, despite several scenes together in the film for the sake of drama. One critic wrote, 'Academic accuracy and spectacular battles are unhappy partners,' but they shouldn't be. They ought to be the essence of historical films.

There is an unpardonable gaffe in the movie's brochure, which claims that Gordon's 'baptism of fire [was] with the Light Brigade at Balaclava'. There was indeed a Captain Gordon who rode with the 17th Lancers, but it wasn't Charles. He didn't reach the Crimea until three months after Balaclava and his role was that of an officer of Royal Engineers, not the cavalry. Gordon's aide, Colonel Stewart of the 11th Hussars, was played with a mixture of integrity and panache by Richard Johnson (sans moustache). To those of us who care about such things, there is no cord boss on the front of his busby – what were they paying costume departments for in the mid-1960s?

The film was shot on location, Khartoum itself a studio rebuilt on the banks of the Nile. Stunt co-ordinator Yakim Canutt who had directed the brilliant chariot race in *Ben-Hur* trained the cavalry and a camel corps, with 70,000 gallons of water sent in daily by tender to combat the effects of the blistering sun. It's interesting to see Major Herbert Kitchener (Peter Arne) as a relatively junior officer before he became the most famous war poster in the world.

Gordon's death at Khartoum was avenged years later. The Mahdi died of natural causes soon after the taking of the city and his grave was destroyed after Omdurman in 1898 and his bones throw into the Nile. And a young officer who rode with the 21st Lancers at Omdurman was Winston Churchill.

Young Winston (1972) was able, thanks to the career of its central character, to link two continents of Empire together. Churchill served with the 4th Hussars in India before he went to the Sudan as a war correspondent. The movie is based on Churchill's *My Early Life* (he was a prolific writer) and inevitably, there is a bias about it. It has all the elements of an 'Our Boys' Yarn', typical of the books and stories that were hugely popular in Britain at the time. Richard Attenborough directed after many years as an actor and in this, as in his later *Gandhi* (see Chapter 11) and *Oh, What a Lovely War!* (Chapter 9) he agonised far too much over the morality of the stories he was telling. The best scene in *Young Winston* is the last one. All his life, Winston had felt a failure because of the exacting demands of his overwhelming father, Lord Randolph. The closing scene has an old Churchill, dozing at Chartwell, surrounded by the oil paintings he took to in later life. His long-dead father comes to see him in his dream, still young, still immaculate in frock coat. We know that the younger Churchill was the man who faced down Hitler's Nazis in the Second World War, but Randolph 'who has been away for some time' doesn't know that. He sees the paintings and asks his boy if this is what he does now. 'Yes, father,' says Simon Ward's voice. 'Well,' sighs Randolph, 'do the best you can.' It is a lovely moment, suffused with regret and the gulf between the generations and, in later editions, Attenborough *cut it out*! Why, I don't know.

The young Churchill is played by Simon Ward, who grows from a diffident cadet into an MP every bit as arrogant as his father (Robert Shaw). Churchill's mother, the American socialite Jennie Jerome, is played by Anne Bancroft at her most engaging. We even get a smooth, womanising David Lloyd George (Anthony Hopkins) and a tetchy General Kitchener (promoted from his *Khartoum* days) portrayed by John Mills.

The touches of family life and humour are marvellous, from Robert Hardy's bullying prep school headmaster to Pat Heywood's 'Womany' (Churchill's nanny). The scene where an average voter (Colin Blakeley) is completely overwhelmed by the beauty of Lady Churchill is a joy to behold. The India scenes looks good – 'Who's the bloody fool on the grey?' – and the uniforms are authentic. The cavalry charge at Omdurman is well-handled, including Churchill's 'Bloody Hell!' at the sight of Dervishes rising out of a hidden trench. He sheathed his sword at that moment and drew his Broomhandle Mauser pistol because an old polo injury was making his arm painful. My one gripe is that, as a lieutenant *attached* to the 21st, he would have ridden serrefile *behind* his troop, not ahead of it close behind his CO, Colonel Martin (Patrick Holt).

I was less impressed by the South African part of the film. In 1899, the Boers (Dutch settlers in Africa) went to war to keep the British out of their affairs. The whole thing was badly handled, world sympathy was with the Boers and it took nearly three years to bring about peace. Churchill found himself caught in an ambush on an armoured train and although his exploits and subsequent escape made him a hero at home, the movie looks as if the whole thing was filmed in North Wales!

And, talking of North Wales, that was also the setting for *Carry On Up the Khyber* (1968). All right, we have gone back to India again and there are no real characters in the film, but the send-up of imperial jingoism is too good to omit. The regiment is a Highland one, the 3rd Foot and Mouth – the 'devils in skirts' – and Bernard Bresslaw is a fanatical Frontier chieftain. The famous Khyber Pass is a field with a gate. Despite hundreds of rounds being fired in the attack on British legation, no one is hurt at all. Wonderful! Even Halliwell gives it three stars.

The other movie set in the Boer War was *Breaker Morant* (1981) starring Edward Woodward in the title role. Accused of mistreating and killing Boer prisoners in a war that got ever more vicious as it went on, three Australian cavalry officers were court-martialled and two of them were executed. It's a reminder of the way that sons of Empire were expected to serve anywhere, which was to cause problems fifteen years later at Gallipoli. The film is a solid courtroom drama, even if the script is a little too kind to Harry Morant and his comrades. The execution scene, in which Woodward and Kilgore Trout sit in chairs and hold hands as the bullets fly, is heartbreaking.

In the year that *Breaker Morant* is set, all hell was let loose in Peking (today's Beijing) with a monumental clash of empires. China was at the heart of the mysterious East, an ancient culture that didn't set well with an increasingly western world. While thousands of Chinese emigrated to the United States to become virtual slave labour on the railroads, millions more stayed at home behind centuries of difference.

As ever, European nations were anxious to gain as much territory and trade as they could and the various foreign legations in Peking eyed each other with suspicion. In the meantime, a fierce nationalistic fervour exploded in June 1900 when thousands of fanatics, calling themselves the Fists of Righteous Harmony attacked the legations, earmarking Christian missionaries and foreign buildings. The nominal ruler of China, the dowager empress Tzu Hsi (a former concubine) made placatory noises but was powerless to control the fanaticism of the Boxers.

Almost 3,000 civilians, women and children among them, were suddenly under attack throughout the fifty-five-day siege that dominated that summer. Starving legation occupants ate horse meat washed down with champagne and all milk for the babies came from the one cow available. On 14 August, a relief column entered the city, driving out the Boxers and the empress.

When Samuel Bronston produced *55 Days at Peking* (1963) it was already too late to film on location. China had become communist and was – and is – highly suspicious of the West. Spain had to stand in instead. The imperial palace, the Forbidden City and the Tartar Wall were all recreated by an army of technicians and construction workers and covered 250 acres. The buildings themselves were the result of months of research through old photographs and architects' plans. There were more actors, extras and technicians (6,500 of them) than were allowed into the Forbidden City at the time. In 1963, there was still a handful of people who remembered the Boxer rebellion, so authenticity was vital. Actual tinned produce from British museums was borrowed for the legation sets, as were real copies of newspapers from 1900.

Spain had only 350 Chinese nationals in 1963, but a further 1,200 were imported for the filming. Astonishingly, the actual robes worn by the empress and her advisor, Prince Tuan, were made available and were insured for $150,000. The clothes had been appropriated by a member of the Italian legation after the siege and had remained in the family's hands ever since. Not to be outdone, composer Dimitri Tiomkin produced a rousing score using Chinese instruments dating back to the fourteenth century.

As far as possible, the minor rules were played by the relevant nationals, but today, the central casting seems a little odd. Charlton Heston was fine as the fictional Marine major, Matt Lewis. So was David Niven as the British ambassador. Ava Gardner was thrown in as the love interest, playing a Russian aristocrat, but the 'Chinese' leads were anything but. Flora Robson, who has form in playing rulers (she was Elizabeth I in *Fire Over England* – see Chapter 4) was a sinister empress. Leo Genn was the honourable, upright General Jung-Lai who is contemptuous of the Boxers and the endlessly creepy Robert Helpmann is Prince Tuan, secretly organizing the rebels behind the scenes. No amount of 'oriental' make-up can disguise the western-ness of these actors, all excellent though they were.

A superb film about a little oddity in imperial adventures was *The Wind and the Lion* (1975), which told the (almost) true story of the kidnapping of an American citizen by a Moroccan bandit chief in 1904. In reality, the citizen was Ion Perdecaris, a Greek-American who was living in Tangier with his son by a previous marriage and his new English wife, Ellen Varley. Out of the blue, a band of Berbers led by Mulai Ahmed er Raisuni of the Riffs kidnapped Perdecaris and demanded $70,000 and territorial rights for his release. The US president at the time was the belligerent 'cowboy' Teddy Roosevelt and he ordered seven warships and several companies of Marines to the area to sort the problem out.

The movie is a rattling good yarn, with excitement, humour, an excellent music score and some superb performances. The Raisuni (Raisuli in the film) is played by that famous old Berber warrior Sean Connery. He looks so right in the desert robes that we can forgive him anything. His captive is not the 64-year-old bearded Perdecaris but his wife Candice Bergen and their two adorable children. In reality, only the stepson, Cromwell, and Perdecaris himself were taken prisoner; Mrs Perdecaris contacted the authorities. At the time, the whole thing was blown out of all proportion. Congressman John Hay (John Huston in the movie) publicly claimed, 'This government wants Perdecaris alive or Raisuni dead.'

In essence, Roosevelt's government coughed up the money (even in 1904 $70,000 was small change) and father and son were released unharmed. As for the mini-invasion by the Marines that we see in the film, only four soldiers were involved, armed only with pistols. There was no German involvement at the time, rendering the haughty behaviour of the beastly Hun irrelevant.

Brian Keith is superb as the president, giving anybody who will listen his views on just about everything, but the scene I loved was the one in which the Japanese ambassador is enjoying an al fresco meal at the White House. John Hay turns to him and asks with all the racial superiority of the American empire, 'You likey forky?'

A moment later, the ambassador thanks the president in perfect English, for his hospitality, sits back down next to Hay and says, 'You likey speechy?'

Priceless.

Presiding over nearly all the films of empire, at least from the British point of view, was Queen Victoria. She was very short, perhaps 4ft 11in, and grew increasingly stout as she aged. A breath of fresh air when she became queen of England in 1837 at the age of 18, she proved to be a stubborn monarch but at the same time overly reliant on men to give her guidance. Her marriage to the German prince Albert of Saxe-Coburg Gotha was a genuine love match but his premature death in 1861 left her 'the widow at Windsor', temporarily, at least, deranged by grief. Her children married into the royal families of Europe and in that sense, she is a very important figure politically, even though she was the first monarch not allowed to choose her own ministers. She reigned for sixty-four years, until recently the longest in British history and the 'empire on which the sun never sets' was seen as her greatest achievement.

Looking at movies from Victoria's reign chronologically, the first is *Young Victoria* (2009) starring Emily Blunt as the queen and Rupert Friend as Albert. Ms Blunt, who was largely unknown before this, described Victoria as 'a very twenty-first-century sort of woman', which is the kind of comment that is the death knell of historical movies. The screenwriter was Julian Fellowes, himself a member of the British aristocracy, whose *Downton Abbey* was an inexplicable success on both sides of the Atlantic. He 'sought to make the film as historically accurate as possible' so it is a pity that Prince Albert is present at the queen's coronation (he wasn't) and that the prince was wounded in an assassination attempt on the queen (again, he wasn't). Producer Graham King brought Martin Scorsese in as director, on the grounds that the American knew 'pretty much all there is to know about British history'. Let's hope he was being ironic!

Paul Bettany was too young to play Victoria's first prime minister, Lord Melbourne, but King explained 'We couldn't find a 58-year-old actor who was sexy and good-looking enough.' This is odd – I can rattle off at least seven British actors who would have fitted the part perfectly. Some critics found the chemistry between Friend and Blunt non-existent so the love-match element of Victoria and Albert made little sense. 'Where was the tang,' wondered *The Guardian* critic Peter

Bradshaw, 'and the zing and the oomph of Fellowes' cracking script for *Gosford Park*?' Such things are in the eye of the beholder in that I don't remember *any* of those in *Gosford Park*, which couldn't decide what it wanted to be.

There was a curious modern royal link with *The Young Victoria*. Sarah, Duchess of York, had a hand in production and ensured that her daughter, Princess Beatrice, had a walk-on part, the first royal to appear in a movie. The late Elizabeth II had a private screening and was not impressed by Fellowes' reworking of the assassination attempt and found the British army uniforms too German.

For the next depiction of the 'great queen' we have to go back to *Victoria the Great* (1937) made a century after she came to the throne. Anna Neagle was too tall and elegant for the always-dumpy Victoria, but Anton Walbrook was a more dashing Albert than Friend *and* he was German! Sadly, he appears in the wrong Rifles uniform, in terms of both time and regiment. Do such things matter? In historical films, oh yes!

Two later films on Victoria focus on her last years, when the headstrong young girl has become an irritable and stubborn old woman. *Mrs Brown* (1997) dealt with the unknowable relationship between the queen and her dead husband's ghillie (servant) John Brown. When Victoria largely withdrew from public life after Albert's death, Brown was one of the men who talked her out of semi-retirement. As such, he was detested by Victoria's children, especially 'Bertie', the Prince of Wales, and by palace staff and officials generally. Victoria and Albert had bought a country estate at Balmoral and regarded it as their hidey-hole away from the cares of government.

Judi Dench played Victoria – at last someone of almost the right height – and Billy Connolly was Brown. They were both excellent. As one critic said, Connolly 'has the reserve and self-confidence that most stand-up comedians lack almost by definition'. Geoffrey Palmer was a coldly pompous Henry Ponsonby of the royal household, horrified that the queen-empress was being called 'Mrs Brown' behind her back. The sexual element, which *may* have existed, was kept subtly in the shadows, which is what made the film work. Almost lost in the goings on was Anthony Sher's performance as prime minister, Benjamin Disraeli. By the 1870s, although still a dazzling and mercurial politician, his gout was crippling and we see him staggering across the heather trying to keep up with the royal party.

Disraeli (1929) is, as far as I know, the only talkie with the 'arch seducer' (the description is rival William Gladstone's) in the title role. George Arliss played him, the only man in the cinema whose upper lip was on a par with the prime minister's! The work is virtual fiction however. As critic Clive Hirschhorn wrote in 1982, 'Those seeking a fuller assessment of the man and his work would have been better off in a library.'

Nineteenth-century royals and the queen's household were again annoyed by her some years after John Brown over Victoria's relationship with her Indian 'munchee' (servant) Abdul Karim. The film *Victoria and Abdul* (2017) again starred Judi Dench and the (to western audiences) unknown Ali Fayal as Abdul. Eddie Izzard (like Connolly, a comedian who is an excellent straight actor) was a grumpy Bertie and Michael Gambon was Salisbury, Disraeli's replacement as leader of the Conservative Party and prime minister. Most of the filming took place at Osborne House in the Isle of Wight, another of Victoria and Albert's hideaways, complete with its elaborate Durbar Room and paintings of Abdul himself. Victoria was made Empress of India by parliament in 1877, a title she loved and she spent fourteen years learning Urdu. As with Brown, once the queen was dead, Bertie destroyed all relevant correspondence in an ongoing act of vandalism still happening today.

Reviews were mixed. On the one hand, it was a touching love story in the mould of *Mrs Brown* and for the same reasons. Even if there was any sexual chemistry between Victoria and either man, it could never be expressed in real terms. Critic Christopher Orr wrote, 'Just don't mistake [the film] for actual history.' And, true to form, Amrou Al-Kadhi criticized the Abdul role for 'offensive two-dimensionality'.

Someone else found Abdul 'disappointingly servile', which is, after all, what nineteenth-century servants were supposed to be! As ever, from Emily Blunt to Al-Kadhi, twenty-first century mores have to be grafted on to stories set in the past, destroying not only perfectly good movies, but losing our understanding of the past.

The British Empire might have been the largest in the world, but there were others where imperiousness was all. In the tortuously complicated history of Mexican politics, the Mexican assembly offered its crown to Ferdinand-Joseph Maximilian, younger brother of the Austrian emperor in 1864. The locals didn't approve of this and revolted under their populist leader Benito Juarez, a reforming republican lawyer who became president of Mexico in 1861 before Napoleon III's plot to put Maximilian on the throne. In the event, with objection coming from every quarter, especially the United States, Napoleon withdrew his troops and Maximilian's heroic defence collapsed. He himself was shot by firing squad on 19 June 1867.

The only movie dedicated to this ugly piece of imperialism is *Juarez* (1939) with Paul Muni in the title role. 'See it now!' screamed the film's posters, 'Remember it always!' Critic Otis Ferguson wrote, 'A million dollars' worth of ballroom sets, regimentals, gauze shots and whiskers.' Muni was a big star at the time, but the moment that stands out in the film is Brian Aherne's noble death in front of the execution squad. With his sandy hair and huge beard, he is an extremely good lookalike for the misguided emperor-wannabe.

The First World War was the death knell of empires. The Turkish (Ottoman) empire had been the 'sick man of Europe' for decades and fell apart in 1914–18. So did the huge Austro-Hungarian empire. But none went down in such a blaze of horror and destruction as the 300-year rule of the Romanov family in Russia.

Despite the modernizing government of Tsar Peter the Great, Tsarina Catherine the Great and the less dramatically reformist Alexander II, Russia in the early twentieth century was a backwater. It had plenty of artistic culture among its tiny middle class but the overlarge empire was ruled by the tsar and his obscenely rich boyars and the vast majority of the people were agricultural peasants barely existing on the breadline. Since Karl Marx and Friedrich Engels produced their *Communist Manifesto* in 1848, there had been a growing number of dissidents in Russia who believed that a Marxist utopia could be created there, without any real idea of the insuperable practicalities involved. Speaking fluent English, French and German, with family ties to all the major royals in Europe, Tsar Nicholas II was the worst possible figure to manage change and bring his empire kicking and screaming into the twentieth century. Those who knew him described him as a turnip farmer rather than the God-appointed ruler of the second largest empire in the world.

Nicholas and Alexandra (1971) was a glitzy, ambitious attempt to explain what happened. Rex Harrison and Vanessa Redgrave were initially earmarked to play the hapless tsar and his pushy wife but the roles went instead to Michael Jayston and Janet Suzman, both excellent. The script was based on the superb history book by Robert K. Massie. Sam Spiegel produced and Franklin J. Schaffner directed. The screenplay was by James Goldman who won an Academy Award for his work on *The Lion in Winter* (see Chapter 3). The camera took us from marble-floored, gilded palaces to the impossibly backward factories in Russia's struggling industries, pointing up what a broken society Russia was.

The royal children – four princesses and the haemophiliac tsarevitch, Alexei – looked adorable in their summer finery at the tsar's summer residence at Tsarskei Selo and a series of A-list actors filled the roles of household and political advisers. Laurence Olivier was the prime minister, Count Witte, and the royal doctor, Botkin, was played by Timothy West. Plotting behind the scenes were the murky revolutionaries – Michael Bryant as an excellent Lenin-lookalike, Brian Cox as the mad-haired Trotsky and John McEnery as Kerensky, who led the first of two revolutions in 1917, which toppled Nicholas from his throne. Too much was made of Stalin (James Hazeldine) who was still very much a foot soldier in 1917.

The standout role, however, was Tom Baker as Rasputin. The self-styled holy man and womanizer who had an almost hypnotic hold over the tsarina (and any number of ladies of the court) had appeared on celluloid five years earlier, when horror star Christopher Lee played him in *Rasputin the Mad Monk* (1966). As someone pointed out at the time, Rasputin (the name means 'debauched') was neither mad nor a monk, but the focus of *that* film was the mystic's horrific death. Prior to *that* version, *Rasputin and the Empress* (1932) covered the same ground but ran into all sorts of problems. Three of the over-hyped Barrymore family – John, Ethel and Lionel – starred, but the problem was an historical one. The holy man was believed to be having far too much influence over the tsarina, claiming to be able to cure her son's haemophilia (there was no cure) and two aristocrats lured him to their St Petersburg home and killed him, using cyanide and bullets before dumping his chained body into the River Neva. The claim was made in the film that Rasputin had raped the wife of one of the princes, Youssoupoff, and MGM lost their nerve, paying out $1 million. Not a bad payout for a self-confessed murderer!

In *Nicholas and Alexandra*, Rasputin fascinated all and sundry. In his pre-Dr Who days, Tom Baker's eyes were *far* too large for the smelly, unpleasant Grigori, but they worked wonders on the screen. A friend of mine went to see the movie in the cinema. He had no idea of the history of the Romanovs and expected, Hollywood-style, that a regiment of White Russian Cossacks would ride to the rescue of the royal family. In the event, the prisoners of the Bolsheviks in the sinisterly named House of Special Purpose, the entire family, as well as Dr Botkin and two servants, were murdered in a half-cellar room. The wallpaper, riddled with bullet holes and running with blood, used in the film, is an exact copy of the original at Ekaterinburg.

It's perhaps fitting that the last movie discussed in this section on empires should be one in which an empire was destroyed so bloodily. Ironically, the 'empire' that followed the Romanovs' in Russia, that of the 'Red Tsar', Joseph Stalin, produced *far* more deaths than anything that happened under Nicholas.

Chapter 8

Westerns: Heading Them Off at the Past

He was always clean-shaven and usually handsome. He rode tall in the saddle, was courteous to ladies, let someone else (the 'baddie') draw first and he never started a fight. He didn't drink, smoke or swear and he had an unerring sense of right and wrong. He was the cowboy, the greatest hero that Hollywood ever produced.

And he didn't exist.

One of the many oddities about the choice of movie subjects by Hollywood producers is that they focused on a theme that only covered the geographical area from the Mississippi to the West Coast and a time period that barely covered forty years; in the nineteenth century, the average man's lifespan. In the heyday of Hollywood, the studios were churning out hundreds of Westerns a year, distributed all over the world, which had an effect on several generations. In my childhood in the 1950s, the only game in town was Cowboys and Indians, in which we galloped out of the cinema on imaginary broncos, shooting down our friends and foes with invisible Winchesters and Colt 45s. If girls asked to play, they couldn't because women in the Westerns just got in the way of the action. At best, we let them be Indians and tied them up so that us lads could get on with the shoot-outs.

It took Hollywood decades to admit that the real West wasn't like that and by the time they began to make realistic Westerns, the West itself had long vanished and most Westerns were made for television episodes; 'soaps' starring men in funny hats.

The romantic image of the West upon which film-makers drew was the fiction of men like Ned Buntline, Owen Wister and later, Zane Grey. Those writers in turn were captivated by the haunting photographs, largely of native Americans, taken by Edward Curtis and financed by the banker J.P. Morgan. They in turn were influenced by the extraordinary sculptures and paintings of Frederic Remington and George Catlin.

The West was the final frontier (whatever Captain James T. Kirk tried to tell you in the television *Star Trek* series) and it conjured up endless romance. Horace Greeley, founder of the *New-York Tribune* may not have originated the phrase, but he certainly popularized it – 'Go West, young man, and grow up with the country.' Eventually, the settlers came in their covered wagons, grabbing land from the cattle barons who in turn had taken it from the Indians. Then came the railways, the telegraph and the twentieth century and the West was gone. But there was *so* much movie excitement on the way.

The Mountain Men

I have taken Hollywood's coverage of the West from 1865 when the Civil War ended and a hurt and disheartened nation tried to find a fresh start west of the Mississippi. In fact, of course, white Europeans had crossed the wilderness that would become the United States, since Lewis and Clark in 1804. Most of these travellers were hunters and fur traders, finding their way with the help of native guides. They were a hard-bitten race, living with the Indians and speaking a patois of their own. In Canada, they formed an entire race apart, then called half-breeds or Metis, a mix of the Cree tribe and French immigrants.

Meriwether Lewis and William Clark, financed by President Thomas Jefferson, paddled up the Missouri in canoes with thirty followers, meeting the Mandan and Minnetarce tribes on the way. Crossing the Rocky Mountains with the help of the Shoshone woman, Sacagawea, they reached the West Coast in November 1805. Including the return journey, they travelled 8,000 miles and lost only one man. *The Far Horizons* (1954) put them on the celluloid map. Fred MacMurray played Lewis and Charlton Heston, in his pre-*Ten Commandments* days, was Clark. This is the only major motion picture to tackle the expedition and, in 2011, *Time Magazine* placed it in the top ten most misleading historical films, if only because Sacagawea was played by eminently Caucasian Donna Reed. The other unfortunate element was the love interest (essential in a 1950s Hollywood production) between Sacagawea and Clark. Nothing of the kind happened, if only because Toussant Charbonneau, a fur-trapper, was with the expedition and happened to be Sacagawea's husband!

'Liver-eating' Johnson was a perfect example of the breed of men who followed in Lewis and Clark's wake. John Johnson married a Flathead woman who was killed by the Crows, a reminder that warfare among native Americans was endemic, in 1847. He vowed revenge on the entire nation and may have killed as many as 200 of them. Whether or not he ate anybody's liver is unrecorded! He became the hero of a novel in 1965, which translated to the screen as *Jeremiah Johnson* (1972) with Robert Redford in the titled role, filmed mostly in Utah. Redford may seem an odd choice for what was essentially a gritty and unpleasant role; that was because it was first offered to Lee Marvin (who could easily have been a mountain man) and then Clint Eastwood. Interestingly, the role of Johnson's wife was taken by Delle Bolton, not a native American, from a pool of nearly 200 who were.

Filming was delayed by snow, a reminder of just how tough life was for the early pioneers and consequently, there was no opportunity for retakes, relying on heavy editing instead. The natural element underscored the whole thing, with 'rhythms and moods', as director Sydney Pollack said. In what is surely a praiseworthy appraisal of an historical film, Charles Champlin of the *Los Angeles Times* wrote, 'Making fire with flint and steel looks the miserably frustrating job it is; hunting and fishing look as exasperating as they are; snow looks as cold as it is and hands have the numbed and purple looks it gives them.' And we can fully believe the film's end credits which tell us that somewhere in those mountains, Jeremiah Johnson is out there still.

Jim Bridger is difficult to explain in terms of Hollywood non-appearance. He was perhaps the most famous of the mountain men, working in the fur trade in the Rockies and probably knew more about the geography of the West than any other white men and most Indians, who tended to keep to their own tribal lands. He features in a number of Ned Buntline's dime novels but the only movie of any credit in which he features is *Pony Express* in 1952. This extraordinary organization, carrying mail on horseback to way stations in the middle of nowhere, was the brainchild of Messrs Russell, Majors and Waddell, none of whom appear in the film. The two stars are Charlton Heston as 'Buffalo Bill' Cody and Forrest Tucker as 'Wild Bill' Hickok, both of whom are dealt with below. The love interest is Jan Sterling as a faux Calamity Jane (ditto). It is possible that Cody rode for the Pony Express for a while, although Hickok was too heavy. Porter Hall played Jim Bridger.

A mountain man who sat on the fringes of Western celebrities was Grizzly Adams, who kept a menagerie, largely of bears, in California in the 1850s. Ten years later, he was showing them in Phineas Barnum's circus on Broadway. He was the hero of a television series in the 1980s – *The Life and Times of Grizzly Adams* – starring Dan Haggerty, but he also appeared in the peculiar *The Life and Times of Judge Roy Bean* (1972). John Huston played Adams, as eccentrically as the real man probably was. Adams was all but scalped during a fight with a grizzly, which left him with brain damage and a silver plate in his skull. Roy Bean, with no qualifications whatsoever, set himself up as a judge and 'the law West of the Pecos'. He fell in love with a photograph of actress Lily Langtry, the mistress of Edward, Prince of Wales, and renamed his saloon in Vinegaroon the Jersey Lily. As if to point up the general wackiness of the movie, Bruno the bear had a role as Zachary Taylor (named after an American president). Scriptwriter John Milius wanted Warren Oates for the part of Bean and found Paul Newman altogether too 'cutesy-pie' for a man who actually hanged people on a whim. He also thought that Huston 'completely ruined the movie', not for his performance as Adams but as director. The film was essentially a comedy, never actually getting inside the mind of a man like Bean.

'It has the air,' wrote one critic, 'of an elaborate mistake – overblown, tedious and over-emphatic.'

Indians versus Cavalry

The mountain men were the first whites to make contact with native Americans and to deal with them, but what followed was a classic piece of cover-up by successive American governments and Hollywood itself. The change in names reflects the trend. In the heyday of Westerns, the 'baddies' were always Indians (wrongly identified of course by Christopher Columbus – see Chapter 4). They were invariably white men in bad wigs, couldn't shoot straight and spent most of their time dancing and chanting to drum beats or riding their pintos pointlessly around circled wagons or army forts. The first Western I saw that tried to challenge this stereotypical drivel was *The Run of the Arrow* (1957), but it was twenty years later that Hollywood began to show empathy with what were now called native Americans.

Pitted against the 'baddie' Indians were the United States cavalry, always outnumbered, galloping to the rescue of pioneers and settlers, wearing white (of course!) Stetsons and nearly always travelling to the annoyingly catchy tune of Custer's 7th, the *Garryowen*.

Today's anthropologists and sociologists estimate that before the arrival of the white man, there were perhaps 18 million people divided into between 300 and 500 tribes, bands and nations. These were extraordinarily diverse, in terms of economies, habitats and language. There were probably about 200 languages in what would become the United States, including the famous 'smoke signals' of the Plains, which the US army developed into semaphore. In Hollywood terms, however, we have the garbled, grunted Injun-talk of the torturing, scalping savage or the drunk 'friendly' hanging around the army fort. In appearance, the Indians depicted in Chapter 6 concerning America up to 1865, are uniformly shown as Mohawks, with shaven heads and central crests, bare-chested and wearing breech-clouts (loin cloths). The post-1865 Indians are the Plains tribes, with eagle-feathered war bonnets (and the occasional buffalo horns), moccasins, tomahawk, lance (with feathers) and fringed buckskin shirts. The sneaky ones have acquired repeating rifles, either from unscrupulous Indian agents (who also provide them with rot-gut whisky known as 'fire water') or from the bodies of dead cavalrymen.

As for the multiplicity of tribes, the Hollywood Indians beyond the Mississippi are either Apache (in forty-three movies analysed by Ralph and Natasha Friar in *The Only Good Indian*) or the Sioux (eighty-one). The term Sioux itself is an indication of the Eurocentric attitudes of Hollywood – Sioux is what French settlers/trappers called them; the native American name is Lakota.

It's difficult to separate Indians and army in Hollywood movies because no major studio has yet made a film *exclusively* about a tribe from an insider's point of view. As with all other movies discussed in this book, however, we are concerned with real characters only and a sensible way forward is to concentrate on named native Americans and to see how they have been treated.

Sitting Bull's real name was Tatonka Iyotake and the translation is a bad one. He was a chief of the Hunkpapa, a subdivision of the Teton Lakota and is often referred to as a shaman or medicine man. The religion of the Plains Indians is complicated, dismissed or ridiculed by whites as so much superstition and mumbo-jumbo. Certainly, it featured visions experienced during what might be called transcendental states and Sitting Bull may have had a reputation as a prophet. He was an outspoken leader of his people against the whites from 1862 and became an overlord of all the Lakota by 1874 when the whites discovered gold in the Dakota Black Hills, which were sacred to their Lakota owners. He took no part in the battle of the Little Big Horn (see below) but had predicted Custer's defeat in his visions. He surrendered to the American authorities in 1881 and turned into something of a celebrity, touring with Buffalo Bill Cody's Wild West Show with whatever dignity he could maintain. He was shot dead by Indian police during the Ghost Dance religious revival of 1890. Sitting Bull appeared in movies from 1914, usually as a war-painted, war-bonnetted savage, later as something of a caricature.

Crazy Horse (Tashumca-uitco) is often depicted as Sitting Bull's Number Two. In fact, he was the chief of the Oglala Lakota and took part in many of the battles of the Indian Wars. He gave General Crook a bloody nose on the Rosebud in June 1876 before destroying most of Custer's 7th on the Big Horn. Always regarded as a troublemaker, his surrender a year later was treated with suspicion. He was fatally bayonetted at Fort Robinson in 1877. Anthony Quinn played him in *They Died With Their Boots On* (see below) and Victor Mature in *Chief Crazy Horse* (1955). Two native Americans have also portrayed him. The first was Iron Eyes Cody, a Cherokee whose father worked (rather frustratedly, we must suppose) on several Indian Westerns. He played Sitting Bull too and his last role was in *How the West Was Won* (1978). The oddest portrayal, however, was by Will Sampson in *The White Buffalo* (1971). Sampson was a full-blooded Creek who played an Indian in the non-Western *One Flew Over the Cuckoo's Nest* and the oddity of his portrayal of Crazy Horse is nothing to do with him but with the surreal nature of the film itself. Described today as a fantasy Western, it is difficult to see it in any category. The storyline is lifted vaguely from Herman Melville's *Moby Dick*, but the white whale has become a 'spike' (buffalo), equally albino and terrifying. The monster (we only ever see it as a studio-bound creation of the Special Effects Department) has killed Crazy Horse's daughter and he is out for revenge. The movie was panned, described as a turkey by most critics. Incidentally, it also featured Tom Custer (George Armstrong's kid brother played by Ed Lauter) as a thoroughly unlikeable racist and 'Wild Bill' Hickok (see below) played by Charles Bronson. It is true that Crazy Horse and Hickok were both in the Dakotas in the 1870s and both men were murdered within a year of each other, but there is no historical link between them at all.

To find the Apache, we have to move south. In the Hollywood version, the men wear unbraided hair hanging loose over their shoulders and a variety of vague European shirts/waistcoats as a result of a long tradition of living alongside (and dying alongside) Spanish/Mexican colonists. There were at least six tribes, one now extinct, covering what is today New Mexico, Arizona and Texas. The Chiricahua and Mescalero are the best known, the latter because of their association with the hallucinogen mescal. Of all the Hollywood tribes, the Apache and the Comanche are regarded as the most barbarous and untrustworthy. Two Apache leaders have provided the focus of most movies. The first is Cochise, the 6ft-plus chief of the Chiricahua who fought the American army during and after the Civil War. He was persuaded to surrender by an army scout, Tom Jeffords, and lived peacefully on a reservation for the rest of his life. The relationship between the two men, with Jeffords as a virtually unique liberal American and Cochise as a virtually unique 'good Apache' was the theme of *Broken Arrow* (1950). The choice of actors was interesting. James Stewart, known for his honest, upright characters, was Jeffords, but Cochise was played by white man, Brooklyn-born Jeff Chandler. This, along with *The Run of the Arrow* (see above) was one of the first to portray Indians in a human light, but in 1950, it could only go so far. The 'baddie' in the film was Geronimo (see below) and the death of an Indian love interest (played by 15-year-old Debra Paget) releases Jeffords/Stewart from any ongoing mixed-race relationship, which might have proved awkward. Director Delmer Daves had a real affinity with Apache culture, but 1950 was simply too early to remove the old mores. Some of the extras are actual Apaches, living on a reservation south of Flagstaff, Arizona. Interestingly, Canadian Mohawk actor Jay Silverheels (actually Harold J. Smith) better known later as Tonto in the hugely popular *Lone Ranger* television series, played Geronimo. This was one of the first movies in which native Americans didn't have the speech impediment imputed to them by early producers/directors. To promote the new liberal approach, native American activist Rosebud Yellow Rose toured

American cities, sponsored by 20th Century Fox to explain Apache culture. She wanted to reach 'a new generation of children [who are currently] learning the old stereotypes about whooping, warring Indians, as if there weren't anything else interesting about us.'

Geronimo was everybody's 'baddie' in the heyday of the Western. Whereas Cochise, Sitting Bull, Joseph of the Nez Perce, Gall of the Lakota and several others (there are no photographs of Crazy Horse) are striking in their physical appearance, Geronimo is a shrunken little old man with weasel eyes. He could never have played a hero. His real name was Gogathlay, at first a warrior under Cochise, then a chief of the Bedonkohe Apache in his own right. He broke out three times from reservations (to Hollywood, always the mark of a 'bad' Indian) and he was only brought to heel by General Nelson Miles in 1886 after a long pursuit by forty-two companies of the American army and 4,000 Mexican troops. Like Sitting Bull, he hit the celebrity trail towards the end of his life, however reluctantly, selling photographs of himself and more bows than any one man could possibly own!

A number of native Americans have portrayed him in the movies. He even had a walk-on part (played by Charles Stevens) in television's doggie-saga *Rin Tin Tin*. Perhaps the worst portrayal was that by Chuck Connors in *Geronimo* (1962). In the two films released in 1993, he was played by native Americans Wes Studi and Joseph Runningfox.

What of the men who fought these tribes in the post-bellum period? Today, the Indian Wars are often regarded as the most shameful in American history, the sharp end of carrying out the Manifest Destiny of white expansion that was the cornerstone of Federal policy. More liberal presidents promised native Americans free rights to all the land west of the Mississippi, but as gold was discovered in California in 1849 and the Black Hills in 1874 and 'land rushes' became the gimmick of the day, all this was forgotten. As the Lakota chief Red Cloud said, '[The whites] made us many promises, more than I can remember, but they never kept but one. They promised to take our land, and they took it.' And the men tasked with carrying this out were the army.

After the Civil War, as after any war in any country at any time, there were pacificist demands for cost-cutting. So by 1874, the huge army of the Union was slashed to 27,000 men (actually only 19,000 fighting operatives) scattered all over the continent. Many of the troops seen in Hollywood Westerns should not be cavalry at all; they were infantry, and occasionally artillery. But the sheer size of the West meant that all soldiers had to be mounted to cover the vast distances involved. The pay was appalling – $13 a month in the 1870s, and the food was worse; beans (that produced chronic wind), hardtack (that cracked teeth) and bacon (often maggot-ridden). There was plenty of coffee, but on campaign that was just beans soaked in hot water. Milk was non-existent. Training was poor and most men had to make do with the single-shot Springfield rifle (while many Indians had repeating Winchesters). Disease was commonplace; in the famous 7th Cavalry (made so only by their destruction on the Big Horn) between 1866 and 1868, six men drowned, two went missing and fifty-one died of cholera. Only thirty-six were killed by Indians. Drunkenness, especially among Irish and German recruits, was commonplace and discipline harsh. In the 7th, a third of the command deserted between 1867 and 1891. The Indians knew their own territory like the backs of their hands and rarely gave battle. They were light cavalry par excellence, using the hit-and-run tactics of guerrilla warfare and their mustang ponies were far superior in hardiness to the government's Quarterhorses.

Although there are any number of cavalry heroes in Westerns (especially those of John Ford and usually played by John Wayne) the central real character in the cavalry genre is George Armstrong Custer. There are numerous photographs of the 'boy general' of the Civil War: at West Point; on safari with the Grand Duke Alexei of Russia; with doting wife Libbie. He even managed (although there is no photograph) to inveigle himself into Appomattox Court House to watch Robert E. Lee surrender to Ulysses S. Grant in 1865. That was where Custer excelled – self-publicity. As a soldier – not so much!

He was a disaster at West Point, dressing up in flamboyant theatrical uniforms and earning demerits for bad behaviour. He impressed as commander of the 3rd Cavalry of the Potomac, leading reckless charges with his 'Wolverines', the Michigan Cavalry, at his back. When peace came, there was a hiatus. As the awful lyrics of the song that accompanied *Custer of the West* (1967) had it – 'What does the mighty general do, when the war is up and the war is through?' The answer was he became commander of the 7th Cavalry, carrying out a massacre of men, women and children on a Cheyenne camp on the Washita (in today's Oklahoma) in November 1868. He wrote an autobiography, *My Life on the Plains*, which was followed up by Libbie with a woman's take on the whole thing.

The first movie in which Custer appears is *The Santa Fe Trail* (see Chapter 6) in which he is wrongly portrayed (by Ronald Reagan) as a West Point classmate of future Confederate cavalry officer, J.E.B. Stuart. The two never met. The film is riddled with errors as we have seen, but one thing is surprisingly accurate. We are so used to seeing Custer with long blond ringlets (he was known as 'Fanny' at school) and neat moustache and goatee, it comes as something of a surprise to see clean-shaven, short-haired Reagan in the role. West Point photographs tell a different story.

They Died With Their Boots On (1941) has to be the best-known Hollywood version of Custer, even if the title is truly awful. The plotline is rubbish, with Custer fighting corruption from the White House to the Great Plains and having a grudging soft spot for the Indians. Like virtually every other army officer of the time, by the standards of today, Custer was incurably racist. Apart from that, of course, Flynn is Flynn, as he always was. Put him in a different costume and he could be Captain Blood (see Chapter 5), the Earl of Essex (ditto) or the fictional Captain Carruthers in *The Charge of the Light Brigade* (see Chapter 7).

A minor role in the film is that of George Winfield Scott, commander of the Union army at the start of the Civil War. Actor Sidney Greenstreet is perfect, in size and attitude, depicting the obese dinosaur quickly out of his depth in ever-changing military technology. The movie was hit with accidents. Three men were killed; one broke his neck falling from a horse; another had a heart attack; and a third was impaled on his own sabre during a cavalry charge. Flynn himself collapsed with exhaustion during shooting. According to legend, all-American (actually Sac and Fox native American) Olympic gymnast Jim Thorpe (Wa Tho Huk) had a row with Flynn off set and knocked him out with a single punch. Incidentally, Warner Brothers made a film about him – *Jim Thorpe – All-American* in 1951; he was played by Caucasian Burt Lancaster.

The last stand at the Little Big Horn was woefully wide of the mark, but it was based on innumerable paintings of the battle. According to eyewitness accounts on the days leading up to it, Custer had his hair cut short and usually rode with the famous buckskin jacket rolled behind him on his saddle. A short-haired Flynn in shirt sleeves would not have impressed anybody. There was no sabre-wielding cavalry charge at the Little Big Horn; sabres had been left behind as being of little use in an Indian campaign. The only man known to carry one was Miles Keogh, commander of I Company. Sixteen actual native Americans were extras; the others were Filipino.

The movie did well at the box office, but by 2009 the cracks had well and truly appeared. Alex von Tunzelman of *The Guardian* wrote, 'More errors riddle this biopic of General Custer than bullets flew at the Little Bighorn.'

It all got rather worse in 1967 with Robert Siodomak's *Custer of the West*. The whole thing was shot, for financial reasons, in Spain, including the use of Spanish Barb horses rather than the rangy old Quarterhorses of the nineteenth-century cavalry. Many of the characters in the movie were real – Libbie Custer (Mary Ure); Major Marcus Reno (Ty Hardin); Captain Frederick Benteen (Jeff Hunter, complete with correct prematurely grey hair); General Phil Sheridan (Laurence Tierney) and even the Grand Duke Alexei (played by Spanish-Hungarian Barta Barri). The central role was played by British actor

Robert Shaw and that was where it all went wrong. Shaw was given far too much scope in screenwriting and direction. He played Custer as a 'Shakespearean sadist' despite the fact that the real man was neither. It was panned at the box office and failed to make money. If there was any attempt to be liberal towards native Americans, it didn't show; Dull Knife of the Lakota was played by Irish actor Kieron Moore.

Three years later, the posters for *Little Big Man* said it all – he was 'either the most neglected hero in history or a liar of insane proportions'. It was a clearly revisionist Western, in which the cavalry are the 'baddies'. Like many films of the 1970s, it was a satire on America's increasingly unpopular war in Vietnam. In the movie, the hero, Jack Crabb, played by Dustin Hoffman, claims to have been a gunslinger buddy of 'Wild Bill' Hickok (see below), a scout for Custer and the sole survivor of the Little Big Horn (in Custer's actual command, there weren't any). Custer was played by Richard Mulligan as a 'borderline psychotic' (which probably isn't far from the truth). Even so, his raging at Hoffman, as he is about to die, believing Crabb to be his old nemesis, Ulysses S. Grant, now president, is little short of absurd. By the time *Little Big Man* was made, the myth of the Custer Massacre had been exposed. Custer brought the disaster on himself with bad intelligence and a refusal to wait for the back-up of generals Crook and Miles. At the time (1876) the American press would have none of this. Far and away the best scene in the movie is the arrival of the 7th out of a dawn mist (clearly, recreating the Washita attack of years earlier) with a creepily haunting, minor-key version of the normally rousing *Garryowen* playing. Quite brilliant is the appearance, not commented on, of the regimental band of the 7th on their (absolutely accurate) grey horses.

The real Little Big Man was involved in the arrest and murder of Crazy Horse in 1877. The writers simply borrowed the name. The real Indian scout with Custer was a Crow called Curly, sent away from the battle scene but able to watch from a distance. His account, too, has been called into question. The movie was filmed in Montana, not far from the actual battlefield. All the extras except two were native Americans and Chief Dan George, playing the fictional Old Lodge Skins, was nominated for Best Supporting Actor.

Westward the Women

If Westerns over the years have produced little more than stereotypes, this goes in spades for women. Traditionally, they are: pioneer mothers in awful bonnets; cavalry officers' wives, sometimes with Southern belle accents; schoolma'ams trying to educate scruffy little frontier kids; saloon girls and prostitutes, with or without a heart of gold, showing as much flesh as the film-makers could get away with; and, very occasionally, wearing pants and toting guns to ape the men. Their primary role, however, is the love interest and arm candy without which, it was feared in Hollywood, Westerns would become a 'boys only' club and women wouldn't even go to the pictures.

Because women in the West were an afterthought, both in Hollywood and the real thing, famous women are thin on the ground. When they exist at all, they are almost always the associates of known criminals. We'll look at them in a broadly chronological context.

Belle Starr was a piece of work. She was born Myra Maybelle Shirley in Carthage, Missouri, in February 1848. A famous photograph shows her as 'Queen of the Oklahoma Outlaws' in a fashionable velvet gown with a Stetson on her head, a holstered pistol at her waist and another in her hand. Like a surprising number of girls-gone-bad, Belle had a private school education and was an accomplished pianist. Her family were caught up in the violence and complexity of Missouri during the Civil War, although stories of Belle being a spy are simply part of her dime novel fictionalized life. She married James Reed, a gang member associated with the James and Younger gangs (see below) and when he was killed, married a Cherokee, Sam Starr, and continued her life of crime. Sentenced by 'Hanging Judge' Isaac Parker in Arkansas in 1883 for horse theft, she served nine months in Detroit Penitentiary.

After Starr's death in a gunfight, Belle drifted from crook to crook and was ambushed and killed in February 1889, two days before her forty-fifth birthday. Extraordinarily, there is a statue to her in Woolaroc, Oklahoma, gun in hand.

In the movies, Belle was portrayed in 'B' feature Westerns starring Roy Rogers and Hopalong Cassidy (Bill Boyd) or as a walk-on in more serious films like *The Long Riders* (1980 – see below). One of the few films to have Belle as the lead character was *Belle Starr* in 1941. The male lead was everybody's favourite cowboy Randolph Scott, but Belle was portrayed by Gene Tierney, *far* too attractive and sultry for the gaunt, grizzled real Belle, with the bad hairdo and bristling with firearms. None of the portrayals of Belle comes close to the reality but include snippets of the legends that grew after her (still unsolved) murder.

'Big Nose' Kate Fisher is not as deformed as the nickname implies. Her nose is long, but, judging by group photographs, this was a family trait. She was a mistress of John 'Doc' Holliday (see below) a friend of the Earp brothers in Tombstone, Arizona. Mary Horony was born in Hungary in 1850, a reminder that many of the personalities of the West were recent immigrants at the time. Her parents were middle class but both died in 1865 having settled in Iowa. Mary ran away from her foster home at 16 and by 1874 was working in a 'sporting house' or brothel in Dodge City, Kansas. It was here that she met Holliday and they moved to Tombstone via a circuitous route in 1880. Claims that she witnessed the famous shoot-out at the OK Corral (see below) are almost certainly fiction, but it is likely that she saw at least one participant, Ike Clanton, the day before. Most of her time with Holliday was spent roving – both had fierce tempers and liked a drink. When the 'deadly dentist' died of tuberculosis in 1887, 'Kate' as she had long since become, took up with a blacksmith and died in what was effectively an old people's home in November 1940. She was 89.

Jo Van Fleet played Kate in what is still the best-known version of the shoot-out, John Sturges' 1957 *Gunfight at the OK Corral*. The portrayal is probably very true to life – she loves Holliday, but life with him, his mood swings, his alcoholism and his coughing, must have been unbearable.

Every little boy in the 1950s – and a lot of big ones too! – fell in love with Calamity Jane. That was because she was played by Doris Day in the movie of the same name. Martha Jane Cannary was born in Princeton, Missouri, in May 1852 and the family travelled all over the West, looking for that elusive fresh start much popularized by Horace Greeley. She cooked, washed dishes and drove ox teams to make a living. Stories of her acting as a scout, complete with buckskins and rifle, for General Crook appear to be complete fiction. In 1904, an officer who *had* ridden with Crook wrote that Jane 'never saw service in any capacity ... She never saw a lynching and was never in an Indian fight. She was simply a notorious character, dissolute and devilish, but possessed of a generous streak that made her popular.'

In the rough mining town of Deadwood, Jane worked as a part-time prostitute and claimed later that she and 'Wild Bill' Hickok, hanging out in the saloons, had not only a relationship but a child. Hickok was at the time married to Agnes Thatcher, who appears in none of the films about him. After Hickok was murdered, Jane spent an increasing amount of time in the Dakota Territory, building up her legend as frontierswoman, Indian fighter and girlfriend of the man who was known as the fastest gun alive. She died, of an alcohol-related illness, in August 1903 and was buried (some said as a joke) next to Hickok.

Annie Oakley belongs squarely in the Western celebrity category. Before the cinema was created, 'Buffalo Bill' Cody glamorized and glorified the West with a series of shows which toured the United States and Europe in the 1880s and 1890s. At that time, the West was only known through the dime novels and few people in the cities of the Eastern seaboard, still less Europe, had ever seen an Indian or even a real-life cowboy. Phoebe Ann Mosey was born to a farming family in Ohio in 1860 and by the age of 15 was a crack shot. Her speciality from 1885 was shooting cigars out of hands and splitting the edge of a playing card at thirty paces. In the Wild West Shows, only Buffalo Bill earned more than Annie.

'Little Sure Shot' performed for many of the crowned heads of Europe, including Kaiser Wilhelm II of Germany who let her shoot the ash off his cigarette. When the Spanish-American War broke out over Cuba in 1899, Annie offered a fifty-strong regiment of female sharpshooters, but the offer was declined. She taught over 15,000 women how to shoot. Annie became a film star in her own right when she appeared in a twenty-one-second 'short' in November 1894 filmed by Thomas Edison. The name 'Sure Shot' was allegedly coined by Sitting Bull, who also rode with Cody and bonded with the girl, believing her ability was supernatural.

In 1904, newspaper tycoon William Randolph Hearst wrongly accused Annie of drug-dealing (cocaine had made its first serious appearance in the United States) and she spent six years fighting no less than fifty-five lawsuits. She died of pernicious anaemia in November 1926.

There have been at least eleven movies featuring Annie Oakley and she was the heroine of the Irving Berlin musical *Annie Get Your Gun* (1946). Barbara Stanwyck played her in 1935, but a more dependable version was *Buffalo Bill and the Indians* (1976) with Paul Newman as Cody. In this revisionist Western, the sharpshooter was played by Geraldine Chaplin – none of the actresses who took on the role looked much like her.

The last famous female west of the Pecos was also the most enigmatic. Whereas most of the women were nothing like as glamorous as the stars who played them, almost the opposite can be said of Etta Place. She was portrayed by Katherine Ross in *Butch Cassidy and the Sundance Kid* (1969) and the real Etta (with no disrespect to Ms Ross who is both lovely and talented) was a *little* more attractive! We only have one photograph of Etta, a studio portrait taken with Sundance (Harry Longabaugh) shortly before they sailed to South America in 1905.

Jacqueline Bisset was earmarked to play her, along with Paul Newman and Robert Redford as the Wild Bunch/Hole in the Wall gang leaders (see below). Ross played her with the same enigmatic qualities we have in Place's real life. We can understand why Katherine would take up with Newman and Redford, but the motivation of an apparently refined young woman going on the run with two men with prices on their heads, is more difficult to fathom.

Unless, that is, we factor in reality. The Pinkerton Detective Agency described Etta in 1906, when she was 27 years old. She had 'classic good looks, [was] 5ft 4in in height, weighing between 110 and 115 lbs with medium build and brown hair'. The Agency gave her several other names – Ethel, Eva and Rita – and, contrary to the myth of her being a music teacher, she was almost certainly a prostitute. High-class call girls on both sides of the Atlantic in the nineteenth century often had musical accomplishments; they were also good riders with linguistic talents. Three aliases are linked with her – Ethel Bishop, Ann Bassett and Eunice Grey – all of them known associates of the Cassidy/Sundance alliance.

The last we hear of Etta Place is in 1909 when a woman matching her description was trying to obtain a death certificate for Harry Longabaugh. She has appeared in another five movies apart from the Newman/Redford film, mostly made for television.

The Gunslingers

There is a convention in Westerns that the 'goodies' (in white hats, clean-shaven etc.) are called gun*fighters*, whereas the 'baddies' (black hats, swarthy etc.) are gun*slingers*. The merest look at the *real* gunmen of the West, whether they wore a star or not, is that they all belong to the latter category.

Gunfight at the OK Corral

The central, climactic moment in any Western is the shoot-out, where one man outdraws another with his six-gun in the middle of Main Street. Such iconic confrontations happened extremely rarely and never as depicted in the movies. One that has all the basic ingredients, however, and involving real people, is the clash between the Earps and the Clantons at the OK Corral in Tombstone, Arizona, in October 1881. The simplest version of the story is the 1957 movie version of the same name, starring Burt Lancaster as lawman Wyatt Earp and Kirk Douglas as his gambling friend, 'Doc' Holliday. It's a brilliant film, with a superb score (in the glory days when Westerns had songs) and became the definitive version, eclipsing an earlier movie with Randolph Scott.

It comes as something of a shock, if you've been brought up with the movie as I was, to find that not only were all the Earps heavily moustachioed, but that 'Doc' Holliday was a borderline psychopath and it's difficult to tell, from actual events, whose side we should be on in the gun battle.

Wyatt Earp, in particular, thanks to writer Stuart Lake, the 'story book' marshal, featured in at least thirteen films to date. Let's look at these before we decide what *really* happened at the Corral. *Law and Order* hit the big screen in 1932, starring Walter Huston. He is clearly supposed to be Earp, but the name in the movie is Frane Johnson and no real characters are included in the cast list. Ten years later, *Tombstone, the Town Too Tough To Die* (!) featured actual characters for the first time – most of the Earp brothers are there, as well as the Clantons, the thug 'Curly Bill' Brocious and 'Doc' Holliday. Wyatt was played by Richard Dix, a hugely popular cowboy star. *My Darling Clementine* (1946) was a bad title for a good film. John Ford directed with his usual mastery of the genre and the always watchable Henry Fonda was Wyatt. Victor Mature is miscast as Holliday and, as with almost all other versions, the script plays fast and loose with reality. According to Ford, who was a prop boy in the silent days, Earp, who had become a wealthy oilman in California, entertained film crews with tales of the gunfight. Ford's version in *My Darling Clementine*, is, according to the director, exactly as it happened.

Unfortunately, it isn't. As well as portraying the Earps as cattlemen, we have the murders of two of the brothers before the Corral confrontation and 'Doc' Holliday dying of his wounds. About the only thing that is accurate about the incident is that there is no intrusive Hollywood music! Despite the Clementine love interest, Wyatt was married to Mattie Blaylock and later to Josephine ('Sadie') Marcus. Sadie was, at the time of the shooting, living with John Behan, a rather shady sheriff of Cochise County, Arizona, who does not feature in the Ford version. This, Ford claimed, was because Sadie threatened him with legal action (which fits other evidence about her). 'Old man' Clanton (Walter Brennan) died before the OK Corral and it's doubtful whether he met the Earps. Holliday, of course, was a dentist, not a surgeon. James Earp, the 'kid' brother murdered by the Clantons early in the film, was the oldest of the family and lived on until 1926. Typical of Ford's Westerns, most of the locations were in Monument Valley, Utah, 500 miles from Tombstone. *My Darling Clementine* was President Harry S. Truman's favourite movie and many cinematic greats have praised it. As a piece of historical re-enactment, however, it is awful.

Hour of the Gun (1967) is much better. John Sturges directed; James Garner at his most taciturn was Wyatt; Jason Robards was Holliday and the reliably malevolent Robert Ryan was Old Man Clanton. This one has in its credits, 'This picture is based on fact. This is the way it happened.' Sturges had also directed the 1957 *Gunfight* in which the shoot-out lasted seven minutes, as opposed to the seconds it actually took. Intriguingly, *Hour of the Gun* begins with the OK Corral and the rest is the aftermath, living proof that very little is actually properly sorted out by violence. Again, however, errors occur. In this version, Wyatt kills Ike Clanton, who was actually shot dead by Jonas Brighton six years later. Holliday as a Civil War veteran wasn't true either – he was younger than the Earps and too young to fight in the war. Real characters abound – the Indian agent John Clum (mayor of Tombstone); Sheriff John Behan ('Jimmy' in the film) and cowboy Frank Stilwell. As evidence that, in the Hollywood game, you can't win, one critic complained that Edward Anhalt's script was *too* historical, constraining the actors' talents.

In the mid-1990s, that thing happened which is infuriating for everybody concerned – two films released within months of each other on the same theme. First was *Tombstone* (1993) with Kurt Russell as Wyatt. This was the decade of the duster coat, showing three Earps and Holliday, all in black and wearing outsize hats walking ominously towards the camera. Correctly, 'Doc' Holliday brandished a shotgun on that October afternoon. The film was hit by personality clashes and a cumbersome and overlong script had to be pared down. Everybody grew their own moustaches and Val Kilmer, highly praised for his tuberculous Southern gentleman as Holliday, practised regularly with his six gun off set. *True West* magazine hailed the piece as 'one of the 5 greatest Westerns ever made'. President Bill Clinton loved it. Six months later, Kevin Costner's *Wyatt Earp* came out, by comparison with *Tombstone*, a box office failure. The film covered much of Earp's career, rather than focusing on the Tombstone period and it lost direction as a result.

So what *really* happened at the OK Corral? The two sides, contrary to virtually every movie made on the subject, were both murky in terms of law-abiding behaviour. Virgil Earp was the local marshal, but the post was appointed by election and honest and upright behaviour were not considered necessities for the job. With him that October afternoon were his two brothers, special policemen Morgan and Wyatt, and temporary special 'Doc' Holliday. Ranged against them were a group of outlaws called the Cowboys – brothers Ike and Billy Clanton, brothers Tom and Frank McLaury and Billy Claiborne. Virgil was the central character, as marshal, not Wyatt, and tension between the two groups had been building for weeks. The actual site of the shoot-out was in an alley alongside C.S. Fly's photographic studio in Fremont Street (shown in the 1957 movie) six doors down from the Corral itself. According to witnesses who watched from safe(ish) vantage points, about thirty shots were fired in as many seconds, some from a range of 6 feet. Both the McLaurys were killed, as was Billy Clanton. The others ran. Virgil and Morgan Earp were wounded and Holliday's hip was grazed by a bullet.

In what sounds like a very modern move (more or less faithfully retold in *The Hour of the Gun*) Ike Clanton filed murder charges against the Earps, but the killings were deemed lawful. Two months later, Virgil was ambushed and crippled and Morgan was murdered in the March of the following year. In the 1957 version, Morgan's death happens *before* the OK Corral. The Cowboys responsible had alibis and were hunted down by Wyatt Earp, now a US Marshal (as in *The Hour of the Gun*) and he killed Frank Stilwell.

Tombstone was not the hick mining settlement in the middle of nowhere as depicted in all the movie versions. It had a school, an ice house, two banks, three newspapers, four churches, an opera house and (as we have seen) at least one photographic studio. Unfortunately, for law and order, it also had 14 casinos, 110 saloons and an unknown number of brothels.

The bottom line on the OK Corral is that we have no way, after all this time, of knowing who drew first. The Earps contended they were trying to get the guns off the Cowboys (it was supposedly illegal to carry firearms in the town limits) and the Cowboys swore that the Earps opened fire on them. Even when dealing with real people, Hollywood Westerns cannot sit on a fence like this and the Earps will always be the 'goodies' in this context.

The Kid

There is only one Hollywood actor who should have played Billy the Kid and that was the young Dustin Hoffman. With his boyish looks, sloping shoulders and the quizzical look he had on his face in *The Graduate*, he could easily pass for the 'left-handed gun' who had killed twenty-one men by the time of his twenty-first birthday. But of course, he wasn't and he hadn't.

Henry McCarty was born in New York in autumn 1859 of Irish descent. When his father died, the family moved to Indianapolis and McCarty's mother married William Antrim. For a time, young Henry used his stepfather's name but the man abandoned him when he was 15 and his mother died. Stealing horses and in trouble with the law, he came to be known as Kid Antrim. At the age of 17, he killed his first man, Francis 'Windy' Cahill in a fist-fight that got out of hand. By this time, McCarty was in New Mexico, rustling cattle in Lincoln County, most of them belonging to the cattle baron John Chisum. McCarty worked as a ranch hand for the English rancher, John Tunstall, and when Tunstall was murdered by rivals, McCarty was up to his neck in the ongoing feud called the Lincoln County War. In 1878, he was offered a pardon by Lew Wallace, the state governor. The man has a link with another chapter in this book – he was the author of *Ben-Hur* (see Chapter 1).

Mistrusting Wallace, McCarty broke out of jail and killed Joe Grant, reason unknown, in 1880, by which time he called himself William H. Bonney. There was a $500 price on his head and newspaper articles building up his homicidal tendencies began to appear across the United States. He was sentenced to death for the murder of Sheriff William Brady but escaped again and killed Deputy Bob Olljer in the process. He was eventually killed by Sheriff Pat Garrett in July 1881, with rumours of his survival rife for the next fifty years.

The only *authentic* photograph of McCarty shows a moronic-looking young man holding a Winchester rifle with his pistol on his left hip, hence the title of one movie about him, Paul Newman's *The Left-Handed Gun* (1958). In fact, the photograph is a ferrotype, which reverses the image; McCarty was actually right-handed and, as will be evident from the historical evidence above, killed four men, not the twenty-one usually alleged.

It wasn't until the 1920s that Billy the Kid was converted, first into a misunderstood victim of circumstance, then a hero. That was the context that Hollywood has always followed. King Vidor directed *Billy the Kid* in 1930 and eleven years later, MGM reproduced the piece with heart-throb Robert Taylor dressed in black to hint that he was a 'baddie' in the title role. Taylor looks too old for Billy (he was 30 in

1941) as did Paul Newman, aged 32, in 1958. At least, in this version, the Kid is on the prowl for the four men (the correct tally) who killed his friend in Lincoln County. *Chisum* in 1970 featured John Wayne as the rancher, complete with rousing song narrated by William Conrad, but it contains Billy, Pat Garrett (Glenn Corbett), John Tunstall and a number of other real-life characters. Billy himself (Geoffrey Dueul) is shown as a psychopath (which he may well have been) but we are encouraged to feel sorry for him. *Pat Garrett and Billy the Kid,* three years later, explored the relationship between the two men (there wasn't one). Kris Kristofferson was miscast as Billy and James Coburn didn't look comfortable in a handlebar moustache. One critic said, 'Shows what [director Sam] Peckinpah can do when he doesn't put his mind to it.' It was one of the first Westerns (see *The Assassination of Jesse James* below) to have actors mumbling in fake realism, which actually confuses most of their audience. For those who still regard the Kid as a hero, Garrett got his come-uppance; he was shot in the back in 1908 while urinating on a country road.

Young Guns (1988) was a movie intended to make the dying genre of the Western appeal to the young, whose grandfathers had been brought up with the genre. The 'background authenticity' to which Halliwell alludes only goes as far as long hair and duster coats. It starred Keifer Sutherland and had Jack Palance in there somewhere for a bit of gravitas.

The Prince of Pistoleers

Being shot in the back was also the fate of 'Wild Bill' Hickok and, rather like the surname Bonney, the moniker has no links with the man at all. He was actually James Butler Hickok, known to his family as James or Jim. He drove freight wagons for Russell, Majors and Waddell (hence the confusion over his being a Pony Express rider), served as a scout for the US Army, both in the Civil War and after it, and shot more than his fair share of buffalo. He was 6ft tall, softly spoken and a striking-looking man with shoulder-length hair, flowing moustaches and a natty taste in formal dress. He was photographed often, as a friend of 'Buffalo Bill' Cody and 'Texas Jack' Omohundro, buckskin-clad showmen of the Old West in the 1880s and 1890s.

Briefly a marshal in Hays City and Abilene, his speed with his ivory-butted Dragoon Colts (later Navy specials) was legendary. He was a brilliant shot, slow to anger, but deadly. And he was prone to exaggeration. In a famous fight with the McCanles gang in Rock Creek, Nebraska, in 1861, he killed three men but claimed to have despatched ten. Recently, a number of historians have gone beyond his dime novel adventures, like *The Scouts of the Plains* and *Wild Bill, Indian Slayer* to the truth behind them. A realistic tally of his kills is seven definite, with a possible five more. This still puts him ahead of any other figure in the West.

He was sacked by Cody for firing too close to Indian extras on tour with the Wild West show and drifted to the ghastly mining town of Deadwood where he gambled, drank and married Agnes Thatcher five months before he was shot in the back at a poker table by a psychotic drunk, Jack McCall, who would never have taken Hickok on face to face. His supposed romance with Calamity Jane (see above) was largely a figment of her imagination. Legend has it that Hickok was holding aces and eights at the time of the shooting and that this came to be known as the dead man's hand. His murder – McCall was duly tried and hanged – took place soon after the destruction of Custer's 7th Cavalry on the Big Horn and perhaps because of that, it didn't get the coverage it deserved.

Hickok first appeared on celluloid in *The Pioneer Peacemaker* in 1913 (though he was neither a pioneer nor a peacemaker) but reached greater prominence ten years later as portrayed by William S. Hart. In 1936, Gary Cooper played him. The only thing correct about the movie was Cooper's taciturn performance (not much of a talker was Wild Bill) – the rest of it was about Calamity Jane. In fact, the film's posters referred to it as 'grandest love story ever told' whereas of course, it was nothing of the sort. Graham Greene must have been having an off day too; he called it 'perhaps the finest Western in the history of film'. Perhaps he didn't get out much.

In *Pony Express* (1952) he was played by Forrest Tucker, but since Hickok never rode for the company, the whole thing was based on a myth. He was a bit player in *Little Big Man* (see above) in which Jeff Corey portrayed him as a neurotic oddball, who has *far* too much to say to Dustin Hoffman in his dying moments, considering he had a bullet in the back of his head.

One of the oddest movies featuring Hickok was *The White Buffalo* (1977). Critic Jonathan Rosebaum quipped, 'The dried husk of a Moby Dick allegory seems to be rattling around here amidst all the other dead wood.' We have discussed this film already in the context of Crazy Horse (Will Sampson) but if we shift our attention to Hickok (Charles Bronson) it is still unsatisfactory. The man's hair colour is wrong (the real Hickok was blond/auburn) and too much is made of the syphilis that was sending him blind. It's true that when a marshal in Abilene, Hickok killed his own deputy by mistake, but that was at night in a darkened street and at a moment of high tension when the marshal was in the thick of a gunfight. In *The White Buffalo*, Bronson wears thick glasses and blasts away at spectral figures that don't exist.

A similar portrayal comes from Jeff Bridges (whose eyebrows are *far* too bushy for the real Hickok) in a remake of *Wild Bill* (1995). Remake is the wrong word, because Bridges' version is a drug addict (more 1990s than 1870s) and the whole thing is depressing and disappointing, as if all those actors, actresses, directors and producers have been lying to us about Westerns for all those years.

The Gang's All Here

One of the things that never struck me about Westerns I watched as a child was the *psychology* of the gangs. What made the Hole in the Wall Gang and the Jameses, Youngers and Daltons want to hang around together, just to rob banks, rustle cattle and shoot up trains? And what the Sam Hill did they do when they *weren't* doing that? I still have no answers, sixty years later.

Jesse James is a fascinating character, one of the first professional criminals to blame society for his own misdeeds. He also elicited a great deal in sympathy and popularity. His gravestone in Mount Olivet Cemetery reads, 'Jesse James, murdered by a coward whose name is not fit to appear here.' For the record, it was James' cousin, Bob Ford, and for anyone robbed by the James/Younger gang, he did society a favour. In their day, the Jameses and the Youngers were the most famous infamous men in America and after their robbery spree was over, their legend spread worldwide. Ironically, Jesse and his older brother Franklin were the sons of a Baptist minister but they had the genuine misfortune to be teenagers in Missouri at a time when the war between the states was building to fever pitch over the issue of slavery. They rode with William Quantrill, a vicious pro-slavery guerrilla who used the tensions in the area to rob and murder at will.

The end of the war saw the James boys begin a notorious crime spree, hitting bank after bank in the mid-West with or without the Younger brothers, Cole, James and Robert. They also tackled trains, recklessly running along the roofs of moving carriages to get at safes carrying payrolls. Pursued by the Pinkerton Detective Agency hired by the railway companies, the James boys weren't at home near Laurence, Kansas, in 1875 when detectives threw a bomb into their mother's house; it blew her arm off.

By the 1880s, the James/Younger exploits featured in dozens of dime novels, none of them true, which painted them as heroic Robin Hood figures, robbing from the greedy banks and railroads and giving the money to the poor, hard-pressed pro-Southern farmers. It all went wrong in Minnesota in September 1876 when the inhabitants of Northfield got wind of a raid and shot it out with the robbers. Three gang members were killed and two of the Youngers were wounded and caught. The James boys got away. In the interests of lying low, Jesse changed his name to Howard and bought a house in St Joseph, Missouri. According to reports, he was standing on a chair straightening a picture on 3 April 1882 when Bob Ford shot him dead. 'The dirty little coward who shot poor Mr Howard' was pardoned for the killing and even went on a stage tour proclaiming his deed. He in turn was shot dead in his own saloon in Colorado in 1892. Frank surrendered to the authorities on Jesse's death and also toured in a Wild West Show. He ran guided tours of the James home for 50c a head – 'Kodaks bared [sic]'.

It wasn't until 1939 that the James brothers made it to central roles in the Westerns. *Jesse James* was filmed on location in Missouri and Jesse's granddaughter was technical adviser. Tyrone Power was Jesse and Henry Fonda was Frank, with the ever-reliable pioneer mother, Jane Darnell, as Mrs James. The boys are the heroes, no questions asked, and cinema audiences cheered. As the Halliwell entry says, 'The life of an outlaw turns into family entertainment when Hollywood bathes in sentiment, soft colour, family background and warm humour.' History isn't quite like that.

A whole series of 'B' features in the late 1940s and 1950s dealt with the James/Younger gang, but most merely borrowed the names and gave historical reality a miss. *The True Story of Jesse James* (1957) and *Cole Younger, Gunfighter* (1958) wasn't exactly what the title promised. *The Great Northfield Minnesota Raid* (1972) starring Cliff Robertson, was one of the new 'gritty realism' Westerns in which town main streets were a sea of mud, nobody shaved (except the saloon girls) and everybody wore long duster coats; even so, the script was poor. *The Long Riders* (1980) was fascinating because the gangs of brothers were played by actual brothers; the Carradines, the Keaches and the Quaids were everywhere. It was violent in an attempt to recreate the atmosphere of the time, but there was essentially nothing more to say.

The Assassination of Jesse James possibly has, but the dialogue is so garbled as to make the movie incomprehensible. 'Perhaps the least western Western ever made – and that's not a good sort of singularity,' said one critic. 'Not only one of the best Westerns ever made ...' began another. All of which proves what Abraham Lincoln once said – you *can* fool some of the people all of the time.

It's notable that people who liked this one are largely aficionados of 'mood' Westerns. Unfortunately, moody landscapes and dull colours don't recreate the America of the 1880s. As another critic said, 'The movie is merely a long, empty exercise in style.' Notably, there is nothing online about the accuracy of the thing. At least, the murder weapon is right.

The only other gang of family outlaws worthy of film mention is the Daltons, brothers Frank, Grattan, Robert and Emmet. With a similar post-Civil War Kansas-Missouri background to the James/Younger boys, Frank was killed serving as a police officer. The other brothers took to horse stealing and gravitated to banks and trains. Their Northfield Minnesota was Coffeeville in Kansas where an overly ambitious plan to rob two banks simultaneously went disastrously wrong. Robert and Grattan were killed along with two other gang members, their bodies laid out on a sidewalk for anybody (children included) to gawp at.

Emmet was released from prison in 1907 and campaigned for penal reform. He also had a serious hand in early movies. In 1912, he produced *The Last Stand of the Daltons*, which he remade in a larger format six years later under the title *Beyond the Law*. Emmet played himself and all his brothers! The best of the later versions is Universal's *When the Daltons Rode* (1940) with the usual whitewashing of the boys.

Which leaves us with the granddaddy of them all, the loose group of misfits who captured the imagination of several generations. They were called the Wild Bunch (nothing to do with the hugely overrated Sam Peckinpah movie of that name) and the Hole in the Wall Gang, but to cinema-goers of a certain generation, they are usually referred to as Butch Cassidy and the Sundance Kid. We've come across them before, because the mistress of probably both of them was the enigmatic Etta Place (see above). The movie *Butch Cassidy and the Sundance Kid* (1969) kept the Western alive when it was on its last legs and made Paul Newman and Robert Redford into the most dynamic heart-throb pairing of all time. It was funny and beautifully filmed and the final freeze frame lingers in the mind forever.

Both men knew that the West was vanishing, less than fifty years after it had begun, and the mood was one of nostalgia. It's all about trains and steam and bicycles and the good bad men have to end their days in Bolivia because the West itself doesn't want people like them any more. The fatuous song *Raindrops Keep Falling on my Head* jarred horribly and should have been taken out (with all due respect to the late Burt Bacharach who wrote it); other than that, it's excellent. 'Not that it matters,' read the film's poster, 'but most of it is true!' If only!

Cassidy was born Robert LeRoy Parker in Utah. His parents were Mormons. Cassidy was the name of a family friend and he *may* have worked as a teenager as a butcher. Sundance was Harry Longabaugh. The Pinkerton Detective Agency's file on him tells us almost all we know about him. He was 35 to 40 years old (in 1901); his complexion was dark 'looks like a quarter breed Italian' (oops, Robert Redford); he was 5ft 9in tall, 165–170lbs. His occupation was listed as 'cowboy, rustler'. His *criminal* occupation added 'highwayman and bank burglar, cattle and horse thief'. One of the many myths of the Old West is that horse stealing was a hanging offence, but Sundance, like many others, did a short gaol stretch for it as a teenager. The Pinkerton file links him with Cassidy, 'Kid' Curry, Tom O'Day and Walter Putney, a reminder that the Wild West was, by and large, a fluctuating group of outlaws who sometimes operated singly, sometimes in groups. The Newman/Redford film is a classic 'buddy' movie, focusing on the two of them.

As the film more or less faithfully records, Cassidy, Longabaugh and Etta Place checked into Mrs Taylor's boarding house in West 12th Street, New York, on 1 February 1902 on their way to Argentina. They were on the run from just about everybody and were carrying an estimated £30,000 in stolen cash in their baggage.

In South America, the *'bandidos Yanquis'* assumed various identities, worked for a mining company and became popular with the locals. There is little doubt that both men were as personable as their Hollywood counterparts and the confession in the film from Cassidy that he never killed anyone is probably true. Eventually, Santiago Maxwell (Cassidy) and Enrique Brown (Longabaugh) were surrounded by a troop of Bolivian cavalry in a hotel near La Paz. Longabaugh made a run for it after hours of fighting and was shot dead. Cassidy killed himself. Contrary to the movie's haunting final frames, all this took place in the dark.

Cassidy's sister maintained that both outlaws returned to the United States and lived happily, if anonymously, for years. It's a rattling good story, in the Hollywood tradition, but it's not true.

The Cowboys

The game we all played as children, fed by countless Hollywood movies, was 'Cowboys and Indians'. The Indians were usually imaginary (who wanted to identify with the losers?) or girls (see above). The whole economy of the West seemed based on the cow and the hard-riding, hard-drinking men who, in the days before extensive railroads, drove them along trails like the Sedelia, the Chisolm and the Goodnight-Loving. It was along those trails that the lawless cattle-towns grew up – Dodge, Abilene, Wichita and Hays where dime novels and Hollywood asked us to believe that gunfights happened daily and tall, taciturn strangers walked into saloons through batwing doors and the piano stopped playing. According to actual statistics, the death-rate in Wichita was less than two a year.

The cowboy dress of Stetson, bandana, chaps and boots (all essential for men working long hours outdoors in all weathers) was augmented by a revolver, a rifle and a lariat. Roping, branding, driving cattle was hard work and the pay was poor. Some of the leading cattlemen of their day have found themselves in the movies, but only as a backdrop to violence. John Wayne was John Chisum in *Chisum* (1970); rancher John Tunstall appears in the same film. The cowboys themselves, drovers and ranch-hands, are usually anonymous and we only know of them when they break the law to a sufficient extent to become notorious.

In the context of Hollywood, no other period in history or place in the world has provided more hours of entertainment than the American West.

Chapter 9

To Hell and Back: War from the Trenches to the Killing Fields

War runs through all the chapters in this book because warfare is as old as human civilization. Historically, man has been at war more often than he's been at peace. It may be desirable and preferential to avoid fighting; 'jaw, jaw', rather than 'war, war' as Winston Churchill said, but it is not the historical norm. So most of the movies covering the ancient world are littered with wars, Middle Eastern peoples fighting each other, Greeks invading Persian territory, everybody against Rome. The slave gladiator Spartacus was fighting a war. So was the oddball peasant girl, Joan of Arc. Oliver Cromwell rose to prominence because of his military ability and Napoleon Bonaparte was called by the military theorist Karl von Clausewitz the 'god of war'.

In the context of this book, war films refer to the conflicts of the twentieth century, from the First World War to Cambodia. The Great War, as it came to be known, broke out in August 1914 as a result of a build-up of tension between the various European powers. They formed cliques and alliances like playground bullies and when a deranged nationalist, 19-year-old Gavrilo Princip assassinated Franz Ferdinand, the heir to the Austrian Empire, all hell broke loose. Within a month of the murder, two armed camps confronted each other – Britain, France and Russia (later augmented by Italy and the United States) versus Germany, Turkey and Austro-Hungary. What began as a war of movement, which would all be over by Christmas, slowed to the stalemate of the trenches of the Western Front with horrendous slaughter on a scale never seen before. By the time it was over, four years later, Britain had lost 1 million men, France over 2 million, Germany nearly 4 million. Russia's numbers were never fully calculated before the Bolshevik Revolution of 1917 pulled the country out of the conflict.

Very few movies about the First World War feature real people. They all contain stereotypes – the fanatical general leading from the rear; the crusty old sergeant looking after his boys; the boys themselves transformed from eager, flag-waving school children to battle-hardened veterans, broken in body and spirit. The best of these is possibly Erich Maria Remarque's *All Quiet on the Western Front* (made by Hollywood in 1930 and recently remade) but seen from the German point of view. The book and the movie showed Germany in too weak a light at the time, and both were banned by the Nazis from 1933. But there are no real characters in the film. As one of the leads says, 'Me and the Kaiser, we are both fighting. The only difference is, the Kaiser isn't here.' He does appear in the tame 1970s remake, but is a distant figure, removed from the action and intensity of war.

All Quiet on the Western Front and *Journey's End*, told essentially the same story from the Central Powers and Allied point of view, but only one movie had real characters associated with the Western Front, and that was so surreal that some people don't class it as a war film at all. *Oh, What a Lovely War!* was directed by Richard Attenborough, from Joan Littlewood's stage play. Out went the marionettes of the stage version, but Field Marshal Haig's HQ is still at the top of a helter-skelter on Brighton seafront and the film is a musical with rousing and haunting songs of the period. It is not remotely bloody, the symbol of the poppy substituting for gore. Reception to it was mixed. The *New Yorker* said (in 1977), 'This musical lampoon is meant to stir your sentiments, evoke nostalgia and make you react to the obscenity of battles and bloodshed, and apparently it does that for some people.' It is worth pointing out that the United States did not join the war until 1917 (because of German U-boat attacks on their shipping) and that, by the time of the armistice in November 1918, there was still only one American Division in France.

We see the surreal, music-hall war through the eyes of the fictional Smith family, a cross section of British society and what happens to them all (spoiler alert – all the men are killed!). The last scene, showing their ghosts and their widows and children playing in a vast graveyard of crosses, is heartbreaking.

The vignettes of the statesmen who so willingly sent millions of young men to their deaths, are superbly done. The Kaiser is played by Kenneth More, complete with upturned moustache and pickelhaube helmet. John Clements is Field Marshal von Moltke, his chief of staff. Ian Holm is the vengeful Poincaré, the French prime minister. Paul Daneman is Tsar Nicholas II. The ancient Austrian emperor, Franz Joseph, is portrayed by Jack Hawkins, who plays his organ, clearly with no idea of what's going on. Ralph Richardson is a careful diplomat, Sir Edward Grey, but hovering over them all is the duplicitous John Gielgud as Count Bertholdt, the Austrian foreign minister, who is falsifying reports to ensure that war breaks out.

The generals of the British High Command are portrayed as the donkeys they were. Laurence Olivier is Sir John French, Commander-in-Chief, completely out of touch and pledged to fight this war the way he fought the last one (that was the Boer War, so badly). His pushy Number Two is General Douglas Haig, played by John Mills, who has equally no idea how to break the deadly stalemate of the trenches. While the numbers of casualties are written up in their thousands on cricket scoreboards, Haig is heard offering up a prayer (taken from the actual man's diaries) for victory 'before the Americans arrive'.

In that context, Haig's family complained to Attenborough about what they considered to be an unfair portrayal. Attenborough (see *Young Winston*, Chapter 7) apologised. There has been a move recently among revisionist historians to paint the high command in a more positive light. I don't accept that; the British Tommies of 1914–18 were indeed 'lions led by donkeys'.

The one scene in the film that jarred for me was Vanessa Redgrave as militant suffragette, Sylvia Pankhurst, making an anti-war speech to an indifferent crowd. The suffragettes were indeed being more militant pre-1914, but they officially stopped their activities and supported the government until the war was over. Ms Redgrave's rant seemed out of place.

Other movies that covered the First World War feature action that takes place away from the trenches of the Western Front. *The Light Horsemen* (1988) was a remake of *Forty Thousand Horsemen* (1940), it dealt with the extraordinary charge of the Australian Light Horse at Beersheba in the Middle East in 1917. The first version was written and directed by Charles Chauvel whose father had led the actual charge itself. The astonishing thing about the Beersheba action is that the Light Horse were equipped as mounted infantry, so they carried no swords. In attacking the fortified positions of the Turks (successfully too!) they used their bayonets. In the 1988 version, the most interesting character is almost a sub-plot. Anthony Andrews played Richard Meinertzhagen, who, despite the German-sounding name, was a British officer who was incredibly shady, a spy who claimed to have got at least one of the tsar's children out of Ekaterinburg (see *Nicholas and Alexandra*, Chapter 7). We now know this is untrue. Incidentally, Meinertzhagen was also an ornithologist and artist of some repute – his paintings of birds fetch a fortune today.

In terms of exotic locations for First World War movies, however, none can come close to *Lawrence of Arabia* (1962). After the failure of the Gallipoli campaign (the Allied withdrawal was the most successful thing about it), the idea occurred to hit the Turks in the Middle East by encouraging an Arab uprising. Enter Thomas Edward Lawrence, an odd, homosexual archaeologist who was attached to British Intelligence in North Africa until 1916 when he joined the tribes under Emir (later King) Faisal in co-ordination with General Edmund Allenby, attacking and taking Turkish-held Aqaba and entering Damascus in October 1918.

It would be difficult to find an actor more different from the real Lawrence (5ft 5in, slim build, dark, rather shy) but director David Lean managed it with the unknown Peter O'Toole (6ft 1in, blond, extrovert). *Lawrence of Arabia* is one of the most beautiful films ever made, from O'Toole's white robes against the sand, to the first appearance of the equally unknown Omar Sharif, as a tribal chief, he and his camel wobbling in the heart haze. Much of the action takes place in the Wadi Rum in today's Jordan and I can confirm that the area is a lot scruffier and more built-up than it appeared in 1962. As Halliwell says, 'a sprawling epic which manages, after four hours, to give no insight whatsoever into the complexities of character of this mysterious, historic figure'. In the film, Lawrence works himself almost to death in the Arab cause and is outspoken in his criticism of his British superiors. He was allegedly sexually molested by the Turks (although this is kept under early 1960s wraps) and apparently enjoyed shooting people. So excited was he in leading the charge at Aqaba that he shot his own camel in the head!

Apart from O'Toole and Sharif, Jack Hawkins is a perfect uptight Allenby, even down to the bald head, and Anthony Quinn has to be the Arab bandit leader, Auda Aba Tayi. As ever, Alex Guinness steals every scene as the composed, almost mystical King Faisal. We should be grateful, though, for small mercies; the part of Lawrence was originally offered to Marlon Brando!

As for Lawrence himself, he felt he had betrayed the Arabs in that the British reneged on the promises they made to Faisal and stayed in control of Palestine. Bitter, Lawrence left the army, briefly joined the RAF under another name and was killed in a motorbike accident in 1935.

For all the American involvement in the First World War was limited, Hollywood made the most if it. Standing tallest in the military hall of fame was Sergeant Alvin York, immortalized by Gary Cooper in 1940. *Sergeant York*, wrote *The New York Times*, 'has all the flavour of true Americana, the blunt and homely humor [*sic*] of backwoodsmen and the raw integrity peculiar to simple folk' (which sounds rather patronising today). York was a shy man, who, despite winning the Congressional Medal of Honor, turned down umpteen Hollywood requests to make a movie out of exploits. Warner Brothers eventually won him over but only on the condition that he supervise every aspect of the production and that Cooper got the starring role. The action scenes were applauded, but the Warner Brothers lot couldn't pass muster for the backwoods of Tennessee. Ward Bond, Walter Brennan and Margaret Wycherley (as York's mother) all received Academy Award nominations for supporting performances.

Alvin York single-handedly captured 132 German soldiers in the Meuse-Argonne sector during the war and it was fitting that Cooper won Best Actor for his performance. The irony is that York, a hellion in his youth, became a religious convert and suffered agonies of indecision whether he should enlist in the army or not. He was, also, of course, a crack shot. Since *Sergeant York* was released in 1941, the year of Pearl Harbor, such decisions were centre-front in the United States as the time.

What about the other branches of the service? Spectacular naval actions are thin on the ground in the First World War. The heroes of the Battle of Jutland (1916) and the posthumous VC awarded to 'Boy' Cornwall didn't attract film-makers. The air was a little different, *Von Richthofen and Brown* that had the much better British release title, *The Red Baron,* was made in 1971. Manfred von Richthofen was a stereotypical Prussian aristocrat and cavalry officer who became Germany's top ace in the First World War with eighty accredited 'kills', the highest of any pilot in the war. He commanded Jagdgeschwader I, known as Richtofen's Flying Circus and flew a scarlet-painted Fokker triplane (hence the Red Baron). When the war started, it had only been eleven years since the inaugural flight at Kitty Hawk Beach by the Wright brothers and the planes of all countries were decidedly works in progress, held together with glue and rope. The first pilots fired at each other from the cockpits with pistols, and aircraft were mostly used for reconnaissance. Von Richthofen was shot down on 21 April 1918 near Vaux-sur-Somme and buried with full military honours by the

Australian Flying Corps, the nearest unit to where his crashed plane and body was found. The ace had been wounded in the previous July and possible brain damage may have contributed to his death.

Director Roger Corman, best known for his horror movies, wanted to make a film based on von Richthofen by portraying him as an anachronistic, chivalric 'knight of the air' brought down by the ruthlessness of modern warfare. Nothing could be further from the truth; von Richthofen was fully au fait with every aspect of modern warfare and actually didn't see war as some sort of surreal game. There is a tendency in many films about fighting aircraft (almost all from the Second World War – see later) to assume this same uncertainty, with slow-motion, dream-like aerobatics, complete with overblown music. John Philip Law was an indifferent von Richthofen and Don Stroud was Captain Arthur 'Roy' Brown of 209 Squadron, Royal Flying Corps (morphing at the time into the Royal Air Force) who was credited with shooting the Red Baron down. The movie had a string of real characters: Kaiser Wilhem II; Ernst Udet; Oswald Boelcke; Hermann Göring (all flying aces); Anthony Fokker, the aircraft designer, and Lanoe Hawker VC, a British pilot. None of them is given much character and the movie made no claim to be historically accurate, which is just as well because Brown did not bring down the Red Baron; Australian anti-aircraft gunners from the ground did.

The film itself ran into difficulties. During production, in September 1970, stunt flyer Charles Boddington was killed when his SE5 flipped over and crashed. Undeterred, shooting went on the next day and Don Stroud was hurt along with his cameraman when their plane crashed too. Production was temporarily grounded. Incidentally, a sex scene between Law and Karen Huston was edited out after preview audiences laughed at it!

One unusual film that related to American aviation was set *after* the First World War. This was *The Court Martial of Billy Mitchell* (1955) with Gary Cooper in the title role. Mitchell, a much-decorated war hero, is often credited with being the 'father of the United States Air

Force' because of his almost fanatical championing of aerial warfare as the military element of any future wars. All governments in power are keen to reduce expenditure on the armed forces and since interwar America retreated into a period of 'splendid isolation' it seemed unnecessary to waste time and money on storing up defences. Hence, the air force was falling into decay with far too few (and obsolete) aircraft to do their job.

Mitchell criticized the hidebound high command of both the army and the navy, who could see no real need for an air force at all. He was tried by a military court in 1925 for insubordination, accusing his superiors of neglect of duty bordering on treason. Cooper was excellent as the reasonable but stubborn Mitchell, and Charles Bickford suitably unpleasant as the leading judge in the tribunal (only his name was changed, presumably to avoid legal action). Rod Steiger was a particularly nasty prosecution lawyer (fictional) but a whole host of real characters flitted across the screen, most of them speaking on Mitchell's behalf. Fiorello La Guardia, the reformist mayor of New York; President Calvin Coolidge ('Silent Cal' spoke more words in this movie than he probably did in office!); and air ace Eddie Rickenbaker – all had their day in court. Mitchell was defended pro bono by Congressman Frank R. Reid (Ralph Bellamy). One of the thirteen judges who spoke for acquittal was Douglas McArthur, who would make his name in the Second World War, telling the press that being told to be on the panel was 'one of the most distasteful orders I ever received'.

Even though Mitchell lost his case and left the army, the bomber B-25 was named after him in 1941 and he was granted a posthumous Congressional Gold Medal five years later. Interestingly, the movie made nothing of his heavy drinking, nor of his wife and children. In fact, in several scenes, Cooper keeps turning up at the house of Jack Lord and his wife, Elizabeth Montgomery, like some sort of embarrassing visiting bachelor. Such was the strain imposed on his marriage by the court martial, that he and his wife divorced.

Two extraordinary women, both of whom were executed during the First World War, have rightly made it on to the big screen. The first was Edith Cavell, a British nurse saving lives in a hospital in Brussels. In August 1915, she was charged by the Germans with helping 200 of the wounded to escape over the border to neutral the Netherlands. She was tried by military court martial and shot. *Nurse Edith Cavell* (1939) starred Anna Neagle. It was the fourth film about Edith – the second was nine years earlier (*Dawn* with Sybil Thorndike), and critics found the whole thing too documentary in its approach. Graham Greene, writing for *The Spectator* was waspish as ever. 'Miss Neagle looked nice as Queen Victoria; she looks just as nice as Nurse Cavell.'

If Edith Cavell was a tad too saintly for some tastes, the same couldn't be said of Mata Hari. Unlike Edith, Mata was a genuine spy, although most of the exploits attributed to her were pure fiction. She was actually Margarete Zelle, from the Netherlands and became an exotic dancer in Paris in 1905 when the city was full of them. She had a string of lovers, of various nationalities, including army officers and politicians. She was interrogated by the British secret service, found guilty of espionage on behalf of the Germans and shot in Paris in 1917. Movies about her have been uniformly bad. The 1931 version starred Greta Garbo. According to the film's PR 'Men worshipped her like a goddess, only to be betrayed by a kiss'. There was an Italian version in 1964 and in 1985 Sylvia Kristel stepped slightly out of her usual soft porn role to play the spy. 'Absurd melodrama,' said Halliwell, but with an original character as fake as Ms Zelle herself, it's difficult for it to be anything else.

The Second World War caught the imagination of film-makers like no other. It was a 'just' war, that is the *casus belli* was seen as morally right. Such a vicious, repugnant regime as that of the Nazis could only be destroyed by force. By comparison, the First World War's origins are shrouded in complexity and double think. Secondly, American involvement in this conflict was early and vital – a growing economy and a military organization on a mammoth scale proved too much for Adolf Hitler's regime to survive. Such is the complexity and scale of this war and with so many movies made about it, I have subdivided the rest of this chapter accordingly.

First, though, *The Great Dictator* (1940). Some will object that this is not a war film at all, in that it is a comedy starring Charlie Chaplin. The point however is that this was political satire, made in America before America joined the war *and* it portrayed real people, at least by name. Chaplin was both an innocent Jewish barber and the dictator Adenoid Hynkel, complete with pseudo Nazi uniform, crosses instead of swastikas and, of course, *that* moustache. He had a crowd of henchmen – Hess, Göring (Minister of War Herring), Goebbels (Minister of Propaganda Garbitsch), Himmler – who were pantomime lookalikes. *The New York Times* praised the movie as 'the most significant film ever made'. Just in case the Italians felt left out, Hynkel welcomes Napoleoni, the dictator of Bacteria. For the last six minutes of the film, Chaplin makes a serious and heartfelt political speech that jars with the earlier comedy. The movie won no awards, largely because, before Pearl Harbor, the official government line was one of isolationism.

Battle Stations

The Battle of Britain (1969) was one of those multi-starred extravaganzas that the 1970s delighted in. It is so full of real people that they all have very little screen space, but the overall effect works well. The Wehrmacht had overrun all of western Europe by summer 1940, when the movie action takes place, and Hitler was poised to invade Britain. Historians now take the view that he was never very serious about this (Russia was his real objective) but that certainly wasn't how it was seen at the time. The Blitz was recreated by setting fire to the old London Docks that were being demolished at the end of the 1960s, and the largest number of Second World War aircraft still flyable was assembled for use – Spitfires, Hurricanes, Junkers Ju 52s, Messerschmitt Bf 109s and Heinkel He 111s. Aerial sequences in the skies over southern England were adeptly orchestrated by Freddie Young, although the film failed to capture the mood of the 'Spitfire Summer'.

Laurence Olivier impressed as Air Chief Marshal Hugh Dowding, whose job it was to co-ordinate the island's defences by air. He was ably served by Patrick Wymark as Air Vice Marshal Trafford Leigh-Mallory, head of Bomber Command, and Trevor Howard as Air Vice Marshal Keith Park, in charge of Fighter Command, the pair bickering like schoolboys as to which 'wing' was the more important. Brassey's *Guide to War Films* complains that 'more might have been made of the Polish and Czech contributions in supplementing "The Few",' but this was written in 2000 by which time "inclusivity" was making its presence felt and the criticism is not justified. In fact, two of the best scenes in the film concern the Poles. They deliberately disobey orders in the air to down Luftwaffe planes, claiming that they can't understand English, yet when they get news (in English) that they've been give their own squadron, there are whoops and cheers all round! In another scene, a Polish pilot crash lands his plane and is surrounded by astounded farm labourers armed with pitchforks. 'Good afternoon' the pilot says politely with a thick, foreign accent. Assuming he is a Hun, a farmer answers, 'Good afternoon, my arse!'

The Longest Day (1962) was the first of the big-names Second World War epics to be made, but its events take place four years after the Battle of Britain. Made in wartime black and white, it deals with the invasion of the Normandy coast by the Allies in June 1944. The largest armada ever to leave Britain, it was composed of a huge international force which had been building for months in the south of England. It was the first movie I ever saw that had the French and the Germans speaking their own languages with subtitles, and even today the result is excellent. Thankfully, there is no love story and everybody gets on with the action accordingly. George MacDonald Fraser makes the interesting point that if the scenes in the film were placed in a fictional melodrama, they'd be laughed off the screen, but they actually happened! Red Buttons dangling from the church spire of St Mere Eglise and deaf as a post because of the frantic ringing of the bells; Kenneth More, the beachmaster at Gold with his bulldog called Winston; the anonymous Frenchman ducking bullets to bring a bottle of champagne to the liberating forces – all of it based on fact. Peter Lawford is excellent as the Commando leader, Lord Lovat, with his Highland piper playing as the squad advances. Henry Fonda is just right as the serving member of the Roosevelt family, hiding his walking stick so that his CO doesn't stop his involvement. Werner Hinz is excellent as Field Marshal Erwin Rommel, caught napping by the Allies' timing. But the acting award must go to Hans Christian Blech as the hapless officer Major Werner Pluskat, in a bunker overlooking the huge armada. He calls HQ to say that he has never seen so many guns in his life. 'Which way,' his superior asks haughtily, 'are the guns pointing?' 'At me!' Pluskat shrieks before the balloon goes up.

Patton (1970) was bound to cause trouble because of the 'Marmite' nature of the feisty two-gun General George Patton, known irreverently (behind his back!) as 'Old Blood and Guts', who graduated from West Point in 1909. He led an armoured brigade in the closing months of the First World War at time when tanks were replacing horsed cavalry in warfare and not everybody was happy about that. In 1941 he commanded the 1st Armoured Corps in North Africa against Rommel's Afrika Korps, and took them into Sicily to drive the Italians out of the war. Leading the Third Army after D-Day, he pushed on at amazing speed to reach the Czech border. He was also a deeply flawed character, eccentric and suffering from mood swings. He could be fiercely protective of his men and kind to them, but he outraged most of America when he slapped a wounded soldier recovering in hospital and called him a coward. For this reason alone, it's unlikely that the movie could have been made any earlier than it was. Patton was played superbly by George C. Scott, complete with pearl-handled Colts, and his Number Two, Omar Bradley, was an excellently understated Karl Malden.

One of Patton's less pleasant quotes (he also threatened to get to Berlin before the Russians so that he could personally hang that 'wallpaper-hanging son of a bitch', Adolf Hitler) was the film's tag line – 'Nobody ever won a war by dying for his country. He won it by making the other poor dumb bastard die for *his* country!' The clash of personalities between Patton and his British counterpart, Field Marshal Bernard Montgomery (Michael Bates) get a little lost in Patton's tour de force. There were plaudits all round, but rumour has it that Scott turned down an Oscar.

Two movies covered the valiant efforts of the Norwegian resistance to disrupt the German occupation of their country. In February 1943, a team of Norwegian saboteurs parachuted in from Britain hit the Norsk Hydro power station near Ryukan. The plant was producing 'heavy water' vital to the Germans' atomic research programme. *The Battle for Heavy Water* (1947) was a war-documentary on the operation, starring one of the original combatants, but as this was a Franco-Norwegian film, its release was limited. It was eclipsed in 1965 by the much more box office friendly *The Heroes of Telemark*, starring Kirk Douglas and Richard Harris, awash with real snow and exhilarating action.

A Bridge Too Far (1977) has often been called 'a film too long' which is a shame, because it is very much the flip side of *The Longest Day*. Both the Normandy Landings, and the attempted Arnhem Landing – Operation Market Garden – were meticulously planned, but one worked and the other didn't. That's war. Richard Attenborough directed, and as far as I know didn't feel the need to apologise for anything in this one! Edward Fox was a particularly good lookalike for Brigadier General Brian Horrocks, commanding 30 Corps, the first senior army officer to appear regularly on British television in the late 1950s. Anthony Hopkins was a thoughtful Colonel John Frost of the 1st Parachute Brigade and the street fighting around the Arnhem Bridge was carefully recreated. Laurence Olivier was rather lost as a Dutch civilian caught up in the action, and Attenborough and his screenwriter William Goldman (working from the book by Cornelius Ryan) were far too kind to Lieutenant Colonel 'Boy' Browning (Dirk Bogarde), who mishandled the drop part of the operation. Incidentally, it was Browning himself who came up with the phrase that became the film's title; a pity he didn't express this view rather more forcefully. The results of Arnhem were grim. Colonel Frost had only 100 men of his brigade left when they were finally overrun. Of the nearly 9,000 men who had been pitched into the area, only 2,163 got back. Of the Americans involved, over 3,700 men were killed, wounded or missing, out of 11,000. Browning's phrase, and the film's title, were absolutely right.

A unique addition to this genre is *To Hell and Back* (1955) in that it was essentially the true wartime exploits of a Hollywood star. Audie Murphy, with his blue eyes and clean-cut image, went on to become *the* star of 1950s 'B' Westerns, but he was a real-life hero before that. Murphy was the youngest (at 16), most decorated soldier in the United States army by 1945 and the movie, bearing in mind that he played himself, was desperately disappointing. Historical advisers on movies are routinely ignored if their advice doesn't fit the producer's/director's vision, but to ignore the *star* seems a little ungracious. This was particularly so since Murphy had already been outstanding as a boy soldier in the fictional Civil War movie *The Red Badge of Courage* in 1951.

Wings

If the aerial performance of the First World War was limited by the technicalities and attitudes of the age, the same could not be said of the Second World War. Improvements in technical details meant that both bombers and fighters were well suited to fit Germany's twentieth-century version of von Clausewitz's *Blitzkreig* tactics – aerial assault, followed by pincer movements on the ground effected by tanks with infantry support. Although he didn't live to see it, Billy Mitchell had been right – war in the air was now a fundamental fact of military life. German bombers flattened Guernica in Spain as a preliminary 'warm up', during the Civil War. The same terror was unleashed on Britain in 1940–42, and the Allies replied in spades later in the conflict, with Berlin, Dresden and other German cities blasted into annihilation. Aircraft played a decisive role in nearly all the major operations of the Second World War, but three movies stand out to commemorate the fact.

The first was *First of the Few*, produced in 1942. There is a marked difference between contemporary films like this and later interpretations. Because there was a war on, *First of the Few* had to be made quietly, on the cheap and in black and white. The central character, played by Leslie Howard in his last film, was R.J. Mitchell, who designed and built the Spitfire (the movie's alternative title), the best fighter plane of the war. Much was made in the years after 1945 of Britain's lack of preparedness for war, with Prime Minister Neville Chamberlain appeasing Hitler every which way. In fact, behind the scenes, armaments were being built up and work on the Spitfire was part of that. Ironically, it was Howard's last film because his own aircraft was shot down in 1943. He was flying back from Portugal in a civilian airliner, with a handful of passengers, when it was hit on 1 June by a Junkers Ju 88 bomber, operating out of the agreed fly zone. Rumours have swirled around this ever since, with Howard as the target of the Nazi High Command because he had ridiculed them in his superb, though fictional, *Pimpernel Smith* two years earlier. In that movie, as Howard's elusive spy disappears yet again, in the fog, he voices the narrative, 'I'll be back. One day we'll *all* be back.' It must have made Joseph Goebbels and Co. furious. Prime Minister Winston Churchill said of the loss of Howard, 'The brutality of the Germans was only matched by the stupidity of their agents.' Incidentally, Howard's death was reported in *The Times* in the same edition as that of Major William Martin, *The Man Who Never Was* (see later). Neither Mitchell in this book lived to see fruition of their ideas; Billy Mitchell died five years before Pearl Harbor and Reginald died three years before the Battle of Britain. David Niven plays the dashing RAF pilot who tests Mitchell's machine and goes on to glory, as the man himself, increasingly ill, dies of natural causes.

Reach for the Sky (1956) from the novel by Paul Brickhill, was one of a clutch of black and white films shown for years on British television on Sunday afternoons. It's the story of Douglas Bader, an RAF fighter pilot who had both legs amputated in a plane crash before the war. Kenneth More plays Bader with his usual combination of cheeky, upbeat charm and stiff upper lip. The action of the film is condensed. In reality, there were eight years between the crash and the outbreak of war and in that time, Bader learnt to walk, dance, drive and most importantly, fly, with artificial legs. He persuaded the powers-that-be that he could command a unit in the war and shot down at least fifteen enemy aircraft in the Battle of Britain. Captured after he crash landed in August 1941, Bader spent four years in a POW camp. The Germans let the Allies drop a new leg for him to replace the one damaged in the crash. As squadron leader after the war, he led the victory flypast over London in September 1945. Brassey is dismissive of the movie – 'it is a preening, sentimental and outmoded film – full of stiff upper lips, public school dormitory humour and the supercilious supremacy of the true Brit over the bullying Hun … it's not very palatable.' But it was in 1956 and, to quote a number of comedies since, 'we did *win* the bloody war!'

Two years before *Reach for the Sky*, Michael Anderson produced *The Dam Busters*, the story of Barnes Wallis' bouncing bomb that was dropped by Guy Gibson's 617 Squadron on a series of dams in Germany. As Brassey says, 'A box office favourite in Britain, with schoolboys everywhere whistling Eric Coates' theme as they winged their way across school playgrounds.' Real Lancaster bombers were used in the film but the 'blue screen' technology of the time makes the actual attack seem very amateur by today's standards. The script was written by R.C. Sheriff (of *Journey's End* fame), from books by Guy Gibson *(Enemy Coast Ahead)* and Paul Brickhill. Richard Todd is an excellent Gibson, quiet, confident, good-looking, and Michael Redgrave is an even better Wallis, in glasses and trench coat, wrestling with physics that nobody else believes will work. Modern historians have played down the impact of the raids on the Möhne and Eder dams, but this hardly detracts from the success of the raids or the courage it took to fly them.

There was talk a few years ago of a remake with a screenplay by Stephen Fry; one of the many changes was the alteration of the name of Guy Gibson's black Labrador to Digger, to fit with politically correct sensibilities. If that was a measure of the rewrite's integrity, I am glad, and not at all surprised, that it never got off the ground (pun intended)!

Stalag

Another element in films about the Second World War is the perennial Prisoner of War drama. *The Colditz Story* (1954) was written by Major Pat Reid, who was there, and is one of the British stiff upper-lippers, with more humour than usual in movies like this. Under the international Geneva Convention, men (and women) taken prisoner in war had to be treated humanely. While this was routinely ignored by the Japanese, who had not signed up to it, all European participants generally complied. Colditz was a medieval castle in Saxony from which escape was believed to be impossible. Since it was the duty of soldiers to try to escape however, Major Reid and Co., had other ideas. The movie, said *The News of the World*, has 'all the realism, dignity and courage of the men it commemorates'. A French officer (Eugene Deckers) vaulting over the barbed wire and running to freedom is priceless, but it – and dozens of tunnellers leaking soil from their trousers in full view of the guards – created the completely false impression that the Germans were 'goons' in every sense of the word. This was one of several films in which Anton Diffring played his haughty Nazi role – ironic because he and his family risked their lives by not leaving Germany in 1933; the Diffrings were Jewish!

A film every bit as gripping and enjoyable as *The Colditz Story* was *The One That Got Away* (1957), an account of the only successful escape from a British POW camp by a German – Luftwaffe pilot Oberleutnant Franz von Werra. Everybody is terribly civilised, especially Hardy Kruger as von Werra, to the extent that audiences rooted for him exactly as they did for the Germans in *All Quiet on the Western Front.* Von Werra eventually escaped from Canada and got to the United States, only to be shot down and killed once he was back with the Luftwaffe.

A POW camp with a difference was shown in *Bridge on the River Kwai* (1957), one of the best depictions of any war in cinematic history. The Japanese attacked the US Naval Base at Pearl Harbor in Hawaii on 7 December 1941 (see later) and threw in their lot with Nazi Germany. The British involvement with them came because Britain held Singapore and other outposts in the East. The British army's defeat there was one of the most shameful and incomprehensible on record. While it is true that the RAF could not provide adequate air coverage, the Imperial Japanese army was outnumbered three to one. Despite that, and to the disbelief of his troops, Lieutenant General Arthur Percival surrendered, losing British control of the area and condemning thousands of men to a lingering death on the notorious Burma railway.

Bridge on the River Kwai is rather like *Picnic at Hanging Rock*, which opens this book; it looks as if it is true, but it isn't. The screenwriters took a real premise (British prisoners *did* build bridges) and took a handful of names from the military record. So Colonel Nicholson and Commandant Saito are names only – their actions and characters are fictitious. As such, perhaps, we shouldn't include the film here at all, but I have, because its existence serves as a warning to the unwary!

Probably the oddest Second World War POW film is *Albert RN* (1953) where British prisoners create a dummy in naval cap and duffel coat to fool camp guards into believing that the real man it has replaced is still there, rather than having escaped. This idea has been sent up mercilessly ever since in television spoofs and Halliwell calls the movie 'an archetypal PoW *comedy* drama' (the italics are mine). It really happened, however. John Worsley, an artist, made the original dummy

– and the copy for the film, which is on display in the Royal Navy Museum in Portsmouth. Incidentally, Anton Diffring played a Nazi.

The Cruel Sea

Britain's 21-mile gap between the south coast and France is often all that has prevented invasion. To keep that channel free is the work of the Royal Navy and any number of kings since Alfred the Great (see Chapter 2) have been credited with creating it. Naval operations are notoriously difficult to recreate realistically (all the relevant films we have discussed so far used ship models) and most of the Second World War naval movies suffer from the same problem on studio tanks, wooden models and 'library footage'. One of the worst culprits here was the earliest, the 1942 *In Which We Serve*, directed by and starring Noel Coward. It was, of course, a propaganda piece, shown to naval recruits for years as an example of what life was like on board ship It told the story of HMS *Kelly*, Louis Mountbatten's ship, although for propaganda and security reasons, it was renamed the *Torrin* in the movie. Mountbatten was a personal friend of Coward and provided not only technical advice but 200 real-life sailors as extras. The army extras are genuine too – the 5th Battalion, Coldstream Guards.

Because of Mountbatten's royalty connections, the king, queen and princesses Elizabeth and Margaret visited the Denham studios one day to watch the work in progress. Hopefully, that was not the day when the chief electrician was killed by an explosion caused by director David Lean (who effectively took over from Coward), insisting on a second take using dangerous materials. The *Daily Express* was scornful of the whole production, refusing to believe that Coward, known for his light comedy pre-war, could make a convincing naval officer. He got his own back by putting an edition of the paper in the film with the real headline from 1939, 'No War this Year'. The Hays Commission, whose powerful remit extended across the Atlantic, tried to have 'God', 'hell', 'damn' and 'bastard' censored from the script, but only 'bastard' was removed.

Two other pieces of trivia should be mentioned. James Mason was turned down for a part because he was a Conscientious Objector. Society had been fairly tolerant to those people in the First World War, but in the Second, against the monstrosity of Hitler's regime, such a stance left a nasty taste in the mouth. In one scene in *In Which We Serve* a slim young woman is seen turning towards the camera; she may have been Violette Szabo, who was living near Denham at the time, shortly before she was recruited into the Special Operations Executive (SOE), and would become the heroine of a film in her own right, *Carve Her Name With Pride* (see later).

The Third Reich produced some formidable battleships in the Second World War, none more terrifying than the *Tirpitz* and the *Bismarck*. The first was dealt with by film-makers in *Above Us the Waves* (1955). The *Tirpitz* was the *Bismarck*'s sister ship with a speed of 20 knots and vast armament. She also carried four aircraft and, anchored in Alten Fjord in Norway, emerged as a constant threat to Allied shipping in the North Sea. On 22 September 1943, three midget submarines of the Royal Navy got through the Fjord's boom defences and hit the *Tirpitz* several times with torpedoes. That in effect scuttled her until she was sunk by a squadron of Lancasters in November. Submarine dramas always work well on the screen, whether they are true or fictional. The sense of claustrophobia and the need for quiet create an intensity not matched by surface ship action. The crewmen are fictional in the movie but contained the usual stiff upper lips of John Mills, John Gregson, Donald Sinden and James Robertson Justice.

Sink the Bismarck! (1960) took a different approach, because the most dangerous warship afloat was sunk in the open sea by a combined attack from Swordfish aircraft from the carrier *Ark Royal* and cruisers *Sheffield, Cossack* and *Dorsetshire*. This was at the end of May 1941, but not before the *Bismarck* had sunk HMS *Hood*, with the loss of 800 lives, and damaged the *Prince of Wales*. The sea action in the film is interspersed with naval operations directed by Kenneth More from Whitehall and all the more effective for it. The ships are clearly models but what is interesting is that the admiral and captain on board the *Bismarck* are played by real German Carl Möhner and Czech Karel Štěpánek. For reasons that are unclear, the philosophy of these two officers is reversed. In reality, it was Captain Jurgens who was the committed Nazi, Admiral Lütjens – not uncommonly in the German High Command – not so much. The film's best line is the last one. An exhausted Kenneth More staggers out of the sand-bagged Admiralty buildings, having played his vital part in sinking the *Bismarck* and offers to take his WRNS secretary to dinner. She tells him it's morning, so he takes her to breakfast instead. Overhearing all this is an army guard (Victor Maddern), who says to his mate, 'Typical! Four stripes on his arm and he don't know what time of day it is!'

The Spying Game

As we saw in the First World War section of this chapter, every war in history has had its espionage element. The German secret service, with its headquarters in Berlin, had tentacles that reached into every corner of occupied Europe and beyond. Britain had MI5 for internal affairs and MI6 for overseas work. The United States had the Operation of Strategic Services, forerunner of the CIA. Into the mix in 1940 Winston Churchill threw the Special Operations Executive, which provided arcane 'black' propaganda to undermine Nazism and actual agents who were trained and parachuted into occupied Europe to link up with Resistance organizations bent on sabotage and other mayhem to the same end. Because of their gender and their youth, most interest post-war lay with the female agents and of these, Violette Szabo stands out.

She was born Violette Bushell in 1921, the daughter of a British father and a French mother. Her father, a soldier, taught her to shoot and she was bilingual, two achievements that put her in good stead during the war. At the outbreak of the conflict, she was working in a department store in Brixton but joined first the Women's Land Army (WLA), then the Auxiliary Territorial Service (ATS). She married French Foreign Legionary non-commissioned officer (NCO) Etienne Szabo in 1940 and they had a daughter, Tania. Etienne Szabo was killed at El Alamein and this prompted Violette to volunteer for the SOE. Her cover, like most female agents, was FANY (the First Aid Nursing Yeomany) and she flew two missions before being caught. She was interrogated and tortured by the SS before deportation to Ravensbrück, the female concentration camp; 92,000 women died there during the war.

Violette was executed with a bullet to the back of the head and was awarded a posthumous George Cross (now in the Imperial War Museum in London) in December 1946. *Carve Her Name With Pride* (1958) was a dignified, if sanitized, account of her career and death (in the movie she dies before a firing squad) with Virginia McKenna as the lead. The real Violette was dark and short – 'la petite Anglaise' as she was known – but at least the taller, very blonde Virginia attempted as much of a Cockney accent as was possible for heroines in the 1950s. The poem used in the movie – *The Life That I Have* – was not written for the film as many believe, but by Leo Marks, himself an agent, for his girlfriend Ruth, killed in a plane crash in 1943. Colonel Maurice Buckmaster, head of SOE, was played by William Mervyn, as ever, upper crust and very British, and an uncredited Michael Caine (six years before *Zulu* made him a star) is 'thirsty prisoner on train'.

Eight years earlier, a very similar film was made about Odette Churchill, another female spy with an Anglo-French background. *Odette* in 1950 was Anna Neagle, who had already been cast as Edith Cavell eleven years before that. Marius Goring played the archetypal Nazi and the only difference between Odette and Violette was that the former survived her ordeal.

Dropping agents of either sex into occupied territory was incredibly brave and fraught with danger, but such stories pale into insignificance by comparison with *The Man Who Never Was* (1955). The opening credits show a body washed up by the tide and a creepy voice (Laurence Naismith's) intones the sinister (and very apt) poem – 'Last night I dream'd a dreary [terrifying] dream, Beyond the Isle of Skye. I saw a dead man win a fight and I dreamt that man was I.' Operation Mincemeat should never have worked. After stopping the advance of the Afrika Korps and liberating North Africa, the next step of the Allies would be to invade Italy via Sicily, geographically the nearest point. As a feint to confuse the Germans, 'Mincemeat' would provide evidence that Sardinia or Greece was the real Allied target. Enter Major William Martin of the Royal Marines. His body would be found washed up on the coast of neutral Spain (riddled with German agents) and the briefcase chained to it would specify an Allied attack on Greece. The problem was that even in the Second World War, bodies were hard to come by.

The official story of what happened was outlined in the 1955 movie. The description in Brassey – 'The rest of the picture deviates from the actual events for the sake of dramatic enhancement' – isn't quite true. Deviations occurred because the book on which the movie is based by Ewan Montague (Clifton Webb) was already *completely* different from the truth. In the film version, the body is chosen because he died of pneumonia and his grieving parents give consent for post-mortem usage for the good of the country because they cannot be told the real reason. The always vulnerable Gloria Grahame is the fake fiancée of the fake Marine major and Stephen Boyd is a (totally fictional) Irish spy who senses that something is afoot in Naval Intelligence. The film's tag line read 'The strangest story in British espionage'. It certainly is.

Montague himself wrote the definitive book on which the movie is based and, as a circuit judge, blocked all attempts by researchers to dig further. This he had no legal right to do, but the Official Secrets Act lay heavily over everyone concerned and some things, only twelve years after the events, were considered too sensitive to discuss. Not until 1995 did we discover Major Martin's real identity. He was Glyndwr Michael, a disturbed 34-year-old Welshman living rough in London. His parents were not consulted; the powers-that-be just took his body anyway. Sir Bernard Spilsbury, the Home Office pathologist, told Montague (who was not, by the way, working alone on the corpse ruse) that a pneumonia victim would look most like a case of drowning. But Glyndwr Michael killed himself with rat poison, which would have been obvious in the most rudimentary of autopsies, even in 1943. Very little about Operation Mincemeat makes sense and I suspect there is a lot more to come if today's powers-that-be will actually comply with the Freedom of Information Act.

The Other Side

It still comes as a shock to some audiences to think that the first two versions of *All Quiet on the Western Front*, although made by Anglo-American companies, see war from the German viewpoint. The most recent version (2022) is at least a German production, now freed from Nazi bias. The Third Reich produced hundreds of propaganda movies from Hitler's 'seizure' of power in 1933 to nearly the end of his regime when film-making became impossible. Leni Riefenstahl's monumental *Triumph of the Will* (1935) is arguably the most terrifying propaganda film ever made, featuring thousands of robotic Germans, even children, marching at Nuremberg with a precision that all other countries could only gawp at. Joseph Goebbels' fanatical control of all German media also produced umpteen anti-Semitic films portraying Jews as *untermenschen* (sub-human) and even as rats swarming over the towns and cities they had made their own.

The Desert Fox (1951) saw things from the other side of the Siegfried Line. Arguably, the most impressive German general of the war was Field Marshal Erwin Rommel, played in the film by an intelligent and solemn James Mason. How this played out with his Conscientious Objecting I don't know. Rommel was never a committed Nazi and became more disillusioned with Hitler's regime as time went on. Commanding the Afrika Korps in Libya, he drove the British back to El Alamein where he was defeated by General Bernard Montgomery.

He was associated with the Valkyrie plot (see below) to kill Hitler and committed suicide in 1944. Most of the movie is about this plot and the last weeks of Rommel's life. It was probably the first film to have action happening before the title credits rolled.

There have been more nuanced attempts over the last forty years to bring us movies that tell it like it was. *Der Untergang* (Downfall) (2004) in which Bruno Ganz plays Hitler in the last days in the bunker while the Soviet war machine is pounding the streets of Berlin overhead was outstanding. People complained about 'humanizing' the Reich's inner circle because it showed them as ordinary people; but as the author of *1001 Movies You Must See Before You Die* says, 'the point is that the truly monstrous [people] usually are'.

The backdrop to most Second World War films is just one man – Adolf Hitler. Whether he is in the cast or mentioned or not, it is his existence that the war is all about. The extraordinary life of the Führer has been analysed and reanalysed like no other over the last fifty years and despite excellent research, articles and books without number, we still cannot really see inside his head. In this section, I have selected two films which go to the heart – or try to – of what he really was. He is a bit player in one film – *Valkyrie* (2008) – and in the other – *Schindler's List* (1993) – he doesn't appear at all.

Having taught Nazi Germany at a high school for many years, I took my GCSE and A Level classes to the opening of *List* in the cinema and when it became available on DVD showed it regularly in school. Oskar Schindler remains an enigma. Was he saving Jewish lives by employing them in his metalwork factory near Kraków or was he a sharp businessman using Jewish labour because it was cheap? When I took a school party to Berlin in 2001, I asked the young guide at the Wannsee Villa, where Reinhard Heydrich planned the mechanics of the Final Solution to exterminate Jews, what he thought of the movie and, indeed, of Schindler himself. He merely shrugged and said, 'So the Nazi saved a few Jews,' which I thought rather a sweeping dismissal.

In the movie, Schindler was played enigmatically by Liam Neeson. He's too tall for the real man (Liam Neeson is too tall for everybody!) and we know he likes pretty girls, good wine, nice clothes. We also know he doesn't like hard work, which is why he employs Jewish Itzhak Stern (Ben Kingsley) as his foreman in the factory. 'I feel I should tell you, sir,' a diffident Kingsley says, 'that I am a Jew.' 'Well, I'm a German,' says Neeson cheerfully, 'so there you are.' But Neeson also gives the runaround to Amon Göth (Ralph Fiennes) the local camp commandant, with whom he has dinner and cosy chats. When Göth admires Schindler's silk shirt, the businessman says, 'I'd give you the tailor's name, but he's probably dead by now.'

The violence in the film is terrifying, from the casual sniping of camp inmates by Göth to the lines of Jews walking into the gas chambers at Auschwitz. The little girl in the red coat, wandering lost in the streets as the Einsatzgruppen randomly shoot passers-by, stands out in the otherwise black and white scene, to the extent that several people came forward to say that they *were* that little girl. The movie was based on *Schindler's Ark* by Thomas Keneally and is usually hailed as Steven Spielberg's greatest triumph after a lifetime of excellent movie-making. The reviews say it all – Thomas Rafferty of *The New Yorker* wrote, '[Spielberg] captures images of experience that most of us thought we would never see represented adequately on the screen. This is by far the finest, fullest dramatic film ever made about the Holocaust.' While Will Tremper in *Die Welt* said, 'Indiana Jones in the Cracow Ghetto.' I think we all know whose side Herr Tremper is on. In some ways, it's the last scene of the film that's most moving when the actual survivors of Schindler's factory appear, singing, arm in arm with the actors who played them, placing grateful stones on Schindler's grave in Israel.

There were many attempts on the life of Adolf Hitler, for obvious reasons, but perhaps none came so close as that on 20 July 1944 at his headquarters of the Wolf's Lair in East Prussia/Poland. The story was highlighted for the first time in *Valkyrie* (2008) the codename for the operation in which a number of relatively senior Wehrmacht officers led by Claus von Stauffenberg tried to blow Hitler to pieces with a bomb hidden in a briefcase.

Von Stauffenberg planted the case, then left the building, walking, then driving away on a pretext as the building behind him exploded. He assumed that the Führer was dead and contacted his co-conspirators, who moved to put alternative plans into operation, firstly attempting to come to some sort of truce with Eisenhower, Stalin and the Allies. Then as General Erich Fellgiebel of the Signals telegraphed all concerned – 'Something awful has happened! The Führer still lives!' Hitler was shaken and his left arm useless, but the July plot had failed and one by one, the plotters were identified, rounded up and shot.

Tom Cruise taking on the role of von Stauffenberg caused a circus because the actor is a Scientologist and in Germany Scientology is regarded as a dangerous cult (not unlike Nazism in the 1920s). There were demonstrations where the movie was released, not helped by von Stauffenberg's family who took the anti-Scientology line. The only member of the family to ignore all this was von Straffenberg's grandson, Philipp von Schulthess, who played an ADC to Henning von Tresckow (Kenneth Branagh) in the movie.

The Wolf's Lair was destroyed by the Russians in 1944–45 so a new one was built south of Berlin, taking twelve weeks to complete. The OKW (army) headquarters which is the central location of the film and the actual place where the conspirators were executed was used and is now the HQ of the German navy. A clutch of distinguished British actors played both sides of the high command, notably Branagh, Terence Stamp (General Ludwig Beck) who had lived as a child in Blitzed London and Bill Nighy as General Friedrich Olbricht. Of the filming, Nighy said, 'One of the most disconcerting things imaginable is to put on a Nazi uniform.'

Actual relics from the wartime German Air Ministry were used in the movie, carefully presided over by military expert Professor Peter Hoffmann of McGill University. The use of the swastika in public is illegal in Germany and despite warnings from the film company, some locals complained. Before the filming of von Stauffenberg's execution, Cruise insisted on a minute's silence in honour of the men involved in the plot.

Inevitably, there were mistakes and omissions. Field Marshal Erwin Rommel, as we have seen, was involved indirectly and forced to commit suicide to save his family shortly afterwards. There is no mention of him in the movie. When he was badly wounded in Libya, losing an eye and an arm, von Stauffenberg refused morphine. This was omitted from the film as looking too corny and 'John Wayneish'. The earlier briefcase attempt by the colonel on 11 July took place at Berchtesgaden, Hitler's bolthole in Bavaria, not at the Wolf's Lair. And while Tom Cruise sits enjoying *The Valkyrie* on a scratchy 78rpm record, the real von Stauffenberg hated Wagner!

The Sun Also Rises

While most British films on the Second World War have focused on Europe, the American experience had as much to do with the Far East. The British were there too, as we have seen with *Bridge on the River Kwai*, but for understandable reasons, movie-makers have not been drawn to that theatre of war.

The Japanese attack on the Pearl Harbor naval base on 7 December 1941 was rightly called 'a day of infamy' by President Franklin D. Roosevelt. Attacking another power without the prelude of a declaration of war was – and is – contrary to every military code, except *bushido*, the way of the samurai, Japan's chivalric organization since the early Middle Ages. Two movies, one a dismal remake, cover that day of infamy. The remake, predictable and overblown, is *Pearl Harbor* (2001). It was impossibly expensive to make – $140 million in total – and, unaccountably, did well at the box office. A handful of real characters are there – Admiral Yamamoto, F.D. Roosevelt, Colonel Doolittle – but they couldn't save what should have been a flop. 'Rarely,' wrote Ian Buruma of *The Guardian*, 'perhaps never, in the field of movies about human conflict has so much money, effort and technical expertise resulted in such a vapid piece of schmaltz.'

The first version is *Tora! Tora! Tora!* (1970). 'Tora' is Japanese for Tiger, the codename for the attack and, as with *The Longest Day* and others, all Japanese actors speak their own language with subtitles. 'One of the least stirring and least photogenic historical epics ever perpetrated on the screen,' wrote Gary Arnold. And the ever-dismissive Halliwell – 'calcified war spectacle with much fidelity to the record but no villains and no hero, therefore no drama and no suspense.' And that comment goes to the heart of this book. John Wayne, snapping and growling at his recruits in *The Sands of Iwo Jima* (1949); Randolph Scott being fine and magnificent in *Gung Ho!* (1943); Burt Lancaster rolling in the surf with Deborah Kerr in *From Here To Eternity* (1953) – all this is heroic, gutsy stuff but it is shambolic history and doesn't pretend to be anything else. One of the most exciting Second World War movies has to be *Where Eagles Dare* (1969) but every single bit of it is fiction and it is in fact, boys' comic book drivel. Far from being 'calcified' and studio-based, as Halliwell contends, the outdoor aerial and naval combat scenes in *Tora* are amazing. With the US fleet having to be constructed and then destroyed, it was at the time one of the most expensive blockbusters ever made. More could have been made of the gross incompetence of the American top brass, who didn't see Pearl Harbor coming, but that wasn't what the film was all about. Cynics since 1941 have contended that, thanks to various code-breakings at Bletchley Park, Winston Churchill knew an attack was planned, but didn't tell Roosevelt (with whom he was in constant touch) so that America would be dragged into the war.

They Were Expendable (1945) is an unusually honest movie, directed by John Ford and starring, as usual, John Wayne. It pulls no punches, however, showing the Americans well beaten at Bataan and Corregidor. The hero was Robert Montgomery as Lieutenant John Bulkeley (Brickly in the movie, bearing in mind when it was made). It was propaganda, but not of the later flag-waving kind.

PT109 was made in 1963 while its hero, John F. Kennedy, was still in the White House. The autobiography on which it was based was a runaway bestseller, not because of Kennedy's popularity, but because his father, the obnoxious Joseph Kennedy, bought up all the copies available. The ever-dour Cliff Robertson played JFK who commanded a torpedo boat (the movie's title) in the Pacific and the film was interminably dull.

Clint Eastwood continued the Japanese-angled theme in two extraordinary movies made back to back in 2006. One was *Letters from Iwo Jima*, directed by and starring Japanese nationals (as opposed to Chinese Americans who usually populate US war films), which saw the Iwo Jima attack in February 1945 from the Japanese point of view. The film did better in Japan than in the United States. Although the two central characters are fictional, many of the others are real and the USS *Texas* used in the movie is the original ship in the 1945 engagement. The *Independent* in Britain rather snidely wrote that Japanese characters were 'capable of being decent just so long as they've spent some time in the US'.

Eastwood's other movie, from the American point of view, is *Flags of Our Fathers* surrounding the epic moment when five marines and one navy corpsman raised the Stars and Stripes over the conquered island. It is one of the most iconic photographs of the Second World War turned into an equally famous statue, but frames taken before and after show the reality – and it's very un-Hollywood! First, the men struggle to get the pole upright and once it's up, they stand about, smoking scruffily, hands in pockets – Gung Ho! isn't the phrase. In fact, the flag-raising had to be done twice because there was no cameraman around the first time to catch the moment. All this and more is in *Flags of Our Fathers* (actually filmed in Iceland and California) and it was not until 2016 that the correct names of two of the men involved were found.

Few films made over the last twenty years escape controversy of one kind or another, thanks to the existence of social media. In the case of *Flags*, rival director Spike Lee complained to Eastwood that there weren't any black Marines in the movie. Eastwood replied, quite rightly, that in the Second World War, the American forces were (wrongly) segregated. Black Marines dug trenches and carried out menial tasks, only allowed to fight for defensive reasons. The men who put up the flag on Iwo Jima were white – historical fact – and there were plenty of black extras as marines in both the Eastwood films.

Three months after Pearl Harbor, the Americans retaliated. There is a hint at the end of *Tora! Tora! Tora!* that the Japanese might just have bitten off more than they can chew. The loss of ships and men was serious for the Americans, but the real prizes – the huge aircraft carriers – were out at sea on manoeuvres on 7 December and were ready to fight another day. *Thirty Seconds Over Tokyo* (1944) starred the always-dependable Spencer Tracy as Colonel James Doolittle, an American air ace and Schneider Trophy winner who masterminded bombing raids in Japanese cities. The screenplay was written by Dalton Trumbo (before he risked being shut down for alleged Communist leanings in the McCarthy era) and the camerawork showing B-25 Mitchells taking off from USS *Hornet* was, for the time, magnificent. It was propaganda, of course, but a stunned and hurt America, very much the victim in the Pacific, expected nothing less. Clint Eastwood could never have got away with *Letters from Iwo Jima* in 1944!

Midway (1976) didn't really work. The idea was to recreate the Battle of Midway rather as *The Longest Day* recreated 6 June 1944, but there was much reused footage and little cohesion. *Sight and Sound* said, 'We are under-informed about how the battle was finally won and positively swamped with tedious human interest.' For the record, Henry Fonda was Admiral Chester Nimitz; Robert Mitchum was Admiral William Halsey and Toshiro Mifune was Admiral Isoroku Yamamoto, with almost no attempt to make them 'real' people.

A chance was missed in the movie about how the Pacific War came to an end. Doolittle's 21st AAF, based on Guam, had two aircraft used, in August 1945, to drop atomic bombs on Nagasaki and Hiroshima. In the annals of warfare, this incident is as much a day of infamy as Pearl Harbor. The decision was made by President Harry S. Truman and the bomber *Enola Gay* was captained by Paul Tibbetts (the plane was named after his mother). The results of the bombing were horrendous, with thousands of deaths in seconds, and thousands more from radiation sickness in the weeks, months and years that followed. The 'mushroom cloud' became synonymous with death ever after.

Not that any of that – nor the all-consuming guilt of Robert Oppenheimer, who had built the bombs and Tibbets and the crews who dropped them – was apparent in 1952 in *Above and Beyond*. Tibbets was played by Robert Taylor, strong, determined, manly. It was a flag-waver, as Halliwell says, 'of little interest, then or now'. I don't like remakes, but *Above and Beyond* cries out for one, telling the story like it was.

Nature, they say, abhors a vacuum and into the space after August 1945 stepped the Cold War, rising tensions between the West, spearheaded by the new 'super power' of the United States and the East, personified by Joseph Stalin and the USSR who seemed bent on world domination. There were actual flashpoints in those years – war in Korea for example – but essentially, the next war to interest film-makers was Vietnam and by that time, a very different kind of film-goer – and a different Hollywood – existed.

In the 1950s, the United States took on the role of the world's policeman, checking the 'red menace' of Communism wherever it appeared. The USSR was creeping ever westward. Berlin was a divided city with a wall between East and West and the only game in Hollywood's repertory was the spying game, featuring James Bond and other improbables. Such movies as these *had* to be fictional because every country had its espionage secrets and nothing accurate must be leaked.

Vietnam had been French Indo-China until 1954, a reminder of the days of empire (see Chapter 7) when European powers were cashing in on the raw materials of the most remote parts of the world. In that year, Communists in North Vietnam defeated the French at Dien Bien Phu and a state of tension existed between the North and the US-dominated 'free' South. Throughout the late 1950s and 1960s, the number of American advisers (actually soldiers) expanded into the thousands. John F. Kennedy wanted to pull them out, but his assassination in Dallas in November 1963 put paid to that and his successor, Lyndon B. Johnson, allowed matters to escalate. By the time the Vietnam War ended, 58,000 Americans were dead. 'Hey, hey, LBJ,' ran the protest song, 'How many kids d' you kill today?'

Most Americans were opposed to war and as the body count multiplied, their numbers grew. What could Hollywood do about all this? In 1917 and 1941, it made propaganda movies with handsome heroes and bright young things waving flags and making the 'baddies' back down – the stuff of Hollywood movies since the beginning of the industry. But times had changed and the mood was wrong for all that. Excellent war films were still being made – *The Deer Hunter* (1978); the surreal *Dr Strangelove* (1963); *Apocalypse Now* (1979) but they all dodged the issue. The stereotype of Robert Duvall's colonel in *Apocalypse Now* – 'I love the smell of napalm in the morning' as the Apache helicopters swarm towards the camera to the thunderous *Ride of the Valkyries* – stood for the hawks in Washington who wanted to make war on everybody who didn't envy the American dream.

John Wayne's *The Green Berets* (1968) was an anachronistic embarrassment and, unsurprisingly, featured no actual characters. It was an old-fashioned Second World War movie, only the uniforms had changed. Wayne was 61 at the time and, as critic Penelope Gilliatt wrote, 'A film best handled from a distance and with a pair of tongs.'

A number of films focused on the survivors, the wounded and maimed condemned to lives in wheelchairs. Marlon Brando did it first with *The Men* as early as 1952, as a paraplegic home from Korea – 'I was afraid I was gonna die ... Now, I'm afraid I'm gonna live.' *Coming Home* in 1978 pursued the same theme, with John Voight crippled in Vietnam. Hovering over them all, and the only one based on an actual individual, was *Born on the 4th of July* (1989) starring Tom Cruise as

Ron Kovic, a shattered veteran who co-wrote the screenplay based on his own book. Oliver Stone directed.

We began this chapter with the surreal musical *Oh, What a Lovely War!*, a hard-hitting satire and anti-war film totally devoid of blood. Perhaps it's fitting we should end with *The Killing Fields* (1984) all too filled with blood and the horrors of war. It is set in Cambodia under the regime of the psychopathic Pol Pot and charts the experiences of journalist Sidney Schanberg and his translator/guide Dith Pran. For once, Halliwell gets it right. 'Brilliantly filmed, but probably too strong for a commercial audience to stomach.'

Most of the movies in this book I would cheerfully watch again; but not this one.

Chapter 10

Shoot! Crime Films: From Cain to Bundy

Crime is as old as time itself. The first murder in the Bible is that of Abel by his brother Cain, the sons of Adam and Eve. Technically, it was fratricide (brother killing) and it seems to have been spontaneous, without, in legal terms, 'malice aforethought' which is the definition of murder. The 'fact' that this one took place, according to the Old Testament, in only the second generation of mankind, speaks volumes for how far we had fallen since the creation.

In real terms, of course, we have no idea when the first crime took place, but it must have been early in man's development and it must have been frequent. Societies created laws to control the anarchy that accompanied rampant crime.

Depending on our definition of what a crime is, most of the movies listed in this book contain crimes. The Bible features Cain himself. According to the laws of Moses, large numbers of the Children of Israel were criminals because they worshipped 'graven images', e.g. the god Baal, rather than the God with whom Moses was dealing in *The Ten Commandments*. When Kirk Douglas in *Spartacus* rebelled against the authority of Rome, he was committing treason, and he and his followers paid a hefty price for it. In fact, treason, which is barely heard of nowadays but is still on the statute books in Britain, features in any movie involving a monarch. Anne Boleyn was guilty of it in *Anne of the Thousand Days* because it was alleged that she was having affairs behind the king's back. Thomas More, in *A Man For All Seasons*, was guilty of it because he would not support Henry VIII's break with Rome. Richard Harris was guilty of it in *Cromwell* because he overthrew and executed an anointed king – and got away with it. Of course, he didn't. Even though he was dead by the time the monarchy was restored, his body was dug up and dragged around the streets, his skull displayed to the delight of the crowd.

As to the behaviour of countless marauding armies shown on the big screen, where do we start with them? A common prayer in the English monasteries of the eighth to tenth centuries was 'From the fury of the Northmen, good Lord, deliver us.' That fury included vandalism (named after a whole nation of looters!), assault, murder and rape. Obviously, in what is supposedly family entertainment, this is generally downplayed, with much screaming, rushing about, the clash of iron and burning buildings.

In this chapter, however, we are concerned with films that are actually *about* crime and criminals, not those in which such things and people star anyway. Certain crimes have a modish fashionability about them and the Age of Reason of the eighteenth century became obsessed with highwaymen. To be fair, most of the actual literature comes from the nineteenth century when novelists like Harrison Ainsworth took common felons like Richard Turpin and made them into heroes. The increased wealth of Britain as a result of the Industrial Revolution led to a larger population and more travel than ever before. London was the largest city in the world and rich people travelled in and out of it by coach, creating an irresistible magnet for 'knights of the road' as the mythology called them. On lonely Hounslow Heath, for example, or still wild Epping Forest, a horseman would trot out from the undergrowth, point his pistol at the coachman and demand that his passengers hand over their valuables. With no effective police force before the 1820s, chances of being caught were minimal.

In 1969, all this was shown in Technicolor splendour in *Where's Jack?* Jack Sheppard was probably not an actual highway robber, but he was a burglar with a natural ability to get in and out of buildings at will. He was handsome, with large eyes and a cute stammer and escaped *twice* from the condemned cell of Newgate gaol. In the film he was played by Tommy Steele, the Cockney rock star hailed in the 1950s as Britain's answer to Elvis Presley. The sets are good, the crowd impressively dirty and Steele himself makes a believable 'good baddie'. This immediately raises the moral dimension. In Sheppard's time, nobody much cared what problems a criminal had and there were *no* mitigating circumstances for their behaviour. By the 1960s, all that was changing and, however unconsciously, 'victimology' was becoming a factor. For that to work, we had to have a 'real' baddie. That was Jonathan Wild, the thief taker, played with sneering nastiness by Stanley Baker, dressed in black and carrying a swordstick. Wild was the forerunner of Eugène Vidocq in Paris in the early nineteenth century who set up what would become the Sûreté (the French CID). The problem with both men is that they ran with the hare and the hounds, profiting from crime while handing over other criminals (for money) to the authorities.

In *Where's Jack?* of course, complete with its quirky snatches of song, Sheppard isn't hanged at all, but escapes the noose by the crafty work of his cronies. *Plunkett and Macleane* (1999) were genuine highwaymen and the movie was made thirty years after *Jack* with a very different atmosphere. James Plunkett (the always watchable Robert Carlyle) was a Londoner who took to the roads with William Macleane and they briefly operated on Hounslow Heath. After that, the movie is pure fiction, with the inevitable love interest and far too much swearing. Note to reader – the 'f' word and others were not routinely used in the past and should have virtually no place in historical movies. Identifying with modern audiences does the film industry no credit at all.

Edinburgh is still a creepy old city. Its ghost walks are among the best in the country. It is full of little alleyways, 'winds' and steps that have vanished, thanks to 'progress', in other major cities. It is in fact the perfect setting for murder and never more so than in John Landis' *Burke and Hare* (2010). Comedy doesn't come much blacker than about the bodysnatchers who saw a wonderful opportunity to make money out of the rampant scientific revolution of the time. The law said that only the bodies of hanged felons could be used for dissection purposes (until 1831 when the law was changed), which clearly provided insufficient 'subjects' for medical schools. Edinburgh had several of these and so William Burke (a good lookalike Simon Pegg) and William Hare (Andy Serkis who doesn't look like anybody!) began to dig up unhanged individuals and eventually cut out the digging up bit as being both unpleasant and hard work. They would target a victim, get him or her drunk and Hare would pin the unfortunate's feet to the bed with his body weight while Burke suffocated them (a process that briefly came to be called burking). The body was then sold, no questions asked, to Dr Robert Knox, the eminent Edinburgh surgeon.

Tom Wilkinson was excellent as the smarmy Knox; Bill Bailey gloriously over the top as the hangman. There are delightful moments of realism in this movie and the words on the poster should be written on every historical film ever made – 'This is a true story. Except for the parts that are not.' In real life, the pair of 'resurrection men' as contemporary wags called them, overstepped the mark when they picked on a vagrant who would be missed. 'Daft Jamie' was what in those days was called a village idiot and the whole community looked out for him. When he disappeared, somebody remembered that he had last been seen in the company of Burke and Hare. Their premises were searched and there was Jamie's body waiting to be taken to Dr Knox. Hare turned king's evidence (a scam to avoid the drop) and walked free. Burke was hanged and, according to legend, himself dissected. One of the gaffes in the movie is the efficiency of the long drop for hanging, not invented until the 1870s by William Marwood. In Burke's day, men strangled slowly at the noose, to the delight of the baying mob.

The Great Gold Robbery (or Great Bullion Robbery as it is also known) happened in May 1855. A routine shipment of gold was being sent from London to Paris, according to some to provide pay for British troops in the Crimea. It was carried by the South Eastern Railway and the heist was an inside job (as most robberies of this kind are). Two employees, William Tester and James Burgess, provided duplicate keys to the strong boxes, made from wax impressions, and an ex-employee, William Pierce, who had been fired by the company for gambling, made up a third accomplice. The mastermind was Edward Agar, a professional career criminal.

The crooks soon fell out over how to melt down the gold and how to fence the smaller amounts and over-spending led to their arrests. Tester had already done a runner to Sweden, but he lost his job there and had to return. The trial at the Old Bailey had huge media coverage and the crooks were found guilty after less than ten minutes' deliberation by the jury. Tester and Burgess were transported to Australia, as was Agar, who was last heard of, after his release, in Ceylon (today's Sri Lanka).

The First Great Train Robbery (1978) was directed by Michael Crichton from his novel of three years earlier. Agar was played by Donald Sutherland and Pierce by Sean Connery. The sets, costumes and dialogue were all excellent, but the slick brothel scenes made the whole thing such a romp that few realized the story was based on fact. It was Crichton's decision to add the farcical element and both leads played it for laughs. For those who like this kind of trivia, the film's locomotive was a J15 class 0-6-0 No. 184 of 1880, suitably adapted for an 1850s look. Most of the film's characters were real-life figures (only love interest Miriam played by Lesley-Anne Down is wholly fictional), among them 'Clean Willy' Williams (Wayne Sleep), an acrobatic cat burglar who had escaped from Newgate gaol.

Gangs of New York (2002) is an oddity. Directed by Martin Scorsese, it has reached iconic status without much reason. The now disgraced Harvey Weinstein bought the rights in 1999 after Scorsese had spent years trying to bring it to the big screen. Virtually every studio turned Scorsese down because of the film's excessive violence, a trademark of most of his movies.

Virtually *nothing* of mid-nineteenth century New York now exists, so sets were built in the Cinecittà Studios in Rome and it shows. Even more jarring are the costumes. The tale begins in 1846, but most of the action (largely one enormous street battle) happens amidst the anti-draft riots of 1862 when men refused to join the Federal army during the Civil War (see Chapter 6). The problem was that no one told the costume department that sixteen years had passed and the gangs still wore their 1840s chic. This is perhaps excusable for New York's poorest, but unacceptable for characters like William 'Boss' Tweed (Jim Broadbent) who was richer than God thanks to his financial chicanery.

A great deal of effort went into the many accents of the gangs, from the Irish brogue of Leonardo DiCaprio to the 'Nativist' patois of New Yorkers already in the city. Accurate this may have been, but it jars for modern audiences. Incidentally, Cameron Diaz's Irish accent was dismissed as the worst in the film. The cost of *Gangs* soared to over $100 million.

Historians are fickle people and the PBS channel on US television aired programmes that both praised and shamed the film. Many felt the violence was way over the top and the scale of immigration, especially of female Chinese labour, was greatly exaggerated. The character of William Poole (Daniel Day-Lewis) was known as 'Bill the Butcher' for obvious reasons. He led the Bowery Boys gang and, astonishingly, was elected a member of the Board of Education in the city in 1853. He was the acknowledged leader of the Know-Nothings, a blinkered, racist organization opposed to immigration, especially of Jews and Catholics. He lost the sight of his left eye in a fight in October 1851. Unfortunately, by the time of the Draft Riots, Bill Poole was dead, shot by rival John Morrisey in February 1855. Nor is there any record of his having killed anybody. The riots themselves were real enough, resulting in over 100 deaths and 11 lynchings of black Americans, all of them free men.

The killer about whom most movies have been made is unknown. At the time of his killing spree, he was usually called the Whitechapel murderer, but because of the signature on one of the fake letters sent to the press, he has become known as Jack the Ripper. There have been so many films on the man that film critic Denis Meikle wrote an entire book on the subject in 2003. Briefly told, a blitz serial killer murdered at least five women (I personally believe it was seven) in the 'autumn of terror' 1888. This type of killing was virtually unheard of in Britain and the police 'were baffled'. As Denis Meikle says, 'It always happened to a lady of the night! Sometimes it happened in an alley, sometimes in a dark hallway and sometimes in the middle of a scream!'

All the movies get it wrong. They invariably start, before the credits roll, with an attractive girl, overly made up and usually blonde, bouncing along a dingy street half submerged in dry ice. Her cleavage is more 1970s than 1880s and she smiles at the camera. A shadow crosses her face and the slimy wall behind her. It is a shadow of a man in a top hat and cape and he is holding a knife in his raised hand, the blade-tip pointing downwards. She screams (see above) and the credits roll, almost always blood red.

Why is this wrong? All Jack's victims except one were in their mid- to late forties and looked much older. They couldn't afford the kind of dresses starlets could and looked like bag ladies. There was no fog (dry ice) on any of the nights of the murders. It's most unlikely the killer was a gentleman with good taste in hat and cape. And Jack's knife was plunged horizontally and up, not down in a stabbing motion.

As with all other movies in this book, I have limited analysis to those that feature real people. Obviously, Jack himself was real, but he has been so often and systematically altered to fit a wacky storyline that I am counting him as fictional throughout. The only real character in Laird Cregar's 1944 version was, bizarrely, King Edward, which would place the murders between 1902 and 1910. The 1954 version – *The Man in the Attic* – starring Jack Palance, does have a character called Chief Inspector Melville, probably a garbled version of Assistant-Commissioner Melville Macnaghten who was appointed to Scotland Yard some months after the murders ceased.

The concept of 'the lodger' comes from the commonly held theory that the killer couldn't have been an actual local in the East End, but an outsider, an alien not quite like the rest of mankind. The best-known lodger at the time of the murders, questioned by police, was Joseph Isaacs, who lodged near Mary Kelly's room in Miller's Court, Dorset Street. He played the violin at night and suffered from insomnia. There was no actual evidence against him at all and he was released without charge.

By 1959, serious research was being undertaken, ironically at a time when the actual murder sites were being demolished in Whitechapel. *The Veil: Jack the Ripper* (1958) wasn't very good but it did feature a rugged, believable Clifford Evans as Inspector James McWilliam, head of the City Detective Force. Because Kate Eddowes was murdered on the night of 29/30 September in Mitre Square, the case fell within the jurisdiction of the City, as opposed to the Metropolitan Police. McWilliams' report on the murder was next to useless, prompting the Home Secretary, Henry Matthews, to write, 'They evidently want to tell us nothing.'

By the mid-1960s, film-makers hit upon the idea of putting Victorian England's most notorious killer together with its most famous fictional detective, Sherlock Holmes. *A Study in Terror* (1966) was one of the Ripper classics even if it stuck to the myth that Jack was a member of the aristocracy. The thinking behind this is that only a cover-up by powerful officialdom could have prevented Jack from being caught. The *real* reason, of course, was police ineptitude and a lot of luck on the part of the killer. Both the prime minister and the home secretary were on screen, though unnamed (for the record, they were Salisbury and Matthews) and all of Melville Macnaghten's 'canonical five' – Annie Chapman, Cathy [*sic*] Eddowes, Polly Nichols, Mary Kelly and Elizabeth Stride – are named. The fact that Chapman – 'Dark Annie' – is played by bubbly blonde Barbara Windsor says it all. The last named in the cast list is Emma Smith, not a Ripper victim but an actual prostitute attacked by a gang in the days before Jack struck.

The only genuine character in *Hands of the Ripper* (1971) was Long Liz (Elizabeth Stride) played by Lynda Baron. She was the first victim of the night of the 'double event' which also witnessed the murder of Kate Eddowes. Since at least one victim in *Hands of the Ripper* ends up in a bath, I think we can leave the plot alone and move on.

Murder By Decree (1979) revisited the Ripper versus Holmes theme, but this time there was a new theory on the real Whitechapel murders. Stephen Knight's *The Final Solution* (1976) was hailed as definitive. In fact, it is a piece of hokum riddled with holes. Concerning the 'highest in the land', the storyline involves the queen's doctor, Sir William Gull, murdering women to cover up the fact that the heir apparent (the Duke of Clarence) has married a common shop girl, Annie Crook, and everybody involved must be silenced. None of it makes sense and there is no evidence for any of it. All the victims are there, including Annie Crook, half the royal family and two credited constables of the day – Alfred Long and Edward Watkins – both involved in the Kate Eddowes killing. Another character thrown in is Sir Charles Warren, Commissioner of Police, played by a bluff Anthony Quayle, and the medium Robert Lees (Donald Sutherland) who claimed to have inside knowledge on the killings from the Other Side. In reality, we only have Lees' word for his involvement; if he went to the police at all, they ignored him.

The centenary of the Whitechapel murders produced one of the best of the Ripper films. *Jack the Ripper* (1988) starred Michael Caine as Chief Inspector Abberline and, despite clinging to Stephen Knight's nonsense, focused on the police investigation. Abberline was from Dorset, but Caine played him as a Cockney, using the strongarm, which was more or less accurate for 1880s policemen. Caine's Number Two was Sergeant George Godley (Lewis Collins) and William Gull (aka Jack) was a slobbering maniac when roused, played with panache by Ray McAnally. For the first time, real characters abound – Harry Andrews was Coroner Wynne Baxter; the 'mad pork butcher' Jacob Isenschmid was played by John Dierkes; Hugh Fraser was far too nice for Commissioner Warren and we have a whole range of genuine policemen – Superintendent Arnold (Edward Judd); Inspector John Spratling (Jon Laurimore) as well as a smattering of police surgeons – Rees Llewellyn (Michael Hughes) and George Bagster Phillips (Gerald Sim). My main quarrel with the film is Michael Gothard as local builder George Lusk. It's not the actor's fault, but he is portrayed as a dangerous revolutionary Marxist, whereas the real Lusk was a philanthropic businessman doing his bit to help the police.

The latest blockbuster about Jack was *From Hell* (2001), the title taken from the 'address' on a supposed Ripper letter sent to George Lusk, together with a human kidney which may or may not have been taken from the body of Kate Eddowes. I personally know the historical adviser on this movie and can only say that his sound advice must have been largely ignored because the plotline *still* follows the discredited Knight theory. Abberline is played by Johnny Depp, an Anglophile who admitted at the time that he couldn't do a Dorset accent and so did (excellent) Cockney instead! Virtually everybody in the cast list is a genuine character, including prostitute Martha Tabram (Samantha Spiro), Dr Thomas Bond (Simon Harrison) and the journalist Robert Best (Byron Tear). The silliest point in *From Hell*, however (and it spoiled an otherwise enjoyable romp through the East End's 'Abyss'), was the love interest between Abberline and Mary Kelly and the fact that the inspector commits suicide with a drug overdose while (wait for it) 'chasing the dragon'! The real Abberline lived on for many years after 1888 and probably hardly knew one end of a hookah from the other.

The 1920s in Germany were a harsh time with a defeated country trying to recover after the First World War and being hit hard, in 1929, by the ripple effects of the Wall Street Crash. Peter Kürten's victims were usually, but not exclusively, female and he exhibited the classic traits of the serial killer – an obsession with fire, bedwetting and mutilation of animals. Kürten was an ordinary-looking everyday Joe and no one looked twice at him as he wandered the streets and parks of Düsseldorf.

It was Kürten's crime spree, although his name wasn't used, that sparked Fritz Lang's *M* (1931). The movie has little to do with reality. In it, the police are hopelessly at sea and it falls to a criminal underclass who catch the killer. Peter Lorre (whose first role this was) is too over-the-top for Kürten, but in 1931 *all* German films looked like that –

shadows, close-ups, little movement. It all seems very mannered now, but as a depiction of a society terrified of a monster, has rarely been bettered. In reality, the 'Vampire of Düsseldorf' was convicted of nine counts of murder and seven of attempted murder and was guillotined in July 1931.

But despite the lure of the serial killer, Hollywood was more interested in organized crime, which inevitably focused, in the 1930s, on prohibition and racketeering. As the huddled masses arrived from all over the world via Ellis Island in New York harbour, various nationalities brought their criminality and criminals with them. Foremost among these was Cosa Nostra, the Sicilian gang dating from the nineteenth century and the 1930s were dominated by gang warfare between the Italians and the Irish.

Both groups used violence and threats of violence as a way of life, making money out of protection rackets, gambling, fraud and prostitution long before drugs hit the streets. The most lucrative source of cash for the hoodlums of the day was bootlegging, the supply of illegal alcohol. In what has to be one of the silliest pieces of legislation ever, Congress passed the Volstead Act in 1920, making the supply and drinking of liquor illegal. In response, all over the major cities, especially on the eastern seaboard, 'speakeasies' opened up, illicit, disguised nightclubs where alcohol flowed as freely as ever. In the more remote hillbilly areas, 'hootch' and 'moonshine' was brewed in illicit stills. It is noteworthy that the Volstead Act became law at midnight on 16/17 January and fifty-nine minutes later, six men stole $100,000 worth of liquor from a freight train.

In the 'land of the free' where federal edicts were suspect, the bootleggers became local and national heroes and few people condemned them or were prepared to help the authorities close them down. Many of these bootlegging gang lords have become heroes, portrayed as such on the big screen, but none more so than Alphonse Gabriel Capone. Many of the crime films of the 1930s had ex-crime reporters like Ben Hecht as their creators. They knew the streets and the casual violence of the time and producers were able to find actors who, for the cinema-going public, represented the leading gangster of the day. Jimmy Cagney, Humphrey Bogart, George Raft and a host of others played the swaggering 'wise guys', as handy with their fists as they were with Thompson sub-machine guns.

Capone himself was the prince of hoodlums, although his dominance of Chicago's 'Outfit' lasted only seven years. Despite the Italian connection, Capone was all American, born in Brooklyn, New York. No actor who has played him looks much like him but there have been some excellent portrayals, nonetheless. At the height of his power, Capone was worth $60 million ($5.5 billion today) and he passed himself off as a successful businessman, providing what the public wanted (booze, gambling and women). His list of crimes, for which he was never properly punished, included the murders of gang rivals the Genna brothers, Bugs Moran, Roger Tuohy, Dean O'Banion and most of Moran's heavies in the notorious St Valentine's Day Massacre in 1929. Capone's success lay in the fact that he had over half 'Chicago's finest' in his pocket, not to mention high court judges and prohibition agents. Eventually, he was brought down on charges of tax evasion, carrying an eleven-year sentence. He was released in 1939 suffering from tertiary syphilis and died at his Florida mansion in 1947.

Most of the hugely popular gangster films of the 1930s portray elements of Capone's life or refer to him. In *Little Caesar* (1931) the central figure of Cesar Bandello (Edward G. Robinson) is clearly him. Howard Hawks' *Scarface* (1932) had Paul Muni in the lead role. The character name is fictional (we have to remember that these movies were made while Capone was still alive) but he mixes with high society, loves Italian opera and organizes the St Valentine's Day hit more or less as it must have been in reality. The scarface reference (it emerges again in Neville Brand's portrayal *The Scarface Mob* in 1958) comes from the wounds Capone received in a knife fight during his teens.

It was Robert Stack's television series *The Untouchables* (1957) focusing on the career of exciseman Eliot Ness' role in bringing Capone down that spawned a new interest in the gangster and his times. *Al Capone*, two years later, starred Rod Steiger as easily the best lookalike and *The Untouchables* became a movie in 1987, starring Kevin Costner as stodgily determined Ness. Capone was played as a short-fused homicidal maniac by Robert de Niro and showed the (genuine) scene of the 'big fella' clubbing a dinner guest to death with a baseball bat.

Brian De Palma's *Untouchables* looked good. When Jimmy Cagney was roaring around the Roaring Twenties in black and white, everything was, by definition, correct – the cars, the guns, the homburgs, the suits. When Kevin Costner was sorting Capone out (in colour) we are aware that everything has had to be manufactured from the originals. Cagney fought his gun battle in the studio; Costner used what looked like one street in Chicago. Ness was a real-life agent and the Untouchables were too. The last surviving member of the group, Albert H. Wolff, acted as consultant on the movie, especially in respect of Ness' character. For American purists, the legal terminology of the film was wrong – Illinois has state attorneys, not district attorneys.

The fictional character Jim Malone (Sean Connery) has the best line in the film. 'You wanna know how to get Capone? They pull a knife, you pull a gun. He sends one of yours to the hospital, you send one of his to the morgue. That's the Chicago way! And that's how you get Capone.' Nearly as good is the movie's last line. A reporter says to Eliot Ness, 'Word is they're going to repeal Prohibition. What'll you do then?'

'I think,' says Ness, 'I'll have a drink.'

The Untouchables is excellent, but there is one glaring mistake. One of the most noxious of Capone's heavies is Frank Nitti, played with menace by Billy Drago. Ness throws him off a high building and he crashes through the roof of a parked vehicle, prompting the movie's third best line – 'Where's Nitti?' 'He's in the car.' In reality, despite being called The Enforcer, Nitti was a mild-mannered accountant. He took over from Capone after his imprisonment and was among those charged with trying to extort money from a number of Hollywood studios, including Fox, Paramount, Columbia and Metro-Goldwyn-Mayer. Nitti shot himself in March 1943.

But the 1930s weren't all about Capone. Sticking with the Mafiosi theme that the 'family that slays together, stays together', the Barkers were fascinating, in a dysfunctional, murderous sort of way. 'You gotta believe,' said the *Bloody Mama* posters in 1969, 'You gotta have faith, but first you gotta get rid of the witnesses!' The matriarch of the drug-taking, incestuous family of bank robbers was played with panache by Shelley Winters.

The deeply unpleasant Kate Barker has, in today's forgiving, liberal age, been largely exonerated from actual wrong-doing in her sons' criminal escapades in the American mid-West in the 1930s. It was all the fault of that nasty Mr Hoover, whose FBI 'G men' had the task of bringing the family to justice. Kate and her son Fred were killed in a shoot-out with the FBI in Florida in January 1935. Never the criminal mastermind that Hoover claimed, she was nevertheless complicit in most, perhaps all, of her brood's criminality, from kidnap to bank-robbery to murder.

Hollywood became as obsessed with lone operators as it did with murderous families. John Dillinger was declared 'public enemy number one' by the FBI and the media of the day loved him. With his dimpled chin, Clark Gable moustache and bearing more than a passing resemblance to Humphrey Bogart, he was referred to as a dashing Robin Hood-style hero in newspapers and on radio. It was largely because of his crime spree that the Bureau of Investigation, set up in 1908, morphed into the Federal Bureau of Investigation, with more men, more money and more technology than ever before. In gaol from 1924 to 1933, Dillinger, who was almost certainly unbalanced, hit twelve banks in a single month after his release. He had gone to see *Manhattan Melodrama* at the Biograph Theater, Chicago, on 22 July 1934 with two women. The FBI were waiting for him and Dillinger was shot several times in the back while trying to run. Fifteen thousand people turned out for his funeral to gawp at the corpse in its open casket.

There have been at least fifteen movies depicting some aspect of Dillinger's life and death, although in some, the actual name isn't used. The best known, and least accurate, is *Dillinger*, starring Warren Oates, in 1973. Oates' make-up is very good and Clarence Hearst, the former FBI agent involved in Dillinger's death, was technical adviser. Intriguingly, J. Edgar Hoover, the head of the FBI tasked with bringing him down, was due to deliver a voice-over for the film in his own words. Although he died before he could do so, another actor read his words. 'Dillinger was a rat that the country may consider itself fortunate to be rid of and I don't sanction any Hollywood glamorization of these vermin. This type of romantic mendacity can only lead young people further astray than they are already and I want no part of it.'

But 'young people' and Hollywood weren't listening. In 1967, Arthur Penn directed the movie that became iconic for a generation of teenagers in the 'summer of love' – *Bonnie and Clyde*. The impossibly good-looking Warren Beatty and the smoulderingly sensuous Faye Dunaway were ridiculously romanticized portrayals of the real killers and bank robbers, but they were acted off the screen by Michael J. Pollard as the baby-faced C.W. Moss who aided and abetted the murderous pair. The film was hailed as 'new Hollywood', breaking taboos, especially in terms of violence. The ambush that resulted in the robbers' death, with its slow-motion exploding 'blood' capsules was revolutionary at the time and stunned cinema audiences when they saw it. The posse who actually did the shooting were deaf for hours afterwards and photographs of Barrow's Ford Deluxe V8 show it riddled with bullets, all the windows smashed.

The real Bonnie Parker and Clyde Barrow were very average looking and she was badly burned in a car crash while on the run. In the movie, the shoot-out by the Texas Rangers happens with the getaway vehicle parked, but, in fact, officers opened fire while it was still in motion. Denver Pyle played Texas Ranger Frank Hamer in an act of personal revenge. In fact, there is no direct link between these characters – Hamer was, in the time-honoured lawmen's phrase, 'just doing his job'. Outraged by the movie's depiction, his family threatened litigation against the producers and won an out of court settlement.

When the film was released, two of the gang members were still alive. Blanche Barrow was the widow of Clyde's brother Buck (Gene Hackman) and was consulted during the making of the movie. In the end, she was unhappy with Estelle Parsons' portrayal of her – 'That film made me look like a screaming horse's ass!' Conservative America was shocked and appalled by *Bonnie and Clyde*. Joe Morgenstern in *Newsweek* called it 'a squalid shoot-'em up for the moron trade' and both lead actors were criticized for beautifying two essentially unlovely people. Needless to say, the public loved it, the box office was huge and today it is highly regarded as a milestone in American film-making.

What about the 'good guys'? Over the last forty years, it has been Hoover's creation, the Federal Bureau of Investigation, that has dominated screens both big and small. *The FBI Story* (1959) was an oddity in every sense. Its characters, led by the eminently upright and trustworthy James Stewart, were fictional, as was much of the storyline, but Hoover himself exercised such control over the film that he was virtually co-producer. If he saw a scene that failed to show the Bureau in a good light, it had to be reshot. Two special agents were with producer/director Mervyn LeRoy throughout and one of them, Lewis Greene Libby, starred as an uncredited 'G Man'.

More modern films have focused on Hoover himself. *The Private Files of J. Edgar Hoover* (1977) starred Broderick Crawford as the Director (not a bad lookalike) and was made in response to a negative attitude towards American politics. If that was the point, it failed, because the storyline follows attempts by the media to get hold of the 'black books' that Hoover had on virtually anybody who was anybody in American politics and society, including the Kennedys and Martin Luther King. Inevitably, a number of real-life characters appeared. Michael Parks was Attorney General Robert Kennedy; Dan Dailey was Hoover's friend Clive Tolson; Howard Da Silva was Franklin D. Roosevelt; Raymond St Jacques was Martin Luther King. The film pulled no punches about Hoover's semi-legal use of phone tapping and actual blackmail to coerce people in a particular direction. It was ambivalent, however, about the director's alleged cross-dressing and homosexual relationship with Clive Tolson.

J. Edgar (2011) was produced and directed by Clint Eastwood. The FBI boss was played very well by Leonardo DiCaprio, but the actor looked so unlike the real man that it took some believing. Following years of Hoover's career, the movie features one of the most notorious crimes of twentieth-century America, the kidnap and murder of the child of aviator Charles Lindbergh in 1927. A national hero as Lindbergh was, the case made huge headlines and led to kidnap becoming a federal offence, giving it far more credence than it actually merited.

DiCaprio allegedly dropped his fee from $20 million to $2 million and he needed six hours in make-up to attempt at least to recreate the spoon-faced J. Edgar. DiCaprio apart, the film was not well received. One critic referred to 'cheesy make-up, poor lighting, confusing narrative [it was not chronological] and humdrum storytelling'. Hoover experts were impressed with the film's portrayal of the man who made the FBI professional and up to date in terms of technology, but the fact that the Bureau is often, today, portrayed as the annoying enemy of honest local cops in umpteen television shows, perhaps hints that its days are numbered and the Hoover years best consigned to (controversial) history.

Robert Stroud found his own kind of salvation for a life behind bars. The man was originally jailed for killing a barman in 1909 and, once inside, on McNeil Island in Puget Sound, he killed a guard in a prison fight. There was no doubt that Stroud was a dangerous man, and after a number of trials, he was sentenced to life imprisonment. At Leavenworth, he found a sparrow's nest in the prison yard, tended the fledglings and amassed a collection over time of 300 canaries. He also became a respected ornithologist, bringing out his first book – *Diseases of Canaries* – in 1933. His success and fame amazed prison authorities and he was transferred to Alcatraz, where he was allowed no pets at all.

Undeterred, he wrote a history of the American penal system. Forty-two years of his life were spent in solitary confinement.

The 1962 movie directed by John Frankenheimer and starring Burt Lancaster, became *The Birdman of Alcatraz*. The real Stroud bears no resemblance to Lancaster, who wore glasses in the film presumably to give him a scholarly appearance. The film follows the Bird Man's career quite closely, including his involvement in a prison riot in 1946. The director of the FBI, James V. Bennett, tried to get the movie blocked because of its glamorization of criminals. Insiders claimed that Lancaster was too nice for Stroud, who one author said was more like the serial killer Ted Bundy (see below). A former inmate said, 'He was a vicious killer. I think Burt Lancaster owes us all an apology.'

In the meantime, what was happening 'across the Pond', as no doubt many Hollywood people used to say? While British cinema-goers were more than content to soak up the hail of bullets and 'wise-guy' cracks from American gangster movies, the 1950s provided the setting for two real-life crime films that helped bring about the abolition of the death penalty in Britain. The first to be made was *10 Rillington Place* (1971), starring Richard Attenborough as the serial killer John Christie. The storyline was adapted from the book of the same name by Ludovic Kennedy who was the film's technical adviser. Reggie 'No Dick' Christie was a strange misfit with delusions of his own self-importance. He joined the Special Police Reserve during the Second World War and this gave him a position of authority in which he was able to lure prostitutes to his house at the address in Notting Hill which is the movie's title. He gassed and strangled all his victims, and, after having sex with their corpses, buried them in the garden of his flat and even in the cupboards of the house itself. When his wife became suspicious of him, he killed her too, burying her under the floorboards of his front room.

When new lodgers arrived at Number 10 in 1949, Christie struck again, murdering Beryl Evans. Her husband, mentally challenged

Timothy, was charged with her murder and that of her baby and was hanged. New tenants moving in to Christie's flat after he vacated it discovered the rotting corpses and Christie himself faced the drop. Albert Pierrepoint, the executioner, hanged both men and there was huge public outrage at such a gross miscarriage of justice. Evans was officially pardoned in 1966 and Rillington Place today is Ruston Close.

Attenborough hated playing the part of Christie, but he acknowledged that it was in a good cause. At the time of the filming, the actual house was still there but derelict. Only Attenborough was filmed inside it; other scenes were studio-built and the place was demolished once shooting had finished. John Hurt was a brilliant Timothy Evans, a man (with an impeccable Welsh accent) bewildered by a turn of events he could barely understand.

Someone else out of his depth in a harsh post-war world was 19-year-old Derek Bentley. In November 1952, he and 16-year-old Christopher Craig were caught by police trying to break into a warehouse in Croydon, Surrey. Craig was armed with a revolver, wounded one policeman and killed another. The law at the time (and still today) says that if more than one person is engaged in a 'felonious enterprise', then they are all guilty of any further crime. That meant that the unarmed Bentley, actually under arrest at the time of the shooting, was as guilty as Craig. At 19, despite having an IQ of only 66 (the national average is 100, updated regularly to make sure there is a proper benchmark for all generations) he was old enough to hang; and hang he did, at Wandsworth in February 1953, Pierrepoint again doing the honours.

Let Him Have It (1991) covered the case from a simplistic point of view. The title comes from Bentley's alleged statement on the Croydon rooftop – 'Let him have it' – shouted to Christopher Craig. The prosecution contended that this meant 'shoot'. The defence claimed that Bentley said no such thing. Virtually everybody in the movie (as in *10 Rillington Place*) is a real character – the Bentley family, the police officers of Z Division, Metropolitan Police, the courtroom figures, with a suitably grim and appallingly biased Michael Gough as the judge, Lord Goddard, and a friendly, bustling Clive Revill as Albert Pierrepoint.

Christopher Eccleston played Bentley (a reminder that the lad was 6ft 4in tall) but his response to one interviewer was disappointing. The film he said was 'liberal crap' and he was 'crap' too. It's possible that the film helped the Bentley family's campaigning to have the conviction of Derek overturned, but since that didn't happen until 1998, it's rather far-fetched to assume that. For the record, the last execution in Britain was in 1964. In 1965, the death penalty was suspended until 1969, when it was finally abolished.

An oddity in British true crime was *The Young Poisoner's Handbook* (1995), which catalogued the crimes of Graham Young, working in an office in St Albans in the early 1960s and quietly murdering his colleagues. He cleverly used thallium, a little-known poison whose effects can be confused with natural causes. The movie was played as black comedy (how else?) written by actor Jeff Rawle and starring Hugh O'Connor as Young. Having been released from prison in 1971, the St Albans poisoner went on to kill another six. He died in gaol in 1990.

Back on the international scene, *The Honeymoon Killers* (1970) was described as a 'putrescent version of Norman Rockwell's America', for its documentary style, grubby sets and unpleasant people. The real killers were Martha Beck and Raymond Fernandez. She was an overweight part-time nurse who became involved with a series of dissolute men. In 1947, she placed an advertisement in a lonely hearts column and Fernandez answered it. Seventeen murders were attributed to the pair, but they were charged with only one, that of 66-year-old Janet Fay in Long Island. They were executed at Sing Sing Correctional Facility in March 1951.

Heavenly Creatures (1994) was the unusual story of two schoolgirls who killed the mother of one of them in New Zealand in 1954. The director was Peter Jackson and the girls were Kate Winslet and Melanie Lynskey, all the more believable as potential psychopaths because the cinema-going public hadn't seen them before. Pauline Parker (Winslet) and Juliet Hulme, both 15 at the time, were living in Christchurch and Hulme's parents were about to divorce. She was due to live with relatives in South Africa. The girls had created a fantasy world with characters such as James Mason and Orson Welles and the last thing they wanted was to be separated. On 22 June, while out for a walk, the girls battered Parker's mother Honorah Rieper with a rock at least twenty times. Tried in August, both girls were found guilty but, too young for the death penalty then in place, were imprisoned 'at Her Majesty's pleasure'. That, in practice, meant a mere five years.

Juvenile delinquency became a common theme in the United States too during the 1950s as rock 'n' roll was believed to have marked the end of civilization. One real-life miscreant was Charles Starkweather, the central character in *Badlands* (1973). Only the names have been changed to avoid litigation. So Starkweather (Martin Sheen) becomes Kit Carruthers and his 15-year-old girlfriend Caril Ann Fugate (Sissy Spacek) becomes Holly Sargis. Both stars are excellent as what one critic described as 'the self-absorbed, cruel, possibly psychotic children of our time', but the plot is largely fiction. Starkweather murdered eleven people in Wyoming and Nebraska (the 'Badlands' of the film's title), ten of them inside one week. His accomplice, Fugate, was sentenced to seventeen years in prison, getting out in 1976. A disturbed and psychotic bully, Starkweather went to the electric chair in June 1959 aged 20.

Seventy-four per cent of today's serial killers are American. Four of them stand out in the movies. Albert DeSalvo has featured in two movies, both called *The Boston Strangler* (1968 and 2023). Posing as a workman or technician, he gained entry to thirteen women's apartments between 1962 and 1964 and murdered them, having raped them first. Their ages ranged from 19 to 85. The press first called the killer 'the Phantom Fiend' (did journalists *really* still write like that in 1962?) but the police made the mistake that more than one murderer was involved.

Parapsychologist Peter Hurkos focused on a single perpetrator, however, and DeSalvo was arrested, admitting to his crimes. Tony Curtis played him in 1968, complete with a built-up nose that fooled nobody, and the focus of the most recent effort is not the killer himself but the two female reporters, Jean Cole and Loretta McLaughlin, whose stories led to the arrest.

The New York Times had it in for both films – the 1968 version was 'an incredible collapse of taste, judgement, decency, prose, insight, journalism and movie technique' – come off the fence, now, Grey Lady, what did you *really* think of it? In 2023, it was a 'dreary, painfully stylized slog'. Incidentally, the recent version hints that DeSalvo may not have been guilty, which is interesting because his body (he was murdered in gaol) was exhumed and DNA comparisons with his last victim matched. That was ten years ago and it's inexcusable for film-makers to make mistakes like that.

Henry Lee Lucas makes Charlie Starkweather look like an amateur, although his claim of more than 250 victims is clearly nonsense. He killed his mother (the source of the problem for many serial killers) in 1960 and was still murdering people over twenty years later. Because of his confessions (at one point to nearly 600 crimes) he was for years listed as America's most prolific serial killer. He was eventually sentenced to death for just one murder, that of a Jane Doe later identified as Debra Jackson, a runaway who disappeared in 1977 and was identified as recently as 2019. Arrested in June 1983, Lucas was on death row for years before his sentence was commuted to life in prison without parole in 1998. He died of congestive heart failure in Huntsville, Texas, three years later.

The man had a horrific, abusive childhood thanks to his prostitute mother who pimped him out to men and women. It's very telling that in prison Lucas retracted his ludicrous murder count, but he never denied killing his mother. In *Henry, Portrait of a Serial Killer*, Lucas was played by Michael Rooker, too chunky and personable for the odd-looking one-eyed killer. That said, he plays the role well, showing a lack of emotion, which is characteristic of such murderers, even those who brag about non-existent crimes. The movie became classified as a 'slasher' movie, which is a shame, because it is far more than that. The whole thing was shot in less than a month with a miniscule budget of $110,000, adding to the grubby squalor of the piece. Rooker wore his own clothes, both to cut costume expense and to give the film a reality of its own. Because of the graphic violence involved, sections were cut in the US, Britain and New Zealand, but in terms of true crime, much of what was retained really happened. Lucas' equally depraved 'buddy' was Ottis Toole and he did sexually abuse Toole's 12-year-old niece (played of course by an adult in the movie).

Five people were killed in the San Francisco Bay area between 1968 and 1969 by the killer known as The Zodiac. He got his nickname from a series of letters he sent to the press threatening more violence if they were not printed. He used cyphers and cryptograms, claiming that he was killing courting couples to use as sex-slaves in an afterlife. One of these was not cracked until 2020. The case remains open in Napa Valley and Vallejo and has inevitably attracted all sorts of cranks over the years.

Zodiac was released in 2007, directed by David Fincher based on two non-fiction books on the murders. Jake Gyllenhaal played crime writer Robert Graysmith, perhaps the best-known expert on the case and Mark Ruffalo was leading investigator Dave Toschi. Fincher had grown up in the Bay area and regarded the Zodiac as the 'ultimate boogeyman', admitting to having something of an obsession with him. The film had excellent reviews, avoiding as it did the cliché of the Californian hippy culture of the time, reminding us all that not everyone 'wore flowers in their hair'; nor were they all going to San Francisco.

Female serial killers are a rarity. Female serial killers who kill at close range with a hand gun are rarer still. Such a one was Aileen Wuornos, a Florida prostitute who killed and robbed seven clients, accusing them all of rape or attempted rape. She was sentenced to death for the murder of six and executed by lethal injection in October 2002. The Wuornos murders happened in 1989–90, but the movie *Monster* of 2003 had to reflect the subtle changes that had occurred since those dates. It was extraordinary for a number of reasons. Wuornos was played by the gorgeous Hollywood star Charlize Theron who put on 30lb and ignored make-up to recreate the killer. Her lesbian lover was portrayed by Nina Ricci, whose demonic scowl perfectly encapsulated the real-life Tyria Moore. The movie won umpteen accolades and one critic called Theron's work 'one of the greatest performances in the history of cinema'. Inevitably, there were howls of protest from people who objected to a serial killer being seen as a victim herself.

How can we explain the enduring appeal of Theodore Robert Bundy? He confessed to killing thirty young women in seven states between 1974 and 1978, although experts believe the total is actually higher. A handsome, charismatic law student, he targeted pretty brunettes, picked them up in his infamous yellow VW car on some plausible excuse, bludgeoned, raped and murdered them. A necrophiliac, he often returned to their graves to have sex with their corpses. He twice escaped from custody and his towering arrogance led him to conduct his own defence at his trial; it was a disaster. Sentenced to death, he spent several years on death row, even assisting authorities in their attempts to catch the even more prolific Green River killer, Gary Ridgway. Finally, confessing in detail to his crimes (and others the FBI didn't know about) Ted Bundy was sent to the electric chair in January 1989. Hundreds sang and danced outside the prison and cheered as his body was taken for cremation.

There have been at least eleven films on Bundy's murderous spree in which a series of handsome and plausible actors have taken on the role. Mark Harmon starred in a television mini-series in 1986; Carey Elwes played Bundy in *The Riverman* (2004) and, most recently, Luke Kirby in *No Man of God* (2021). As the screenwriter of this version told the press, 'The deeper you dig into the story, you realize there's nothing to mystify here, there's nothing amazing about him.'

Chapter 11

Ice-Cream and Popcorn

Some movies don't fit into a neat category or any category at all, yet they must be included because they deal with real characters and are all worth watching.

One of the oddest is *Topsy-Turvy* (1999), an account of musical impresarios Gilbert and Sullivan putting on the first production of *The Mikado* in 1885. 'The Egos,' ran the movie's PR line, 'The Battles. The Words. The Music. The Women. The Scandal. Gilbert and Sullivan and So Much More.' It was tongue-in-cheek but nevertheless conveyed the surreal world of the D'Oyly Carte operettas in the bitchy world of high Victorian theatre. W.S. Gilbert (Jim Broadbent) wrote the lyrics; Sir Arthur Sullivan (Allan Corduner) the music. The pair are falling out during the film and eventually did so permanently, not speaking to each other for years. Mike Leigh wrote the screenplay and the London *Evening Standard*'s review, that it was 'an overlong, overdressed and over-indulgent recreation of a familiar story' is ludicrous. Most of the cast was composed of real characters and the costumes and sets were spot on. *The Mikado* came about because of a Japanese exhibition then showing in London.

Around twenty-five years after that exhibition, a cross section of British society went down with the White Star Line's *Titanic*. Hailed as the most advanced ship afloat, she hit an iceberg on her maiden voyage to New York with shocking loss of life. *A Night to Remember* (1958) was the not very good title of a very good film. There are no leads in this movie, although perhaps we identify most with the second officer, Herbert Lightoller (Kenneth More), played with understated professionalism. The sinking has spawned a whole industry on both sides of the Atlantic, with nostalgia, memorabilia and conspiracy theories abounding. All the more disappointing, then, was *Titanic* (1997). Interestingly, although he only gives it two stars, there is a complete column devoted to it in Halliwell's film guide of 2006, a reminder of the movie's real brilliance, its PR. The focus was on a love story (when is it not?) between the fictional characters played by Leonardo DiCaprio and Kate Winslet – 'Nothing on Earth could come between them' said the posters. The relationship was pure 1990s – spoilt millionaire's daughter falls for poor Wisconsin boy. Forget the fact that steerage passengers on board were allowed nowhere near the high-fee-paying punters – you've already heard how love finds a way and you've seen it in thousands of movies.

The visuals are superb – streets ahead of *A Night To Remember* – but the rest of it is risible. 'Do you know Dr Freud?' one character asks. 'His ideas about the male preoccupation with size may be of interest to you' is about as good as it gets. Richard Corliss of *Time* wrote, 'The regretful verdict is: Dead in the Water.' Kenneth Turan of the *Los Angeles Times* was even more direct – 'As James Cameron [writer and director] sails his lonely craft toward greatness, he should realize he needs to bring a passenger with him. Preferably someone who can write.'

The movie cost $200 million, had 550 CGI shots and Cameron forewent his salary to try to make it pay. He also upset a lot of people because of the idiotic idea that steerage passengers were locked in their quarters and threatened at gunpoint. Public Record Office papers proved that this was not the case and the crew member who trains his pistol on the poor was pure fiction. The man's family threatened to sue. Incomprehensibly, the film picked up eleven Oscars (a record shared with *Ben-Hur*) and made a fortune for all concerned.

Darkest Hour (2017) took up the story of Winston Churchill, and Gary Oldman was now playing a beleaguered prime minister. His performance and make-up were both superb (as they always are) and the film had a feel-good sense about it. Even so, there were errors. The scene where Churchill jumps on a tube train and gets to know ordinary Londoners' views on the war never happened; the PM went everywhere by chauffeur-driven car. The raucous House of Commons was depicted very well and we may note cynically that it had not improved since the days of *Cromwell* and *The Madness of King George*. Ronald Pickup was excellent as Neville Chamberlain, the prime minister completely taken in (as many were) by Adolf Hitler.

Churchill turns up again in *The King's Speech* (2010), this time played by Timothy Spall. The abdication crisis, in which the heir to the British throne abandoned it for the sake of a deeply unpopular American divorcee, left his kid brother George as the lad who wears the crown. Unfortunately, George had a dreadful stammer and performing in public filled him with horror. Enter the persuasive Lionel Logue (Geoffrey Rush) whose therapy *just about* works. Colin Firth was excellent as the king, but insiders, of both the 1930s palace set up and speech therapy, pointed out huge holes in the film's authenticity as to who said what to whom and how successful Logue's bullying techniques were anyway.

One of Churchill's many enemies was Mohandas K. Gandhi, one of several populist leaders demanding Indian independence in the twentieth century. A lawyer by training, with a degree from London University, Gandhi practised in Bombay (today's Mumbai) and South Africa where he met racism for the first time. Incidentally, his own racism showed in his reaction to black Africans, although this is not apparent in the movie. Throughout the 1920s and 1930s he led a pacifist movement to remove British control from India (see Chapter 7) and was called Mahatma (great soul) by his followers. He appeared in Britain and elsewhere at high-level conferences in sandals and a dhoti, traditional Indian garb, which led to Churchill referring to him as a 'half-naked fakir in a loincloth'.

Gandhi (1982) was directed by Richard Attenborough at his luvviest and was interminably long, but the lead performance, by Ben Kingsley, was superb. Inevitably, there were protests. Why wasn't an Indian actor given the role? After all, Bollywood had plenty to choose from. It was a fair question. The real Gandhi, as shown in the movie, was shot by a Hindu fanatic (one of his own followers) in 1947.

One of the fakest of fake heroes to be thrown up in the twentieth century was Ernesto 'Che' Guevara. No self-respecting student in the 1960s could get by without a poster of the man on the wall of his Hall of Residence room, complete with 'revolutionary' beret. The man was as artificial as the poster, an asthmatic doctor from Argentina who joined Fidel Castro's revolution in Cuba in the 1950s, trying to foment revolution (it was what he did) in South America. He was captured and shot dead in 1965. The movie *Che!* (1969) cashed in on and helped create the legend of doomed youth pushing the boundaries, like anti-Vietnam protestors in the United States. Omar Sharif was Guevara and Jack Palance an unlikely Castro. 'It goes at the pace of a drugged ox,' said *The New Yorker*, 'and hasn't an ounce of political or historical sense ...'

Another larger-than-life character was Idi Amin, a Ugandan army officer who led a colonel's revolt in his native country in 1971. As one of a long line of African rulers who have governed as dictators, Amin expelled Asians and Jews from Uganda and ordered the murder of thousands of opponents. *The Last King of Scotland* (2006) takes its title from the ludicrous public pronouncements by a man who was not only profoundly ignorant but almost certainly deranged. He claimed, among much else, that he was rightfully king of Scotland and that Adolf Hitler had invaded the United States. Forest Whitaker did an excellent and believable job of playing a man who almost defies explanation.

As scandals go, the 1970s Watergate has it all, spawning a silly 'gate' at the end of every issue, no matter how minor, ever since. The bugging of Democrat offices by Republicans in Washington DC had the full backing of the president, 'Tricky Dickie' Nixon. That fact alone would have brought him down, but the cover-up – and the cover-up of the cover-up – 'There will be no whitewash in the White House', was a scandal of epic proportions. It's true to say that American politics was never the same afterwards. *All the President's Men* (1976) was billed as 'the most devastating detective story of the century' and it's difficult to disagree with that. Frank Rich of the *New York Post* didn't pull any punches when he wrote that the movie was 'a chilling tone poem that conveys the texture of the terror in our nation's capital during that long night when an aspiring fascist regime held our democracy under siege'. The movie was based on the book by its leading protagonists, Carl Bernstein (Dustin Hoffman) and Bob Woodward (Robert Redford). Hal Holbrook, perennially sinister, was Deep Throat, an anonymous whistle-blower whose moniker was derived from a different kind of film altogether! Jason Robards played newspaper boss Ben Bradlee (too heroically, critics said). The film was inevitably romanticized (I doubt that Bernstein and Woodward were quite as 'Butch and Sundance' as the script made out) and I was struck by how easily people in high places were prepared to spill catastrophic secrets over the phone to journalists of *The Washington Post*; surely, it can't have been as simple as that?

And, talking of presidents, Oliver Stone's *JFK* (1991). The assassination of John F. Kennedy in Dealey Plaza, Dallas, in November 1963 marked 'the day the dream died'. With ample evidence that the hit was the work of two, perhaps three, marksmen, the only culprit rounded up was Lee Harvey Oswald, a strange, possibly Communist ex-Marine who was conveniently killed in police custody before he could stand trial. A whole industry has developed over this killing, with die-hard conservatives insisting that Oswald was a 'lone rifle nut' and their opponents equally convinced that there was a conspiracy. Oddly, the mainstream American media have never strayed from the former viewpoint and were quick to rubbish Stone's efforts as a result.

Stone was using the work of New Orleans DA Jim Garrison (Kevin Costner) who had uncovered a macabre organization determined to continue the lucrative 'war' in Vietnam, out of which Kennedy intended to take America. 'Bad history' says by-the-book Halliwell (which it isn't) and a 'bullying [?] movie mixing fact and dubious speculation indiscriminately'. That last line could fit virtually every movie in this book and it does the cause of justice in the Kennedy killing no good at all.

Gary Oldman was an excellent Oswald lookalike. His mannerisms in front of the newsreel cameras are identical with what the world saw in the days after the shooting. Joe Pesci is superb as the slightly deranged David Ferrie (complete with orange wig and fake eyebrows), on the fringes of involvement in the Bay of Pigs, as is Tommy Lee Jones as Clay Shaw, a crooked businessman who was in Garrison's crosshairs. It is noticeable that the American reviews were generally hostile, even the usually sensible Norman Mailer writing that the film, 'is one of the worst great movies ever made'. British reviews, away from the straitjacket of American media, were more honest – 'Courageous, gripping, reckless ... the culmination ... of the paranoid political thriller.'

Long before the slogan 'Black Lives Matter', black American issues formed the basis of a number of movies. One of these, *Selma* (2014) about the violence in Alabama in the 1960s against Martin Luther King and his freedom marchers, was a boring disappointment, probably because it tried to stick to the facts and left little room for drama or characterization. Another, *Malcolm X* (1992) was far better, but again, critics panned it for its blandness and 'subdued treatment that seems anxious not to offend'. Denzel Washington was excellent as the complicated Malcolm Little, the black activist who fell foul of the equally black Nation of Islam who eventually killed him.

When he wrote his *Hollywood History of the World* in 1977, George MacDonald Fraser apologized for the list of historical characters he had to leave out, pointing out that such a book would run to several volumes. That is my problem too, so here, I'll merely list *some* of the people that cinema forgot. Sydney Greenstreet, best known perhaps for *The Maltese Falcon* was the writer William Makepeace Thackeray in *Devotion* (1946), which is actually about the Brontë sisters and their dissolute brother Branwell. The movie is an odd one, giving the vicar's daughters far more interest than they actually deserve, for example, 'Emily [Ida Lupino]; she ruled in that strange quiet house [now a museum]. None could resist her force of will!' 'Charlotte; the sweetness of love and the meaning of torment – she learned them both together!' When Hollywood PR resorts to exclamation marks, you know you're in trouble [!] As for Greenstreet's Thackeray – 'the furious fat man; they couldn't fool him; they couldn't trust him'. The dialogue included the famous chilly exchange between two literary greats – Dickens: 'Morning, Thackeray.' Thackeray: 'Morning, Dickens.' *Mr Turner* (2014) went one better when two artistic giants tied to ignore each other at an art exhibition – 'Turner.' 'Constable' was the extent of the conversation.

As for the Brontës and *Devotion*, Halliwell demolishes it with, 'An enjoyably bad example of a big-budget Hollywood production which tampers with things it cannot understand …'

Clark Gable played Charles Stewart Parnell, the Irish Home Rule leader. Parnell was a force of nature in the 1880s House of Commons, but his career was ruined by his affair with Kitty O'Shea, the wife of an army officer. The American-Irish contingent unfailingly backed their 'broth of a boy' heroes and raised money for him. All the more disappointing, then, that *Parnell* (1937) was such a flop. Clark Gable was miscast as Parnell and Graham Greene wrote, 'Poor though the picture may be, it is pleasing to think how clean a film magnate's wish-fulfilments are, how virginal and high-minded the tawdry, pathetic human past becomes when the Mayers and Goldwyns turn the magic ring.'

Looming far larger than Parnell in terms of politics, Otto von Bismarck with a mixture of animal cunning and force majeure, welded the disparate German states into a single country by 1871. In *Royal Flash* (1975) based on the Flashman novels by George MacDonald Fraser, Bismarck was played for quiet laughs by Oliver Reed. His soft-spoken German accent is highly believable, as in the line as he spins a globe under his fingers – 'I think I shall be rather busy for the next twenty years.' He loses a bare-knuckle boxing bout to real-life fighter Henry Cooper. And Florinda Bolkan pops up as every-royal's-mistress Lola Montez as handy with a sword as is Harry Flashman (Malcolm McDowell).

While Bismarck's Germany was busily building an empire and a navy to threaten the British and while Parnell was forced to hand over the cause of Irish freedom to others, France was undergoing its own crisis. The whole story of 'l'affair' hinged on who was selling military secrets to the Germans in the 1890s. Suspicion fell on artillery captain Alfred Dreyfus, almost totally because he was a Jew. Sent to the terrible penal colony of Devil's Island, he was only released and pardoned when the real culprit came to light. The writer Émile Zola (see below) championed his cause with a book entitled *J'Accuse* in which he blasted the government and the high command. Cedric Hardwicke played Dreyfus in the 1931 version, *The Dreyfus Case*, José Ferrer in 1958. Zola was played by George Merritt and the *real* spy, Major Esterhazy, by Gary Marsh. Incredibly, the original trial and rioting that ensued was captured on camera by Georges Méliès in 1899.

The same ground was covered in *The Life of Emile Zola* in 1937, with Paul Muni in the title role. *The New York Times* raved over this one. 'Rich, dignified, honest and strong, it is at once the finest historical film ever made and the greatest screen biography.' Otis Ferguson had a rather more cynical take – 'It ought to start a new film category – the Warner crusading films costume division.' While Dreyfus went on to fight in the First World War and won the Legion d'honneur, Zola died from breathing in toxic fumes via a blocked chimney in his Paris apartment in 1902.

Inevitably, artists have captured the imagination of film-makers. A trio that couldn't be overlooked were Henri de Toulouse-Lautrec, Paul Gauguin and Vincent van Gogh, all of them the doyens of the Bohemian Left Bank in Paris at the turn of the nineteenth/twentieth century.

Lust for Life (1956) starred two of them, Gauguin and van Gogh. Gauguin was played by Anthony Quinn (who, when he retired from acting became a highly successful artist himself) and van Gogh was a mad-looking Kirk Douglas, complete with spiky auburn hair. Today, the authorities would be looking very hard at Gauguin, who had a thing for under-age Polynesian girls and van Gogh was a tortured soul by anybody's standards. Quinn got an Oscar for his eight minutes of screen time; Douglas, who was only nominated, had to work much harder. 'Two hours of quite shattering and exciting entertainment,' wrote Alan Dent of *The Illustrated London News*. Van Gogh was probably unstable throughout his life, with failed love affairs and violent mood swings. He sliced off his ear after threatening Gauguin with a razor and was in and out of asylums for years.

Actors had difficulty playing de Toulouse-Lautrec because of the artist's physical problems. At the age of 14, he broke both his legs and the limbs didn't grow properly. The rest of his life was spent in pain and with the height of a dwarf. Well known in the Bohemian quarter of Paris, he painted clowns, prostitutes and dancers. A serious drinker, he was committed to hospitals with greater frequency as he got older. He died of a syphilitic stroke in 1901, aged 35. Clever camera angles brought José Ferrer down to the necessary size in *Moulin Rouge* (1954) but the remake in 2001 isn't realistic at all. De Toulouse-Lautrec appears, played by John Leguizamo, as one of a range of colourful grotesques. There is *nothing* in the historical record that fits the movie. As Kenneth Turan of the *Los Angeles Times* wrote, the movie is 'like being thrust into the middle of a loud and frantic party whether you want to be there or not'.

Musicians haven't fared as well as artists on the big screen, no matter how colourful their lives may have been. In fact, the more colourful, the more Hollywood is likely to make a mess of things. *Amadeus* (1984) is a classic case in point. 'The Man ...' screamed the movie poster, 'The Music ... The Madness ... The Murder ... The Motion Picture ... Everything you've heard is true.' Not really. If this was a surreal experience to lure the post-rock 'n' roll generation back to classical music, it failed abysmally. Wolfgang Amadeus [beloved of God] Mozart was a freak. He could write piano pieces when he was 5 and played the violin superbly at 6. He had a tempestuous career in his native Austria, as well as performing for various crowned heads of Europe, like the Empress Maria Theresa and Emperor Joseph II. He became a freemason towards the end of his life and was constantly in debt, quarrelling continually with the men who actually paid his wages. The movie, with Tom Hulce as a deranged eighteenth-century beatnik, concentrated on the claim by Antonio Salieri to have murdered his young rival. There is no evidence for this at all. 'Only the American accents jar the ear,' said Halliwell, but as an attempt to create an accurate historical figure, the movie fails on all levels.

The critics raved over Cornel Wilde as Frédéric Chopin, however. *A Song to Remember* (1945) was, according to the critic James Agee, 'As infuriating and funny a misrepresentation of an artist's life and work as I have ever seen.' Richard Winnington went one better – 'It is the business of Hollywood to shape the truth into box office contours.' It should actually be the business of Hollywood to get history right. Five foot tall, cigar-smoking revolutionary George Sand, Chopin's love interest, with arms like a stevedore, was played by the far daintier Merle Oberon.

In the context of the cinema, two giants from the past have had movies based on them. William Friese-Greene was a British pioneer of the film industry, making his first movie in 1890. He experimented with 3D and colour, but, because of the vagaries of the cut-throat industry, sank without trace and is almost forgotten today. The encyclopaedic *Chronicle of the Cinema*, for example, effectively begins in 1894 and the first entry is that of self-publicist and scene-stealer, Thomas Alva Edison (see below), against whom someone as self-effacing as Friese-Green stood no chance. *The Magic Box* (1951) is a sweet and touching biopic of the old school, with a convincing Robert Donat as the pioneer cinematographer. Interestingly, the movie was made by the British Film Institute to celebrate the Festival of Britain held on London's South Bank that year. The *Daily Express* called it 'an honest and often very moving film'. Moving it certainly was, portraying Friese-Greene's death after a stormy meeting of movie-makers in London 1921, but a re-evaluation in *Time Out* in 1984 said it was 'Patriotic, sentimental, overlong and faintly embarrassing'. A huge array of British acting talent queued up to play cameo roles in the film.

Edison the Man (1940) starred Spencer Tracy and the film's PR said it all – 'The love of a woman ... the courage of fighting America ... lifted him from obscurity to thrilling fame.' If you add up all the plotlines in the films in this book, I am prepared to bet that well over 60 per cent of them will put various heroic exploits down to 'the love of a woman'. I will also bet that that is *completely* irrelevant to the particular exploits involved. Did 'the courage of fighting America' mean the conflict with Spain over Cuba in 1898? In which case, Edison missed the boat and other film pioneers covered that. If it meant the Civil War, he missed that too, working on the railroads as he was at the time. What actually 'lifted [Edison] from obscurity' was his own ability to self-promote and see the opportunities for making a buck, with his kinematograph machines catching on all over America. The movie focuses on the creation of the light bulb (before which, it tells us, he lived in abject poverty). In fact, Edison was a polymath, with interests in almost every aspect of physics. 'Slightly suspect,' says Halliwell kindly, 'in its facts.' The man was undoubtedly a genius, taking out over 1,000 patents during his life, but the Tracy version is pure schmaltz.

I end this section with a look at Hollywood from the inside. *Trumbo* (2015) starred Bryan Cranston as Dalton Trumbo, the producer, director and screenwriter who outraged 1950s and 1960s America with his pro-Communist stance. We've come across him before because he wrote the screenplay for *Spartacus* (see Chapter 1) and fell foul of the establishment because of his left leanings. The movie deals with the *Spartacus* production and the workings of the notorious House Un-American Activities Committee (HUAC), a clique of censorious pedagogues who could not contemplate that there could be anything else other than the 'American Way'. Cranston is excellent as Trumbo, chain-smoking in the bath and bashing away at an old upright typewriter on a tray across the tub. He needles John Wayne (a good lookalike in David James Elliott) by asking the famously non-combatant Wayne where exactly he served in the Second World War. The man who kicked so much Japanese and German backside on the screen actually fought nowhere; he didn't even enlist. Helen Mirren is superb as the fascistic Hedda Hopper, a waspish critic whose word was law in the McCarthy era. 'When did you get to be such a bastard, Kirk?' she asks Kirk Douglas (Dan O'Gorman). As he points out, 'I've always been a bastard, Hedda.' O'Gorman isn't beefy enough for Douglas, but his voice and mannerisms are excellent. Cinematic giants Otto Preminger and Louis B. Mayer waltz in and out of shot, but the area of greatest controversy was the role of actor Edward G. Robinson (Michael Stuhlbarg) in his betrayal of Trumbo, which critics of the movie said didn't happen. We have Robinson's testimony to the HUAC on record. He testified four times and among the names he lists is Trumbo.

I find it a rather sad indictment of Hollywood that a critic could write as recently as 2015 that the movie was 'historically misleading' because it suggested that it was a film 'in which the blacklisted movie folks are all innocent, in every conceivable way'. The movie's script wasn't saying that. What it did say is that the McCarthy-era America was obsessed with 'reds under the bed', which still leaves a nasty taste in the mouth even today.

Chapter 12

The One-Eyed Monster

In 1920s Britain, as Hollywood was still churning out silent movies in black and white, including a version of *The Three Musketeers*, Douglas Fairbanks' *Robin Hood* and DeMille's *The Ten Commandments*, John Logie Baird was experimenting in the London area only, with images from a medium-wave broadcasting station. The pictures were reddish-brown, grainy and flickering, but they were the beginning of television, destined to become the 'one-eyed monster' in the corner of everyone's living room.

As the idea caught on and technology improved, the little 9-in screens that only worked intermittently, got bigger, the programmes more diverse and the broadcasting day longer. The British Broadcasting Corporation obtained a charter and a licence from the government in 1922 and only slowly did independent broadcasters, funded by advertising, enter the field. America, home of Hollywood, had nothing but this sort of programming and, unlike Germany during the Second World War, Britain suspended television programming, missing out on a whole area of propaganda.

The glory days of the Odeon, the Gaumont, the Royal, the Majestic, picture palaces worthy of the name with their plush seating, flock wallpaper and girls selling ice-cream and popcorn, disappeared to become bingo halls and car-dealers' showrooms. Nobody had to queue for the cheap seats any more; nor were they obliged (in Britain) to 'stand for the queen' as the national anthem played at the end of the day's showing.

Movies transferred easily to the telly. Deals were done so that virtually every movie listed in this book and thousands more that haven't been, could be watched at leisure, in the comfort of the family home. My generation watched old black and white films most Sunday afternoons, movies my parents had only seen in the cinema.

As the number of commercial stations increased and the grip of television became ever more hypnotic, film studios began to make movies for television. These were, almost by definition, less grand affairs than the old cinema efforts, although the costs of production are now so sky-high they defy belief. Even so, there is a 'second-rate' attitude to such movies, as though they are made on the cheap and nothing about them is as good as the one-offs made for the cinema. This line of thinking extends to the historical accuracy of the movies you see on television today, in which various commercial giants, every bit as valuable and successful as the old Hollywood studios, are forced to provide entertainment for a new audience.

That audience is ever more difficult to please. There are those who will always believe something because it's on the screen. We saw newsreel footage of the 1969 moon landing by Armstrong, Aldrin and Co., so it must have happened; even though there are thousands around the world who still doubt it. Thanks to the presence of amateur cine-film operator Abraham Zapruder in Dealey Plaza, Dallas, in November 1963 we now *know* that the head shot that killed Kennedy came from the front; even though conservative, die-hard America continues to trot out the nonsense that Lee Harvey Oswald fired from behind. Recently, we have seen a black actress play Anne Boleyn, the hapless second wife of Henry VIII, so there are thousands on social media who believe that the totally Caucasian girl from Kent was from an ethnic minority unknown in England at the time.

The age of streaming had brought with it new problems and new responsibilities. Historical movies have never been about recreating text-book history for classroom use. As we said in the Overture, there has to be a dramatic, usually one-sided, approach for a movie to work as entertainment. Where the whole thing has gone wrong is that audiences have seen it all before and want something new. No one today is going to be astonished by Cecil B. DeMille's parting of the Red Sea in *The Ten*

Commandments, except to find it laughable given today's technology. Impressive as it was at the time, Sergei Bondarchuk's French army at Waterloo is a pathetic imitation of the real thing; now thousands of men can be reproduced with CGI.

Another problem is the series mentality. To make as much money as possible, television companies extend their storylines to encompass a series of, say, ten episodes and watch viewers' response. If they like it, they will commission ten more and on it goes. The highly contentious *The Crown* for example, might have worked well as a one-off, but its wholly inaccurate portrayal of the British royal family is stretched out in agonizing embarrassment. That happened because of the fashion that began in the radio 'soap' like family sagas about really boring people, just like us. Interestingly, as American and British television soaps' storylines have got ever more bizarre and unlikely, there seems to be a deep-rooted urge to get back to the pure escapism of the old cinema.

I have selected five historical series, nearly all of which are still available on various streaming platforms. They have all been covered already in this book by conventional movies made for the big screen.

Britannia (2017–21) is a classic exercise on how *not* to make an historical mini-series. It deals with the so-called Claudian invasion of Britain (the province the Romans later called Britannia) in 43 AD. Claudius was emperor at the time but took no part in the actual invasion, merely turning up at the end when the danger was past. The general who did the work was Aulus Plautius (David Morrissey), a highly competent soldier who became Britannia's first governor. One of the problems of translating this campaign to the screen is that we have very few actual names, so most of the cast are fictional stereotypes. There are lots of skulls and furs and wild-looking Celtic extras who speak Welsh (the rough modern equivalent of the language the Celts actually spoke) but the script is laughable. Two things you should *not* do if you're making a Roman epic is to use the 'f' word (it's 1,400 years too early for that) or use stirrups (not used until the fifth century by the Huns). Caving in to health and safety issues, *Britannia* is awash with the things. Someone vital to Plautius' success was the commander of the II Augusta Legion, Vespasian, who went on to become emperor and died peacefully in his bed in AD 79. In the series, he is killed off. Runes, used extensively in the series, did not appear in Britain until the Vikings brought them over, perhaps as early as the fifth century. And what Donovan's *Hurdy Gurdy Man* (1960s) has to do with the first century AD, I really can't imagine, but it is the soundtrack of the series nevertheless.

From the ridiculous to the nearly sublime. *Vikings* (2013–20) was serious history, researched and worried about, even if, inevitably, it got things wrong and concertinaed time to an alarming degree. The central character, Ragnar Lothbrok (Travis Fimmel), appeared in Kirk Douglas' 1958 film (played by Ernest Borgnine). His name and that of his sons appear in the Viking sagas, which can hardly be called histories, heavily laden with gods and superstitions as they are; but they are the nearest thing we've got. Aelle, the king of Northumberland (Frank Thring in the Douglas version), is played by Ivan Kaye and his grim death, in which his ribcage is broken open in what the Vikings called the blood eagle, is shown in surprising detail on the screen. Nine dragon ships were made for the series, all of them with their steering oars on the wrong (port) side. The army of Wessex (there was no country called England at the time) wore armour recycled from the David Hemmings 1969 version of *Alfred the Great* (see Chapter 2) and it showed. They carried kite-shaped shields, unknown in England before 1066 and burgonet helmets actually worn in the sixteenth century.

Real characters abounded – Ecgberht, king of Wessex was played with gravitas by Linus Roache; Harald Fairhair by Peter Franzén. Hrolf, better known as Rollo (Clive Standen) went on to take Normandy for himself; he was the great-great-great-grandfather of William the Conqueror. Ivar the Boneless (a menacing and unpleasant Alex Andersen) was actually the eldest son of Ragnar. He may have had a condition called *osteogenesis imperfecta*, which effectively made his legs useless, but after all this time, we cannot be sure of that. Viking haircuts and tattoos are very much in the eye of the beholder. They *looked* right, but the archaeological record is unhelpful, despite the existence of hundreds of 'bog bodies' in Denmark in which the skin has been preserved by chemicals in the peat. There was no such stronghold as Kattegat – that is an area of sea between Denmark, Norway and Sweden. Lagertha (Katheryn Winnick), everybody's heroine-queen, doesn't occur in the sagas but she is mentioned in chronicler Saxo Grammaticus' *Gesta Danorum* (the exploits of the Danes).

The dialogue wasn't bad, bearing in mind we have actually no idea how the Vikings spoke. The extras, depending on their own national origins, spoke Danish, Icelandic, Norwegian, Swedish and Finnish. And no one would have called Ragnar's sons by the surname Lothbrok, which was a personal nickname. They would all have been Ragnarsson. My favourite line from what was an engaging and excellent series comes from Floki, played by Gustaf Skarsgård who was the historical and linguistic adviser on set – 'We've been to Hel and back.' Sadly, I have to report – feminists look away now – that the shield maidens, female warriors hacking about them with the men, are pure hokum. There is nothing about them in any historical record.

The Borgias have been done before too (see Chapter 4), that extraordinary Italian family that dominated – along with the Medicis and the Sforzas – Renaissance Italy. The first television series aired in 1981 with Oliver Cotton as a commanding 'heavy' Cesare, Anne-Louise Lambert as Lucrezia and Adolfo Celi as a plump, smiling but nonetheless homicidal Rodrigo who went on to become Pope Alexander VI. A more recent attempt (2011–13) starred Jeremy Irons as the pope, bringing a different kind of nastiness to the role. Holliday Grainger was Lucrezia and François Arnaud was Cesare, although he lacked Cotton's presence, not helped by the fact that he broke his arm during filming and had to appear in some scenes with his cloak covering his sling.

What draws many viewers (and there are many reviews on IMDb) is the incestuous relationship between Lucrezia and Cesare, brother and sister. It is almost totally absent from the historical record, as is the often claimed 'fact' that Lucrezia was a poisoner. For those who like their Renaissance sagas bloody (which, by modern standards, they were) the weapons on display looked, according to one reviewer, as if 'they wouldn't cut butter'.

There were a number of mistakes. Nobody spoke of 'the New World' in 1492. The pope didn't crown Charles VIII of France in Naples; in fact, he refused to do so. Cesare didn't kill Giovanni Sforza, Ludovico Sforza or Prospero Colonna – all three died peacefully in bed. That said, real characters abound – the deranged monk from Florence, Savonarola; the often-banned political commentator Machiavelli, to name but two. The basic problem with either version of *The Borgias* is that history has been brushed aside for centuries on this family and any film-maker today has to provide what audiences expect. Cesare was a killer; Lucrezia a murderess; and they shared a bed; just get on with it. The real weakness of the most recent *Borgias* is that it is based on the novel by Mario Puzo, who also wrote *The Godfather*. So *The Borgias* is simply the twentieth-century mafia in funny clothes, with everybody making everybody else an offer they can't refuse.

Things were a *little* more genteel across the Channel in *The Tudors* in 2007. It was perhaps unfortunate for the television series that some of the best historical films ever made (see Chapter 4) have featured this family and this period. Alongside most of them, *The Tudors* is awful. The problem is one of visual perception. We *expect* Henry VIII to look huge, like the Holbein painting and as portrayed by Charles Laughton, Robert Shaw and Charlton Heston. Jonathan Rhys Meyers as a humourless *slim* young man might have fitted the young Henry (he was only 17 when he became king) but he filled out considerably later as he took less exercise after umpteen jousting injuries. 'Why isn't Henry fat?' one reviewer wanted to know while the series was running. 'Isn't he ever going to be fat?' The answer was 'No', allegedly because Rhys Meyers refused to play him that way. So the superb performances by

Heston, and Keith Michell in a film made for television, showing them slow and suffering from painful ulcers, simply don't fit with the 2007 version. To be fair, the action of *The Tudors* deals with the Anne Boleyn crisis, the 'king's great matter', but surely an auburn wig wouldn't have been too much trouble? The sex scenes went on and on, despite the likelihood that Henry was no great shakes in bed and virtually every female wears her hair long and unbraided – unbelievably scandalous at any sixteenth-century royal court.

And, talking of royal courts, *The Crown*. This is a fascinating Netflix soap tracing the ups and downs of the Windsors over the last forty years. At the time of writing, it is still running, with the death of Princess Diana to come. As a piece of skulduggery, it's up there with *The Borgias* and *The Tudors* and American audiences in particular lap it up. The problem is that very little of it is true; history is not being well served.

We don't have such detailed knowledge of any historical period in the past. If we were able to bring real-life characters back from the past in an H.G. Wells' time-machine, I suspect they would either be outraged at our attempts to portray their lives and period or laugh hysterically at how wrong we've got it. The only people who can do this with complete authority regarding *The Crown* are the royals themselves and with their unwritten motto of 'Never complain, never explain', we are never going to hear from them.

Television has brought historical movies into our homes. We can watch and rewatch movies in a way that was impossible for our parents and grandparents. Increased education over the last century *ought* to have made us more aware of where Hollywood is bending the truth and why they are doing it; but sadly, that is not the case.

A few years ago, I showed bits of *The Battle of Britain* to a quiet, not very bright 13-year-old. When his class had gone at the end of the lesson, he asked me, 'Did we win this one, sir?' I told him that we did, but I was quietly astonished that he didn't know. Every historical film ever made has mistakes in it. Sometimes it is an honest mistake and/or for good reasons. Sometimes it is plain bad history.

But good, bad or somewhere in between, historical movies are out there, thousands of them. Now that you've finished this book, watch one today!

Bibliography

Books

Beare, Emma (ed), *501 Must See Movies*, Bounty Books, 2004
Blum, Daniel, *A Pictorial History of the Talkies*, Spring Books, 1958
Brown, Gene, *Movie Time*, Macmillan, 1995
Buscombe, Edward, *BFI Companion to the Western*, Andre Deutsch, 1988
Cameron, Ian, *Adventures and the Cinema*, Studio Vista, 1973
Cameron, Ian, *Pictorial History of Crime Films*, Hamlyn, 1975
Cary, John, *Spectacular: the Story of Epic Films*, Hamlyn, 1974
Coultass, Clive, *Images for Battle*, Ontario Film Institute, 1989
Dargis, Manohla and Scott, A.O., *The New York Times Book of the Movies*, Universe, 2019
Fyman, Scott and Duncan, Paul (eds) *John Ford: the Complete Films*, Taschen, 2004
Gritten, David, *Halliwell's The Movies That Matter*, Harpeer Collins, 2008
Hammond, Laurence, *Thriller Movies*, Galley Press, 1979
Heston, Charlton, *In the Arena*, Harper Collins, 1995
Heston, Charlton, *The Actor's Life*, Penguin, 1980
Jarvis, Everett G., *Final Curtain*, Citadel Press, 1995
Karney, Robyn (ed), *Chronicle of the Cinema*, Dorling Kindersley, 1995
Leigh, Danny, *The Movie Book*. Penguin Random House, 2022
Lerichan, John, *Showdown*, University of Illinois Press, 1985
MacDonald Fraser, George, *The Hollywood History of the World*, Michael Joseph, 1988
Matthews, Tom Dewe, *Censored*, Chatto and Windus, 1994
McKenzie, Alan and Ware, Derek, *Hollywood Tricks of the Trade*, Admiral, 1986
Medved, Harry, *The Fifty Worst Movies of All Time*, Angus and Robertson, 1978

Meikle, Denis, *Jack the Ripper: the Murders and the Movies*, Reynolds & Harn, 2002

Morgan, Robin and Perry, George, *Sunday Times 1000 Makers of the Cinema*, Thames and Hudson, 1997

Rand, Yardena, *Wild Open Spaces*, Maverick Spirit, 2005

Schneider, Steven Jay, *1001 Movies You Must See Before You Die*, Cassell, 2012

Searles, Baird, *Epic! History on the Big Screen*, Abrams, 1990

Sellar, Maurice, *Best of British*, Sphere Books, 1987

Walker, John, *Halliwell's Fil, Video and DVD Guide*, Harper Collins, 2006

Film Brochures

55 Days at Peking (Samuel Bronston)
Anne of the Thousand Days (Hal B. Wallis)
Ben Hur (Sam Zimbalist)
Braveheart (Mel Gibson/Alan Ladd Jr)
Cromwell (Irving Allen)
El Cid (Samuel Bronston)
Khartoum (Julian Blaustein)
Mary, Queen of Scots (Hal B. Wallis)
Nicholas and Alexandra (Sam Spiegel)
Spartacus (Edward Lewis/Kirk Douglas)
The Alamo (John Wayne)
The Charge of the Light Brigade (Neil Hartley/Tony Richardson)
The Lion in Winter (Joseph E. Levine)
The Ten Commandments (Cecil B. DeMille)
Waterloo (Dino De Laurentiis)
Young Winston (Carl Foreman)

Index

So many people have been involved in the making of historical films that the index to this book should have been as long as the book itself! For reasons of space, we have been ruthless in removing some historical people, actors and actresses who ought to have been included, but who were not central to the theme – our apologies to them. We have kept in all the films, directors and producers.

The People ...

Alexander the Great 13-14, 100
Alexandra 130-1
Alfred the Great 29-30, 183, 238
Amin, Idi 236
Attila 28, 40
Bader, Douglas 180
Barrow, Clyde 213-14
Beck, Martha 218
Becket, Thomas 36-7
Bentley, Derek 217-18
Bernstein, Carl 227
Billy the Kid 21, 154-6
Bligh, William 77-8
Boleyn, Anne xiii, 63-4, 57, 199, 236, 241
Borgia, Cesare 36, 63
Bowie, Jim 90
Bradlee, Ben 227
Bromhead, Lt Gonville ix, 117
Brown, John 127-8
Brummell. George 'Beau' 109
Bundy, Theodore 216, 222
Burke, William 202
Caesar, Julius 3, 17-19
Caligula 24-5
Cannary, Martha 148, 157
Capone, Alfonso 209-12
Cardigan, James Brudenell, Lord 112-13
Cassidy, Butch 150, 161-3
Catherine the Great xi, 64, 87, 102-103, 129
Cetshwayo, King 117-19
Chard, Lt John 117
Charles I xii, 67, 69, 72

Charles II 72-3, 83
Chisum, John 155, 163
Chopin, Frederic 232
Christian, Fletcher 77-8
Christie, John 216-17
Churchill, Odette xi, 186
Churchill, Winston 121-2, 165, 179, 185, 193, 224-5
Clark, William 134-5
Cleopatra xiii, 10, 17-19, 24, 64
Clive, General Robert 114
Cochise 140-1
Cody, W.F. (Buffalo Bill) 1, 136, 138, 148-9, 157
Columbus, Christopher 79-81, 137
Commodus 25-6
Crabb, Jack 145
Craig, Christopher 217
Crockett, Davy 90
Cromwell, Oliver xii, 69-72, 165
Cromwell, Thomas 54-6
Custer, George 93, 137-9, 142-5, 157
David, King 10-11
De Bergerac, Cyrano 68
De Toulouse-Lautrec, Henri 230-1
DeSalvo, Albert 219-20
Diaz, Rodrigo viii, xi, 33-5, 38
Dillinger, John 212-13
Disraeli, Benjamin 128
Dowding, Air Chief Marshal Hugh 175
Drake, Francis 66

Dreyfus, Captain Alfred 234
Dudley, Lord Robert 61
Earp, Wyatt 147, 151-4
Edison, Thomas 1-3, 149, 232-3
Edward I ix-x, 43, 75
Eleanor of Aquitaine xi, 37-8
Elizabeth I xi-xii, 52, 54, 56-61, 66, 73-4, 124
Evans, Timothy 216-17
Fernandez, Raymond 218
Friese-Green, William 232
Fugate, Caril 219
Gandhi, Mohandas K. 225
Garrison, Jim 227-8
Gaugin, Paul 230-1
Gaumont, Leon 2-4
Genghis Khan 40, 100
George III 87, 106, 109-10
George VI 225
Geronimo 140-1
Gibson, Guy 180-1
Gilbert, W.S. 221
Gordon, General Charles 119-20
Göth, Amon 190
Grey, Lady Jane 67-8
Guevara, Ernesto 226
Hamilton, Emma 108-109, 115
Hannibal 14
Hare, William 202
Henry II 36-7, 64
Henry V 45
Henry VIII 52-4, 56, 58-9, 199, 237, 241

Hickok, J.B. (Wild Bill) 136, 139, 145, 148, 156-8
Hitler, Adolf 42, 121, 174, 177, 179, 184, 188-92, 225-6
Holliday, John (Doc) 147-8, 151-3
Hoover, J. Edgar 212-15
Hopkins, Matthew 71
'Jack the Ripper' 204-208
James, Jesse 73, 75
James/Younger gang 146, 159-61
Jesus Christ xviii, 2-3, 5, 9, 19-24
Joan of Arc xi, 47-8, 165
Johnson, John 135
Jones, John Paul 87
Juarez, Benito 129
Karim, Abdul 128-9
Kelly, Ned 3
Kennedy, John F 194, 197, 214, 227, 236
Kidd, William 73-4
King, Martin Luther 214, 238
Lafitte, Jean 89
Lamb, Caroline 109
Lawrence, T.E. 168-9
Lee, Robert E. 95, 142
Lewis, Meriwether 134-5
Lincoln, Abraham 91-2, 96, 161
Little, Malcolm 228
Livingstone, David 116
Lucas, Henry Lee 220-1
Macbeth 35-6
MacCleane, William 201
MacGregor, Robert 75
Mahdi, the xiii, 119-20

Marcus Aurelius 26
Mary I 54, 57-9, 61
Mary, Queen of Scots xii, 2, 60-1
Michaelangelo 64
Mitchell, R.J. 179
Mitchell, William 171-2, 178-9
More, Thomas 56, 199
Moses viii, 5, 8-11, 22, 199
Mozart, Wolfgang Amadeus 231-2
Napoleon xiii, 3, 43, 99-110, 165
Nelson, Horatio 77, 100, 107-109, 115
Nero 24-5, 31
Ness, Eliot 210-11
Nevsky, Alexander 41
Nicholas II 130-1
Northup, Solomon 98
Oakley, Annie 148-9
Parker, Bonnie 213-14
Parker, Pauline 218
Parnell, Charles Stuart 227
Patton, General George 176-7
Pitt, William (the Younger) 106-108, 114
Plunkett, James 201
Ralegh, Walter 59, 62, 66
Rameses II 5, 9
Rasputin, Grigori 131
Richard I 37-9
Richard III 50-1, 63
Robert the Bruce ix-x
Rommel, Field Marshal Irwin 176, 188, 192
Salah-ed-Din xiii, 39

Schindler, Oscar 189-90
Shakespeare, William 45, 62
Sheba 10-12, 24
Sheppard, Jack 200-201
Solomon, King 12
Spartacus 15-16, 18, 165
Stanley, Henry 116
Starkweather, Charles 219
Starr, Belle 146-7
Stroud, Robert 215-16
Stuart, Charles (Bonnie Prince Charlie), 75-6
Sullivan, Arthur 223
Sundance Kid 149-50, 162-3
Surratt, Mary 96
Szabo, Violette xi, 184-6
Teach, Edward 74
Thorpe, James 144
Trotsky, Lev 130
Trumbo, Dalton 15, 195, 223-4
Tubman, Harriet xi, 98
Turner, J.M.W. 229
Van Gogh, Vincent 230-1
Victoria xi, 125-8, 173
Von Stauffenberg, Claus 191-2
Wallace, William viii, x, 43
Wallis, Barnes 180
Washington, George 94
Wellington, Duke of 104-105, 107, 110
Wolsey, Thomas 53, 55-6
Woodward, Bob 227
Wuornos, Aileen 221-2
York, Alvin 169-70
Young, Graham 218
Zola, Emile 230

Played by ...
Arliss, George 128
Attenborough, Richard 61, 121, 166-7, 177, 216-17, 225
Baker, Stanley 7, 50-1, 117, 201
Beatty, Warren 213
Bergman, Ingrid 48
Blanchett, Cate 61
Bonham Carter, Helena 58
Boyer, Charles 102
Branagh, Kenneth 46-7, 51, 191
Brando, Marlon 22, 77, 79, 101, 169, 197
Bridges, Jeff 158
Brynner, Yul 9, 15, 89

Bujold, Genevieve 55
Burton, Richard 13, 18, 21, 37, 55, 109
Caine, Michael ix, xii, 115, 117, 186, 207
Carlyle, Robert 201
Chandler, Jeff 28, 140
Chaplin, Charlie 4, 124
Chaplin, Geraldine 58, 149
Cherkasov, Nikolai 41, 65
Coleman, Ronald 114
Connery, Sean 38-9, 115, 125, 203, 214
Connolly, Billy 127-8

Cooper, Gary 42-3, 86, 157, 169-72
Cranston, Bryan 233
Creager, Laird 74, 83, 205
Cruise, Tom 191-2, 197
Curtis, Tony xii, 16, 29-30, 219
Dafoe, Willem 23
Daniels, Jeff 94
Davis, Bette 58-9
Day, Doris xi, 148
De Niro, Robert 211
Dench, Judi 127-8
Depardieu, Gerard 68-80
Depp, Johnny 72, 208

Index 247

DiCaprio, Leonardo 204, 215, 224
Dietrich, Marlene 103
Dieudonné, Albert 100
Donat, Robert 107, 232
Dunaway, Fay 213
Ecclestone, Christopher 61, 218
Erivo, Cynthia xi, 98
Ferrer, Jose 68, 230-1
Fiennes, Joseph 61-2
Fiennes, Ralph 190
Finch, Jon 36, 110
Finch, Peter 109
Firth, Colin 225
Fonda, Henry 92, 104, 151, 160, 176, 195
Gable, Clarke 77, 229
Gance, Abel 100-101
Garbo, Greta 102, 173
Gibson, Mel ix, 23, 78, 88
Goddard, Paulette 63, 86
Granger, Stewart 7, 58, 109
Guinness, Alec 26, 69, 169
Hardwicke, Cedric 9, 116, 230
Harmon, Mark 222
Harris, Richard 6, 26, 69, 177, 189
Harrison, Rex xiii, 39, 64, 130
Hawthorne, Nigel 97, 107
Hemmings, David 31, 113, 238
Hepburn, Katherine xi, 38, 60
Heston, Charlton xiv, 9-10, 22-3, 33, 35, 41, 57, 64-5, 68, 89, 120, 124, 134, 136, 240-1
Hoffman, Dustin 145, 154, 158, 227
Hopkins, Anthony xiii, 38, 78, 97, 121, 177
Howard, Leslie 179
Howard, Trevor 77, 113, 175
Hulce, Tom 232
Hulme, Juliet 219
Hunter, Jeffrey 20, 144
Hurt, John 56, 217
Huston, John 6-7, 125, 136

Huston, Walter 91-2, 151
Jackson, Glenda 61, 109
James, Sid 19, 54-5
Jayston, Michael 119, 130
Jovovich, Milla 48
Kingsley, Ben 190, 225
Lancaster, Burt 21-2, 118, 144, 151, 192, 216
Laughton, Charles 16, 25, 53-5, 73, 77, 240
Leigh, Vivien 109
Lom, Herbert 35, 104
Lynskey, Melanie 218
Mason, James 41, 184, 188, 219
Masoud, Gassan xiii, 39
Massey, Raymond 91-2
Mature, Victor 8, 14, 21, 139, 151
McDowell, Malcolm 25, 229
McGoohan, Patrick 43, 61, 75
McKenna, Virginia xi, 186
McKern, Leo 56
Meyers, Jonathan Rhys 240
Miles, Sarah 109
John Mills 110, 118, 121, 167, 184
More, Kenneth 167, 176, 180, 185, 223
Morley, Robert 41, 49, 107, 109
Neagle, Anna xi, 127, 173, 186
Neeson, Liam 39, 74-5, 190
Newton, Robert 74
O'Toole, Peter 7, 37-8, 64, 118, 169
Oates, Warren 136, 213
Oldman, Gary 224, 228
Olivier, Lawrence xiii, 16-17, 46-7, 50, 109-10, 120, 130, 167, 175, 177
Pacino, Al 88
Pegg, Simon 202
Phoenix, Joachim 25-6
Plummer, Christopher 25-6, 81, 105, 115
Price, Vincent 67, 71, 83
Quayle, Anthony 53, 55, 207

Quinn, Anthony 28, 139, 169, 230-1
Rathbone, Basil 43, 49, 73, 83
Redford, Robert 96, 135, 149-50, 161-2, 227
Redgrave, Michael 180
Redgrave, Vanessa 57, 60, 113, 130, 168
Richardson, Ralph 110, 120, 167
Robards, Jason 152, 227
Robinson, Edward G. 210, 234
Robson, Flora 61, 66, 103, 125
Rooker, Michael 220-1
Russell, Kurt 153
Sanders, George 38, 72
Schofield, Paul 56
Scott, George C. 176-7
Serkis, Andy 202
Sharif, Omar x, 41, 169, 226
Shaw, Robert 56, 80, 121, 145, 240
Sheen, Martin 95, 219
Sher, Anthony 128
Simmons, Jean 16, 58, 101
Spall, Timothy 225
Steele, Tommy 200-201
Steiger, Rod 105, 117, 211
Suzman, Janet 130
Taylor, Elizabeth 18-19, 109
Theron, Charlize 222
Todd, Richard 57, 59, 75, 180
Ustinov, Peter 15-16, 23-5, 109
Von Sydow, Max 20
Washington, Denzel 94, 228
Wayne, John xii, 21, 40, 90, 142, 156, 163, 192, 197, 233
Welles, Orson 36, 53, 56, 62, 105, 219
Whitaker, Forest 226
Wilcoxson, Henry 38-9, 109
Wilde, Cornell 27, 232
Williams, Kenneth 19, 54
Winslet, Kate 218
Winters, Shelley 212
Woodward, Edward 122-3
Wright, Robin 96

On the Big Screen ...

10 Rillington Place 216-17
300 Spartans 13
300 13
55 Days at Peking 123

Above and Beyond 196
Above Us the Waves 184
Adventures of Marco Polo, The 42

Adventures of Robin Hood, The 38
Agony and the Ecstasy, The 64
Al Capone 211

Alamo, The (1960) 89-90
Alamo, The (2004) 90
Albert RN 182
Alexander Nevsky 41, 43, 65, 103
Alexander the Great 13
Alexander 13
Alfred the Great 31
All Quiet on the Western Front 166, 182-3
All the President's Men 226-7
Amadeus 231-2
Amistad 97
Anne of the Thousand Days 55-7, 199
Annie Get Your Gun 149
Apocalypse Now 197
Assassination of Jesse James, The 156, 160
Attila the Hun 28
Badlands 219
Battle of Britain, The 174, 241
Beau Brummel 109
Becket 37
Belle Starr 147
Ben-Hur ix, 20-2, 120, 224
Bible, The 6
Billy the Kid 154-5
Birdman of Alcatraz, The 216
Birth of a Nation 93
Black Shield of Falworth, The xii, 32
Black Swan, The 74
Blackbeard the Pirate 74
Bloody Mama 212
Bonnie and Clyde 213-14
Bonnie Prince Charlie 76
Born on the 4th of July 197
Boston Strangler, The 219
Bounty, The 76, 78
Braveheart ix-x, 43, 74-5
Breaker Morant 122-3
Bride of Vengeance 63
Bridge on the River Kwai 182, 192
Bridge Too Far, A 188-9
Broken Arrow 141
Buccaneer, The 89
Buffalo Bill and the Indians 149
Burke and Hare 201-202
Butch Cassidy and the Sundance Kid 149-50, 161-2
Calamity Jane xi, 148

Caligula 25
Captain Blood 73
Captain Kidd 74
Carry on Columbus 80
Carry on Henry 54-5
Carry On Up the Khyber 122
Carry on, Cleo 19
Carve Her Name With Pride 184, 186
Charge of the Light Brigade, The (1936) 111-12, 143
Charge of the Light Brigade, The (1968) xii, 31, 114
Che! 226
Chief Crazy Horse 139
Chisum 155, 163
Christopher Columbus 79
Christopher Columbus, the Discovery 79
Cleopatra 18, 109
Clive of India 114
Colditz Story, The 181
Cole Younger, Gunfighter 160
Coming Home 197
Conqueror, The 40
Conspirator, The 96
Constantine and the Cross 27
Court Martial of Billy Mitchell, The 171
Cromwell xii, 61, 67, 69-72, 199, 225
Crossing, The 87
Crusades, The 39
Custer of the West 143-4
Cyrano de Bergerac 68
Dam Busters, The 180
Darkest Hour 224
David and Bathsheba 10
Deer Hunter, The 197
Desert Fox, The 188
Desirée 101-102
Devotion 228-9
Diane 64-5
Dillinger 213
Disraeli 128
Downfall 189
Dr Strangelove 197
Dreyfus Case, The 230
Drums Along the Mohawk 86
Edison the Man 233
Egyptian, The 7
El Cid xiv, 33, 41

Elizabeth 62
Elizabeth; the Golden Age 61
Execution of Mary Stuart, The 2-3
Fall of the Roman Empire, The 26
Far Horizons, The 134-5
FBI Story, The 214
Fire Over England 61, 66, 124
First Great Train Robbery, The 203
First of the Few 179
Flags of Our Fathers 194
Forever Amber 72
Forty Thousand Horsemen 168
From Hell 208
From Here to Eternity 193
Gandhi 225
Gangs of New York 203-204
Genghis Khan 41
Geronimo 141
Gettysburg 94-5
Gladiator 26
Glory 93-4
Go Tell the Spartans 13
Gods and Generals 94-5
Great Dictator, The 174
Great Northfield Minnesota Raid, The 160
Great Train Robbery, The 3-4
Greatest Story Ever Told, The 20-1
Green Berets, The 197
Gunfight at the OK Corral 147-8
Gung Ho! 193
Hands of the Ripper 206
Hannibal 14
Harriet 98
Heavenly Creatures 219-20
Henry V 46-7, 50-1
Henry, Portrait of a Serial Killer 221-2
Heroes of Telemark, The 177
Honeymoon Killers, The 218
Hour of the Gun 152, 154
How the West was Won 139
Howards of Virginia 86
Hudson's Bay 72, 83
If I Were King 49
In Which We Serve 183-4
Ivan the Terrible 65, 102
J. Edgar 215

Index 249

Jack the Ripper 207
Jeremiah Johnson 135
Jesse James 160
JFK 227
Jim Thorpe – All American 144
Joan of Arc 48
Joan the Woman 48
John Paul Jones 86
Juarez 129
Khartoum xiii, 90, 120-1
Killing Fields, The 188
King David 11
King of Kings 20
King Richard and the
 Crusaders xiii, 32, 38-9, 49
King's Speech, The 225
Kingdom of Heaven xiii, 39-40
Knights of the Round Table 32
Lady Caroline Lamb 109-10
Lady Jane 58
Last Duel, The 43-5
Last King of Scotland, The 226
Last Stand of the Daltons,
 The 161
Last Temptation of Christ, The 23
Law and Order 151
Lawrence of Arabia x, 49, 168-9
Left Handed Gun, The 155
Let Him Have It 218-19
Letters from Iwo Jima 194-5
Life and the Passion of Christ,
 The 3
Life and Times of Judge Roy
 Bean, The 136
Life of Brian 5
Life of Christ, The 3
Life of Emile Zola, The 230
Life of Moses, The 4-5
Light Horsemen, The 168
Lincoln 96
Lion in Winter, The 37-9, 43,
 48, 64, 130
Little Big Man 145, 158
Little Caesar 210
Long Riders, The 147, 160
Longest Day, The 175, 177,
 193, 195
Lust for Life 230
M 208
Macbeth 36
Madness of King George,
 The 107, 235

Magic Box, The 232
Malcolm X 228
Man For All Seasons, A 56-7,
 199
Man in the Attic, The 205
Man Who Never Was, The 179,
 186-7
Man Who Would be King,
 The 115
Marie Walewska 102
Mary of Scotland 60
Mary, Queen of Scots xii, 60-1
Mata Hari 173
Men, The 197
Midway 195
Monster 221-2
Moulin Rouge 231
Mr Turner 228
Mrs Brown 127-8
Murder by Decree 207
Mutiny on the Bounty (1935) 76
Mutiny on the Bounty
 (1962) 76, 78
My Darling Clementine 151-2
Napoleon (1927) 100
Napoleon (2023) xiii
Ned Kelly, The Story of 3
Nicholas and Alexandra 130-1,
 168
Night to Remember, A 223-4
No Man of God 222
Nurse Edith Cavell 173
Odette 186
Oh, What a Lovely War! 121,
 166, 198
One That Got Away, The 181-2
Parnell 229
Pat Garrett and Billy the Kid 156
Paths of Glory 16
Patriot, The 88
Patton 176
Pearl Harbor 170, 192
Peterloo 56, 110
Picnic at Hanging Rock viii, 182
Pirates of the Caribbean 72
Plunkett and Macleane 201
Pony Express 136, 158
Prince and the Pauper,
 The (1957) 54
Prince and the Pauper,
 The (1977) 57
Prince of Foxes 63

Private Files of J. Edgar Hoover,
 The 214
Private Life of Henry VIII,
 The 53, 57
Private Lives of Elizabeth and
 Essex, The 58
PT 109 194
Quentin Durward 49
Quo Vadis 23
Rasputin and the Empress 121
Rasputin the Mad Monk 121
Reach For the Sky 180
Red Baron, The 170
Revolution 87
Richard III (1955) 50-1
Richard III (1995) 51
Rise of Catherine the Great,
 The 103
Riverman, The 222
Rob Roy (1953) 75
Rob Roy (1995) 74
Robe, The 21
Robin Hood (2010) 225
Robin Hood Prince of
 Thieves 38
Robin Hood xii, 32
Royal Flash 229
Run of the Arrow,
 The 137, 140
Salome 24
Salome's Last Dance 24
Sands of Iwo Jima 193
Santa Fe Trail 92, 143
Scarface Mob, The 210
Scarface 210
Scarlet Empress, The 103
Schindler's List 189
Sea Hawk, The 66
Selma 228
Sergeant York 169-70
Shakespeare in Love 62
Sign of the Pagan, The 28
Sink the Bismarck! 184
Sodom and Gomorrah 7
Solomon and Sheba 12
Song to Remember, A 232
Spartacus ix, 14-16, 18, 29-30,
 199, 223
Stanley and Livingstone 116
Story of Jesse James, The 160
Study in Terror, A 206
Sword and the Rose, The 57

Ten Commandments, The 8, 10, 134, 199, 235-7
That Hamilton Woman 108
They Died With Their Boots On 139, 143
They Were Expendable 193
Thirteenth Warrior, The 30
Thirty Seconds Over Tokyo 195
Throne of Blood 36
Titanic 224
To Hell and Back 178
To Kill a King 70
Tombstone 153
Tombstone; the Town Too Tough To Die 151
Topsy-Turvy 223
Tora! Tora! Tora! 193, 195
Triumph of the Will 188
Trumbo 223
Twelve Years a Slave 98
Untouchables, The 211
Valkyrie 189-90
Veil: Jack the Ripper, The 206
Victoria and Abdul 128
Victoria the Great 127
Viking Queen, The 31
Vikings, The 29-30
Virgin Queen, The 59
War and Peace 104
Waterloo xii, 104, 106, 110, 227
When the Daltons Rode 161
Where's Jack? 200-201
White Buffalo, The 139, 158
Wild Bill 158
Wind and the Lion, The 124-5
Winstanley 69, 71
Witchfinder General 71
Wyatt Earp 153
Young Bess 58
Young Guns 68, 156
Young Mr Lincoln 91-2
Young Mr Pitt, The 107-108
Young Poisoner's Handbook, The 218
Young Victoria 126-7
Young Winston 121-2
Zodiac 221
Zulu ix, 26, 116-18, 186
Zulu Dawn x, 118-19

... and the Small ...
Borgias, The (1981) 239-41
Borgias, The (2011-13) 239-41
Britannia 237
Crown, The xi, 237, 241
Tudors, The 240-1
Vikings 238

Directed (and Produced and Filmed) by ...
Bondarchuk, Sergei xii, 104-105, 237
Bronston, Samuel 33, 123
Cameron, James 224
Canutt, Yakima 22-3, 120
Cardiff, Jack 104
Corman, Roger 171
Cotton, Oliver 239
Curtiz, Michael 111
Daves, Delmer 140
De Laurentis, Dino 104
De Palma, Brian 211
DeMille, Cecil B. 8-10, 18, 20, 39, 47, 86, 89, 235-6
Eastwood, Clint viii, 135, 194-5, 215
Eisenstein, Sergei 41-2, 65, 103
Enfield, Cy 226-9
Ford, John xii, 142, 151-2, 193
Frankenheimer, John 216
Griffith, D.W. 4, 20, 91-3
Hughes, Ken 69
Jackson, Peter 218
King, Graham 126
Korda, Alexander 54, 76, 103, 115
Kubrick, Stanley 14-15
Laemmle, Carl 4
Landis, John 201
Lang, Fritz 209
Lean, David x
Lee, Spike 194
Leigh, Mike 110, 223
Lester, Richard 68
Lumiere brothers 1-2
Mankiewicz, Joseph 18
Mann, Anthony 34-5
Maxwell, Ronald 94
Mayer, Louis B. 93, 229, 234
Méliès, George 2-3, 230
O'Gorman, Dan 234
Pathé, Charles 2
Peckinpah, Sam 156, 161
Polanski, Roman 36
Pollack, Sydney 135
Ponti, Carlo 104
Preminger, Otto 234
Ray, Nicholas 20
Reeves, Michael 71
Richardson, Tony xii, 112, 114
Riefenstahl, Leni 188
Skarsgard, Gustaf 239
Schaffner, Franklin J. 130
Scorsese, Martin 126, 203
Scott, Ridley xiii, 39, 43-5, 80
Spiegel, Sam 130
Spielberg, Steven 96-7, 190
Stone Oliver 198, 227
Sturges, John 147, 152
Vidor, King 104, 155
Wallis, Hal 55
Wyler, William 23